REPAIR YOUR OWN CREDIT AND DEAL WITH DEBT

Second Edition

Brette McWhorter Sember
Attorney at Law

SPHINX® PUBLISHING
AN IMPRINT OF SOURCEBOOKS, INC.®
NAPERVILLE, ILLINOIS
www.SphinxLegal.com

Second Edition, 2003

Published by: **Sphinx® Publishing, An Imprint of Sourcebooks, Inc.®**

<u>Naperville Office</u>
P.O. Box 4410
Naperville, Illinois 60567-4410
630-961-3900
Fax: 630-961-2168
www.sourcebooks.com
www.SphinxLegal.com

This publication is designed to provide accurate and authoritative information in regard to the subject matter covered. It is sold with the understanding that the publisher is not engaged in rendering legal, accounting, or other professional service. If legal advice or other expert assistance is required, the services of a competent professional person should be sought.

From a Declaration of Principles Jointly Adopted by a Committee of the
American Bar Association and a Committee of Publishers and Associations

This product is not a substitute for legal advice.

Disclaimer required by Texas statutes.

Library of Congress Cataloging-in-Publication Data
Sember, Brette McWhorter, 1968-
  Repair your own credit and deal with debt / by Brette McWhorter
Sember.-- 2nd ed.
    p. cm.
  ISBN 1-57248-344-X
  1. Consumer credit--Law and legislation--United States--Popular works.
  2. Debtor and creditor--United States--Popular works. 3. Finance,
Personal--United States--Popular works. I. Title.

KF1040.Z9S46 2003
346.7307'7--dc21
                                                          002155744

Printed and bound in the United States of America.
VHG Paperback — 10 9 8 7 6 5 4 3 2 1

Contents

In loving memory of Harry Thompson

Many thanks to
Thomas and Kathleen McWhorter

My appreciation also goes out to
Jim and Carol Sember

And as always, for Terry, Quinne, and Zayne, who make it all possible.

Using Self-Help Law Books

Before using a self-help law book, you should realize the advantages and disadvantages of doing your own legal work and understand the challenges and diligence that this requires.

The Growing Trend

Rest assured that you won't be the first or only person handling your own legal matter. For example, in some states, more than seventy-five percent of the people in divorces and other cases represent themselves. Because of the high cost of legal services, this is a major trend and many courts are struggling to make it easier for people to represent themselves. However, some courts are not happy with people who do not use attorneys and refuse to help them in any way. For some, the attitude is, "Go to the law library and figure it out for yourself."

We write and publish self-help law books to give people an alternative to the often complicated and confusing legal books found in most law libraries. We have made the explanations of the law as simple and easy to understand as possible. Of course, unlike an attorney advising an individual client, we cannot cover every conceivable possibility.

Cost/Value Analysis

Whenever you shop for a product or service, you are faced with various levels of quality and price. In deciding what product or service to buy, you make a cost/value analysis on the basis of your willingness to pay and the quality you desire.

When buying a car, you decide whether you want transportation, comfort, status, or sex appeal. Accordingly, you decide among such choices as a Neon, a Lincoln, a Rolls Royce, or a Porsche. Before making a decision, you usually weigh the merits of each option against the cost.

When you get a headache, you can take a pain reliever (such as aspirin) or visit a medical specialist for a neurological examination. Given this choice, most people, of course, take a pain reliever, since it costs only pennies; whereas a medical examination costs hundreds of dollars and takes a lot of time. This is usually a logical choice because it is rare to need anything more than a pain reliever for a headache. But in some cases, a headache may indicate a brain tumor and failing to see a specialist right away can result in complications. Should everyone with a headache go to a specialist? Of course not, but people treating their own illnesses must realize that they are betting on the basis of their cost/value analysis of the situation. They are taking the most logical option.

The same cost/value analysis must be made when deciding to do one's own legal work. Many legal situations are very straight forward, requiring a simple form and no complicated analysis. Anyone with a little intelligence and a book of instructions can handle the matter without outside help.

But there is always the chance that complications are involved that only an attorney would notice. To simplify the law into a book like this, several legal cases often must be condensed into a single sentence or paragraph. Otherwise, the book would be several hundred pages long and too complicated for most people. However, this simplification necessarily leaves out many details and nuances that would apply to special or unusual situations. Also, there are many ways to interpret most legal questions. Your case may come before a judge who disagrees with the analysis of our authors.

Therefore, in deciding to use a self-help law book and to do your own legal work, you must realize that you are making a cost/value analysis. You have decided that the money you will save in doing it yourself outweighs the chance that your case will not turn out to your satisfaction. Most people handling their own simple legal matters never have a problem, but occasionally people find that it ended up costing them more to have an attorney straighten out the situation than it would have if they had hired an attorney in the beginning. Keep this in mind while handling your case, and be sure to consult an attorney if you feel you might need further guidance.

Local Rules

The next thing to remember is that a book which covers the law for the entire nation, or even for an entire state, cannot possibly include every procedural difference of every jurisdiction. Whenever possible, we provide the exact form needed; however, in some areas, each county, or even each judge, may require unique forms and procedures. In our state books, our forms usually cover the majority of counties in the state, or provide examples of the type of form which will be required. In our national books, our forms are sometimes even more general in nature but are designed to give a good idea of the type of form that will be needed in most locations. Nonetheless, keep in mind that your state, county, or judge may have a requirement, or use a form, that is not included in this book.

You should not necessarily expect to be able to get all of the information and resources you need solely from within the pages of this book. This book will serve as your guide, giving you specific information whenever possible and helping you to find out what else you will need to know. This is just like if you decided to build your own backyard deck. You might purchase a book on how to build decks. However, such a book would not include the building codes and permit requirements of every city, town, county, and township in the nation; nor would it include the lumber, nails, saws, hammers, and other materials and tools you would need to actually build the deck. You would use the book as your guide, and then do some work and research involving such matters as whether you need a permit of some kind, what type and grade of wood are available in your area, whether to use hand tools or power tools, and how to use those tools.

Before using the forms in a book like this, you should check with your court clerk to see if there are any local rules of which you should be aware, or local forms you will need to use. Often, such forms will require the same information as the forms in the book but are merely laid out differently or use slightly different language. They will sometimes require additional information.

Changes in the Law

Besides being subject to local rules and practices, the law is subject to change at any time. The courts and the legislatures of all fifty states are constantly revising the laws. It is possible that while you are reading this book, some aspect of the law is being changed.

In most cases, the change will be of minimal significance. A form will be redesigned, additional information will be required, or a waiting period will be extended. As a result, you might need to revise a form, file an extra form, or wait out a longer time period; these types of changes will not usually affect the outcome of your case. On the other hand, sometimes a major part of the law is changed, the entire law in a particular area is rewritten, or a case that was the basis of a central legal point is overruled. In such instances, your entire ability to pursue your case may be impaired.

Again, you should weigh the value of your case against the cost of an attorney and make a decision as to what you believe is in your best interest.

INTRODUCTION

Most people have credit cards and debts. But very few people understand how to deal with both effectively. This book is designed to help you understand your credit report, understand your debt load, help you clean up your credit report, develop a workable budget, avoid scams, and ease your debt situation. All of the forms and letters that you need to do these things are included in Appendix C at the back of this book. It is recommended that you make copies of the forms before writing on them. You may also wish to copy the words from the forms onto your own paper or stationery so that it is not obvious you are using a form from a book. Always keep copies of everything you send, whether it is from this book or something you write yourself.

You probably have concerns or questions about your finances or debts. This book will help you answer your questions, show you your options, and help you make good choices.

Chapter 1 will help you take a look at your financial situation, understand it and deal with any pressing financial problems. Chapter 2 guides you through obtaining and understanding your credit report, which is the report used by all creditors when they decide whether or not to lend you money and also explains credit scores. Chapter 3 walks you through ways to correct errors on your credit report as well as ideas for improving and adding positive items to your credit report. Chapter 4 will help you find ways to cut back and reduce your debt, your expenses and your spending habits.

If you need further help with your financial situation, Chapter 5 will tell you where to find it, with an extensive list of resources. Marriage and divorce are always deeply intertwined with debt and Chapter 6 will help you understand all of the ramifications of your situation. Chapter 7 will explain identity theft and show how you can best protect yourself from this frightening problem. You will receive practical advice about steps you can take to make certain your future credit reports will be positive in Chapter 8.

When you are facing any kind of financial difficulties, budgeting is a tool you need to learn about and incorporate into your daily life. Chapter 9 will show you how to do this. Finally, Chapter 10 will talk about how to go forward with your life and face the future, while putting your financial worries behind you.

You have probably seen ads for companies that promise to erase your bad credit or give you new good credit for a fee. Don't bother! This book will tell you every legal method available for repairing your credit on your own, with no fees. Everything you need to know is contained in this book.

Many consumers find that they use credit cards and end up with more debt than they can handle. This book will help you get a handle on your debt and will discuss how you can actually reduce it. You have probably also seen ads for attorneys or other professionals who advertise that they can reduce your debt and get creditors to stop bothering you. Of course, there is a fee involved for these services. Forget it! You can reduce your debt and negotiate with creditors yourself for no fee if you follow the instructions in this book. You'll also save yourself lots of money.

All of the information contained in this book is accurate as of the time it was written, but laws are constantly changing. You can obtain updated information about current laws at libraries and online.

I ASSESSING YOUR SITUATION

You have already decided that your financial situation either needs help now or will soon need help. Buying this book was an important first step in getting a handle on and solving your financial worries.

To really know what to do to solve your problems, you must first understand the details about your situation. Knowing that you do not have enough money to pay all your bills or that your credit report is unfavorable is not enough information. You must sit down with all of your financial records and all of your bills and get a clear picture of what you have, what you owe and what you can do about the rest. It is also important that you understand how the law applies to the different kinds of bills you have. Spend some time understanding the details about your finances and you will be able to take steps to fix your problems and avoid problems in the future.

Why We Have So Much Debt

Debt is a huge problem in our society. We have developed a culture of debt—it is completely acceptable in the U.S. to have large amounts of debt. In fact, you are expected to. You are not really an adult until you have a car payment, a mortgage and credit cards. In 2002, the average person in the U.S. had almost $9,000 in credit card debt.

While some debt can be useful and even important, having too much can simply overwhelm you and your finances. It is time to stop thinking about debt as something acceptable and common and find ways to control it. Use debt when it makes sense, but never let it control you. It is time to take charge of your finances.

Debt is a problem faced by every age group in the U.S. Children are affected by debt when it affects their parents. Young adults are at high risk for debt problems because very little is done to educate teens about how to manage money and debt. Students go to college and find themselves on their own for the first time, often with a credit card available for use, with no experience in how to use it wisely. Young married couples and new parents find that mortgages, car payments, and credit cards can soon become overwhelming. Middle aged people often take out home equity loans, finance little luxuries and face debt overload. Even the elderly are not exempt as they face medical expenses, low set incomes and rising costs. Debt has permeated every aspect of our society.

Why You Need to Deal with Debt

If you ignore your debts or avoid coping with them, the consequences can be tremendous—tremendously awful. First you will find that you will be denied credit—you will not be able to get a car loan or a mortgage because you are carrying too much debt. Second, you will max out your current credit and will be unable to use your credit cards. You will find that your utilities are turned off, your car is repossessed and your checks are bouncing. If you are a renter, you can be evicted and if you are a home owner, your home can be foreclosed on, leaving you with no place to live. Your creditors can obtain judgments against you, which will give them the right to seize your assets and take part of your paycheck. It is easy to quickly get in over your head with debt. It is easier to deal with your debt before these consequences begin happening. This scenario is frightening, but it does not have to happen to you.

Dealing with Debt Emergencies

If you are experiencing a debt emergency, you need to handle it immediately. An emergency is an eviction, foreclosure, vehicle repossession or other matter that will directly and immediately impact your housing, health or transportation situation. If you are in an emergency, you have to cope with it first, before using the rest of this book to solve your other debt problems. If you are facing one of these problems, contact the creditor immediately and tell them you would like to work out a payment plan. Explain that you are having financial troubles and want to make sure they are paid, but that you need to work something out for the short term. Get the best plan you can and agree to it (see Chapter 4 for more discussion of payment plans). This will give you at least a few months to try to make some permanent changes to your overall situation.

If the creditor is unwilling to work any payment plan out and you are going to lose your home or vehicle and cannot make any other arrangements for yourself, consider *bankruptcy*. Bankruptcy is discussed more fully in Chapter 5. When you file for bankruptcy, at the moment your petition is filed, all creditors must stop any and all collection efforts. All foreclosures and evictions must also stop. Talk to an attorney who specializes in bankruptcies. When you call for an appointment, explain that you have an emergency and need to file as soon as possible. Do not put off this phone call.

If you are having difficulty paying all of your debts and are in a difficult situation, one tactic you can use is to ask your creditors to provide you with documentation of the debt. Under the *Fair Debt Collection Practices Act (FDCPA),* you have the right to request this of any creditor and it often takes several weeks for a creditor to do so, giving you a little extra time to try to pull some money or a plan together. (FDCPA, Section (Sec.) 1692g.)

Other tactics some people use include moving with no forwarding address and not re-registering to vote in the new location, closing bank accounts and opening new ones at a different bank. These tactics are just delaying strategies that make it hard for the creditor to locate you and in no way will reduce your debt. In fact they will increase your debts because interest will continue to build. When it all catches up to you, it is going to be worse than it is right now.

To delay having your credit cards reported as past due, make the minimum payments. This will keep the account current and keep your credit report clean.

Interest will continue to accrue on your balance though, so this is only a temporary solution. You need to find a permanent solution.

If you are facing eviction or foreclosure, you need legal help. If bankruptcy is not a choice, you need an attorney to help with the eviction or foreclosure. See Chapter 5 for information about finding low or no cost legal help.

Remember that though your situation may feel out of control, there is a way out. It means taking the reins, facing the facts and developing a plan to help keep a roof over your head and food on the table. Avoiding the bad news will not help. Stop and develop a plan that includes working with our creditors.

Getting a Clear Picture of What You Owe

Assemble all of your bills, including utilities, mortgage or rent, home equity loans, bank and store credit cards, medical bills, car loans, insurance bills, utility bills, student loans, back taxes and all other bills. Make sure you have the most current statement from each creditor. If you cannot locate the most current bill, call and request one from the creditor.

Next, get together all records of money or assets you have—checking and savings accounts, CDs, retirement accounts, bonds, investments, credit unions accounts, current pay stubs, information on property you own, as well as any vehicles or anything else of value.

Now that you have assembled all of this information and have it in a pile, you need to organize it in a way that will make it easy to work with. Fill out the **DEBT ASSESSMENT** worksheet available at the back of this book. (see form 1, p.176.)

⬥ List each creditor separately.

⬥ Place the total amount owed, monthly payment, address, and contact information in the correct columns for each creditor.

⬥ Total the monthly payment amounts and the total amounts owed at the bottom of the page.

Complete the **ASSET ASSESSMENT** worksheet at the back of the book. (see form 2, p.177.)

⬧ List each account or item separately.

⬧ Fill in the total value for each item.

⬧ For salaries, fill in the monthly amount and the yearly amount earned.

⬧ Be sure to include ALL money coming into your household, including child support, alimony, disability payments, interest, etc. Also include money you can earn or receive from things like eBay sales, garage sales, gifts from family, money from odd jobs, and so on. Total all monthly amounts and yearly amounts. Write those amounts on the respective lines.

⬧ Total all asset values at the bottom of the form.

Next you need to compare your assets and debts on the **TOTAL ASSESSMENT** worksheet. (see form 3, p.178.)

⬧ Transfer the totals you reached on the Asset Assessment and Debt Assessment sheets to the monthly income and monthly debts lines, and the total assets and total debts lines. Your total debt will almost definitely be larger than your total assets. (Don't panic. This even happens to people who are not experiencing credit problems.)

⬧ Compare your monthly income to your monthly minimum debt payments by subtracting your debts from your assets. Write this amount on the respective line.

Thinking About Your Finances
Look at your total monthly income and determine how much of that you would realistically like to have available and not tied up in monthly payments. This is the goal you are going to work towards. After paying for housing, utilities, vehicles and miscellaneous expenses, how much do you want to have left over?

People often ask how much debt is OK to have. There is no good answer to that question. You should only have debt that is necessary (such as a mortgage), that you can manage, and that you can pay off without incurring a lot of unnecessary interest. There is no magic number or magic percentage. It is important to save money so that you can plan for retirement, and also so you can save for emergencies, as well as big expenses like college tuition. Financial experts suggest you develop a cushion equal to six months of your income. For many people this is difficult to do. However, if you can commit to saving some amount each month, you will be on your way there.

In general, debt is bad because, in effect, it increases the cost of the things you buy on it. Instead of paying $29.99 for a sweater, you are paying $29.99 *plus* the interest charges.

However, debt allows you to buy that affordable home and car when, like most people, you are not able to pay cash for them. Debt for these items is often the only way to afford them. Taking out these kinds of debt can be very good if you only take on as much debt as you can handle and you budget for it. Your goal should be to reduce your debt to a manageable level and eventually to eliminate all but home and car loans.

Understanding Your Debts

Before you take any steps to clear your credit rating or get yourself out of debt, you have to look closely at the debts you have and understand what type of debts they are. Different kinds of creditors are treated differently.

Secured Loans

Secured loans are loans where you borrow money or buy a certain item and give the creditor a security interest or *collateral* in an item. An example of this is a car loan. When you take out a car loan, you give the creditor the right to take the car back if you do not pay the loan.

Unsecured Loans

Unsecured loans occur when a creditor lends you money and does not have a security interest in anything you own. Credit cards are unsecured loans, unless you have a card that is secured through your bank account (i.e. the creditor can seize your bank account if you do not pay the amount owed). Personal loans are also usually unsecured.

Student Loans

Student loans are unsecured loans that are usually offered through a bank or loan agency and backed by the government. Student loans cannot be discharged in bankruptcy and are often a source of credit problems.

Mortgage   A *mortgage* occurs when you buy a home and borrow money from a bank. The bank loans you the money to pay for the house, but maintains a type of security interest in the home. You cannot sell the home without paying the mortgage and if you fail to make payments, the bank can foreclose on the home and sell it to pay for the loan. A home equity loan is a type of mortgage.

Taxes   *Taxes* are an amount owed to the state or federal government. Taxes cannot be discharged in bankruptcy.

Dealing with Your Emotions

It is likely that your credit situation or financial problems are causing you a lot of stress. You are worried about how to handle the debt you have or how to clean up your credit history so that you aren't always being turned down for loans, credit cards, or mortgages. It is going to be hard to act rationally if you are panicked. Remind yourself that you are going to come through the situation. Read this book and follow the suggestions. If you take action, you will feel more in control of your situation. If you find that the stress is too much for you to handle, talk to a friend, clergy member, or mental health professional.

A common reaction to credit and debt problems is avoidance. People avoid understanding their situation. If they do not think about it, it cannot be all that bad, they often reason. Ignoring your problems will not make them go away. You need to get a handle on your credit and debt problems. The sooner you face them, the sooner they can be resolved.

Many people avoid dealing with their situation out of embarrassment. They feel too embarrassed to contact a creditor to make payment arrangements or to ask a family member for financial assistance. Just remember that creditors deal with these problems on a daily basis and you are not alone. You must put your feelings aside and deal with this problem as if it were someone else's that you are handling for them. Look at the facts and focus on what concrete things you can do to change the situation. Do not get caught up in your emotions. Take a problem-solving approach.

Your Rights

You have many specific rights provided by the federal government with regard to your debts and credit report. Different states provide for different rights as well. Check your state's laws at your local library or online at **www.findlaw.com**. Chapter 5 lists organizations that can help you understand and exercise your rights. There are two important federal laws that you need to know about to protect yourself and exercise your rights: the *Federal Fair Credit Reporting Act* and the *Federal Fair Debt Collection Practices Act*. Excerpts from both acts are included in Appendix B. Look there for more details about your rights.

Federal Fair Debt Collection Practices Act

This act (abbreviated as FDCPA) sets out specifics about how a collection agency may behave towards you and towards others. Understand that the act applies not just to actual collection agencies, but to people acting as debt collectors.

Contact with You. Debt collectors must speak with your attorney and not you directly unless you give permission. They may not contact you at unusual or inconvenient times (which includes before 8 a.m. and after 9 p.m.) or at work if you are not permitted to accept such calls there. They may not call you repeatedly nor call you without identifying themselves. They may not call you collect nor cause you to be responsible for any costs of the phone call. They may not identify themselves as part of law enforcement or as attorneys. They may not harass, oppress or abuse you. They may not use or threaten to use violence or harm on you or anyone, or to anyone's reputation. (FDCPA, Secs. 1692(c) and (d).)

Obscene language is not permitted. Your name cannot be published on a "deadbeat" list. If you are contacted by a debt collector, you can instruct them not to call you again and they must abide by this request and can only notify you by mail of the status of your account, such as when it is being forwarded to an attorney for a lawsuit. (FDCPA, Secs. 1692 (c) through (f).)

Whenever you speak to a debt collector, get his or her name, name of the agency, business address, and phone number. If you believe you are being treated in a way that violates the law or if your request for no contact is being ignored, write to the agency and complain. Contact your state attorney general about the problem.

Collectors cannot lie about the amount you owe nor can they threaten to take action against you that they do not intend to take. No unfair or outrageous attempts to collect the money are permitted. This includes adding interest or fees not part of the original debt, asking for a postdated check by threatening you with criminal action, or accepting a check that is more than five days postdated unless they notify you three to ten days before cashing it. They may not deposit a postdated check before the date on it. (FDCPA, Sec. 1692(f).)

If you tell a collection agency not to contact you again, they must comply, unless they are giving you notice of their plans to sue or to stop all collection attempts.

Correspondence with You. When you receive correspondence from a debt collector, it must not appear to resemble court documents or correspondence from a government agency. It may not appear as if it is from an attorney. The envelope the correspondence is in must be a plain envelope and may not indicate anywhere on it that it is in reference to collection of a debt or that it is from a collection agency. (FDCPA, Sec. 1692(e).)

Contact with Others. Debt collectors must give their names when contacting other people and state that they are confirming or correcting residence or employment information about you. If asked, they can give the name of the agency they work for. They may not talk about you owing a debt at all and may not call anyone more than once unless they received incorrect or incomplete information the first time. (FDCPA, Sec. 1692(b).)

Your Remedy. If a creditor violates any provision of this law, you can take action against them. Make sure that you keep detailed records and keep all evidence of the violation. If possible, you should have a witness as well, someone who saw or heard the improper act.

Send a letter to the original creditor and your State Attorney General detailing the violation. You should also send a letter to the Federal Trade Commission at your regional office listed in the phone book, or online at: **www.ftc.gov**. Use **LETTER COMPLAINING OF UNFAIR DEBT COLLECTION PRACTICE**. (see form 4, p.179.) You may be able to get the entire debt canceled because of this. If you have been harassed, you could also bring a case in small claims court in your local area for damages for your pain and suffering as well as *punitive damages* of up to $1000 to punish the collection agency for these actions. (FDCPA, Sec. 1692(k).)

Fair Credit Reporting Act This act deals with credit reports and credit reporting agencies. The Fair Credit Reporting Act (FCRA) provides the fee structure for credit reports (see Chapter 2 for more information about this) as well as the situations in which a consumer can obtain a free report if he or she has been denied credit. A report must be requested within sixty (60) days of the receipt of the denial of credit or employment. The act also provides that if you find an error or incorrect information on your report you can inform the reporting agency and they must reinvestigate the matter at no charge to you. You must receive a response from them within thirty (30) days. The information must be corrected or deleted if it is wrong. (FCRA, Sec. 1681(i).)

Credit reporting agencies are required to include on your credit report a record of all inquiries about you received in the last six months. They must also include a listing of all people who have purchased your report within the last two years for employment purposes and within the last year for other reasons. (FCRA, Sec. 1681(g).) Credit reporting agencies are not required to disclose your credit scores or credit risk rating. This is an internal evaluation the reporting agency makes about your creditworthiness. It is like a grade for your credit history and is furnished to employers and creditors. Many credit reporting agencies do release this information, but are not required to do so by law. (FCRA, Sec. 1681(g).)

Creditor Tactics

There are many different tactics creditors can legally use to collect the money you owe.

Wage Assignments/ Garnishments

A *wage garnishment* occurs when a court enters a judgment against you and the creditor is then allowed to have a certain portion taken out of your salary (consult your state's laws to understand how much is permitted) and paid directly to the creditor. A *wage assignment* occurs when a debtor agrees to have part of his or her pay sent directly to a creditor. Never agree to this! Do not let a creditor talk you into this, no matter what. It is vital that you know and understand this before you read further. It will come up early on in your dealings with creditors. You want to have complete control over your income at all times. This can never happen without your knowledge. You must be served with court papers and a court must hear the case before a wage garnishment can be ordered. However, if you ignore court papers, a court can go ahead and order it without your knowledge.

Repossession

Repossession occurs when a creditor has a *security interest* in an item you purchased. This means the creditor has the right to take back the item if you do not make payments on the loan. The most common example is with an automobile. When you purchase the car and take out the loan, you will be given papers indicating the security interest the creditor retains. Repossession is just a way of saying the creditor takes the car away from you for failure to pay. If you take out a loan from an appliance or furniture store, you may be giving the store a security interest in the items you buy.

You can best prevent repossession by making your car payments. If you are going to miss a payment, call the creditor and explain in advance. If you have a continuing problem making payments, you need to speak to the creditor and try to work out a payment plan that will work for you. This may include several months of reduced payments of an extension of the life of the loan to give you longer period of time to make the payments. If you are still unable to make the payments, it is likely the car will be repossessed. Some people avoid this by keeping the car someplace where the creditor cannot find it. This means you will not be able to use it though, since your creditor knows where you live and work.

If your car is repossessed, you should contact the creditor immediately and try to work an arrangement for you to make some payments in order to have the car returned to you. You have to understand though that once the car is repossessed, the creditor does not have much incentive to return it to you.

If you decide to just give up and allow the car to be repossessed, you must know that this is not as simple as it sounds. If your car is repossessed, the creditor can (and usually will) charge you additional fees. You will also still owe them the remaining loan amount minus the current value of the car.

If you find you can no longer make car payments, you are better to negotiate a surrender, where you turn the car over to them. It will cost you less than repossession.

Foreclosure   *Foreclosure* occurs when a bank takes possession of real property (such as your home) that you have failed to make mortgage payments on. Foreclosure is a long process and banks usually prefer to help you find a way to make payment. Just as with repossession, there are costs and fees associated with the process that you will be responsible for. Additionally, repossessed homes are usually sold at auction for a fraction of their value. You will be responsible for the difference between the sale price and the amount of the mortgage.

Dealing with Collection Agencies

Collection agencies are businesses that earn money by collecting debts. This can work in one of two ways. Either the creditor forwards your debt to the collection agency and agrees to pay the agency a percentage of the amount collected, or the creditor sells the right to collect on your debt to the agency and the agency gets to keep whatever it collects from you. The individual collection agents who work for the company do so on commission. They are paid a percent of what they collect from you, so they are highly motivated to get you to pay. Collection agencies have a bad reputation and some people see them as sharks who bother people at home and at work and collect money any way they can. In reality, the law is quite clear about what collection agencies can and cannot do. See the discussion of Your Rights on page 8 of this chapter for more information about what collection agencies may do to collect a debt.

When you decide to talk to a collection agency, you must remember that you are dealing with a professional debt collector. Do not let yourself be talked into paying more than you are able. Know what your *bottom line* is (the most you can agree to pay monthly) before talking with the agency. Realize that the agent may act friendly and seem as if he or she is on your side and wants to help you. Never believe this. Collections are a big business and you are the only one who can safeguard your financial situation.

2 UNDERSTANDING YOUR CREDIT REPORT

When people talk about having *bad credit* what they mean is that they have an unfavorable credit rating or unfavorable items on their credit report that makes it difficult to get new credit. When you find yourself falling behind on payments or you are rejected for credit that you apply for, you should review your credit report. It is also wise as a general policy to review your credit report at least every two years. There are many things you can do to improve your credit report, but you cannot do any of them unless you have your credit report. Your credit report is like your report card in school. It sums up who you are in the eyes of the bureaucracy. To improve your situation, you have to have all the information that is available about you financially. You cannot fix it if you do not know what is broken.

When you get your report, you are going to want to update accounts that have been paid in full or closed and get as many existing accounts listed with a positive rating as is possible. You ideally want to eliminate all negative ratings. You also want to try to upgrade neutral ratings to positive if possible and keep as many positive ratings as you can. Chapter 3 discusses what you need to change in your report in more detail, as well as how to go about doing it.

Credit Reporting Agencies

Credit reporting agencies are large corporations that make money by compiling financial information about consumers and selling it to potential lenders and employers. Anyone who has ever applied for a loan or credit of any kind will have a credit file with each of the major credit reporting agencies. People who pay cash for everything may not have anything in their credit report. A credit report lists personal data, employment, credit cards, and debts in a person's name.

How did these people get all of this information about you? The information is taken from credit applications you have completed as well as from reports your creditors make about how well you meet your obligations to them.

There are many small credit reporting agencies who are often hired to examine and investigate credit histories by banks or loan agencies. However they all obtain their information from the same sources—the big three credit reporting agencies. The three agencies are:

Equifax
P.O. Box 740241
Atlanta, GA 30374
800-685-1111
www.equifax.com

Experian
P.O. Box 2104
Allen, TN 75013-2104
888-397-3742
www.experian.com

Trans Union, LLC
Consumer Disclosure Center
P.O. Box 1000
Chester, PA 19022
800-888-4213
www.tuc.com

Why Your Credit Report Matters

Your credit report shows your entire financial life on paper. It lists your Social Security number, current and past addresses, employment, loans, credit cards, mortgages and all other debts. It shows what accounts are paid in full, which are late, which are in collection as well as any liens against you and any bankruptcies you may have filed. Whenever you apply for a loan or a credit card, your credit report is examined by the potential creditor. The report rates your financial status and the creditor uses it to decide how likely it is you will pay back the money you want to borrow. If your credit report shows many delinquent (late) accounts, a bankruptcy, or more loans than you are capable of paying, you are a bad credit risk. Employers, insurance companies, and child support agencies can obtain your credit report. Since you are judged almost solely on the basis of your credit report, you need to make sure that it is accurate and that it is as positive as possible.

Your Credit Report

Obtaining Your Credit Report

The simplest way to obtain your credit report is to contact the credit reporting agencies by telephone or via the Internet. You may order your report online. You will want to obtain your credit report from each reporting agency since errors may appear on reports from one agency but not others. You will be required to provide information such as your full name, date of birth, spouse's name, address, Social Security number, credit card account numbers and birth date to verify your identity. Use the **LETTER REQUESTING CREDIT REPORT** to request your report by mail. (see form 5, p.180.)

You must remember that when you request your report you will only receive your own report. If your spouse would like a credit report, he or she must request it separately. You are not authorized to obtain your spouse's report. If either of you are experiencing credit problems, you should obtain reports for both of you so that you can correct all errors.

If you have been denied credit, employment, rental housing, or insurance based on your credit report, you can obtain a free report from each agency within sixty (60) days of the denial.

To otherwise obtain your basic credit report, consult the chart below to determine the cost of the first copy in your state:

State	Cost
California	$8
Colorado	one free report per year
Connecticut	$5
Georgia	two free reports per year
Maine	$3
Maryland	one free report per year
Massachusetts	one free report per year
Minnesota	$3
New Jersey	one free report per year
Vermont	one free report per year
Virgin Islands	$1
All other states	$8.50–$9.00

NOTE: *Applicable state sales tax may also be included.*

Ironically, you can pay for your credit report with a credit card or you can send a check.

What Is in a Credit Report

Your credit report contains personal information about you, including your Social Security number, your past and current addresses and employers, your past and present mortgages, loans, credit cards, installment agreements, and public records about you, such as bankruptcies and liens. The report will list if your accounts are current or 30, 60 or 90 days past due. It will also indicate if you have moved without notifying a creditor (the usual designation for this is SCNL).

The items listed can be positive, negative or neutral. Items that are negative such as an overdue account, can only remain on your credit report for seven years. Bankruptcies may remain on your report for no more than ten years. However, if you apply for a job that pays over $75,000, for credit of $150,000 or more, or life insurance for $150,000 or more, then these previously mentioned negative items will appear on the report without regard to how old the items are. (FCRA, Sec. 1681(c).)

Reading and Understanding Your Report

The three credit reporting agencies present credit information in different ways on their reports. If you request your report from all three companies, you will probably find that none of them contain exactly the same information. Often certain debts are included in one company's report, but left out of another's. To completely review your credit history, you will need to obtain all three reports.

Look at the sample reports reproduced in this chapter starting on page 19. Read the following descriptions to help you interpret them. All three agencies must accept phone calls from consumers with questions about information in a report. Customer service employees are available to help you if there is something you do not understand in your report.

Credit Score

Your credit score or rating is a number between about 150 and 900 that summarizes your credit worthiness. The score is based on all the information in your credit report and is a quick rating to sum up your overall credit health. The score is calculated by looking at your payment history, amounts currently payable, how long you have had a credit history, the type of credit accounts you have, how many open accounts you have, how many inquiries there are on your account, and how new your accounts are. A good credit score starts around 680.

Your credit score directly impacts loans and credit you apply for in the future. You may not qualify for a loan if your score is not high enough. Or, you may be charged a higher interest rate because of your credit score.

You may have to pay an extra fee to receive your credit score when ordering your credit report. It is possible to order just your credit score, from companies such as FICO (**www.myfico.com**). FICO offers several packages that allow you to track your credit score throughout a year. It also offers an interesting simulator that lets you see how certain actions can potentially affect your credit score. All of this costs money however and in general it is sufficient to see your credit score once a year when you order your credit reports.

Reading Your Reports

NOTE: *At the time this book was written, the following descriptions were accurate based on the way the agencies were reporting information at the time. However, companies are constantly updating their forms so the forms used by the agencies may change* *at any time. The forms always contain the same basic information and if changes are made they are usually done to make the forms easier to read and understand.*

Equifax   This chapter contains two examples of Equifax credit reports. One is an example of an online credit report and the other is an example of a credit report you would receive by mail. First let's look at the report that you receive if you ordered it through the mail. (See the example on page 22.)

- ✪   The first part contains your basic identification information, previous addresses, and employment history.

- ✪   All public records about your debts, including bankruptcies, liens, judgments, garnishments, secured loans, marital status, financial counseling you have participated in, foreclosures or any non-responsibility entries are listed next.

- ✪   The next part lists all of your accounts that have been turned over to a collection agency and gives account number, balance, date the balance was given, the last activity that happened, the date it was turned over to collection, and the collection status.

- ✪   You will find a list of creditors next. They are listed with company name, account number, account balance (the total amount owed), account status and details. The account status will show whether the account is paid as agreed, the number of days delinquent, or is in collection. Use the codes at the bottom of the sample to understand status.

- ✪   The next part is the "Credit Inquiry" section. This lists all the companies who have requested information about you, either because you currently have an account with them, you applied for an account or a job with them, or because they wanted basic information in order to try to solicit your business. Before the name of each business is the date the request was made.

How to Read Your Credit File

This section includes your name, current and previous addresses and other identifying information reported by creditors.

This section includes public record items obtained from local, state and federal courts.

This section includes accounts that creditors have turned over to a collection agency.

This section contains both open and closed accounts.

1. The credit grantor reporting the information.
2. The account number reported by the credit grantor.
3. See explanation below.
4. The month and year the credit grantor opened the account.
5. Number of months account payment history has been reported.
6. The date of last payment, change or occurrence.
7. Highest amount charged or the credit limit.
8. Number of installments or monthly payment.
9. The amount owed as of the date reported.
10. The amount past due as of the date reported.
11. See explanation below.
12. Date of last account update.

This section includes a list of businesses that have received your credit file in the last 24 months.

Please address all future correspondence to: Equifax Credit Information Services
123 Street Address
City, State 000000

SAMPLE CREDIT FILE

Personal Identification Information

Your Name
123 Current Address
City, State 00000

Social Security #: 123-45-6789
Date of Birth: April 10th, 1940

Previous Address(es)
456 Former Rd. Atlanta, GA 30000
P.O. Box XXXX Savannah, GA 40000

Last Reported Employment: Engineer, Highway Planning

Public Record Information

Lien Filed 03/93; Fulton CTY; Case or Other ID Number-32114; Amount-$26667; Class-State; Released 07/93; Verified 07/93

Bankruptcy Filed 12/92; Northern District Ct; Case or Other ID Number-673HC12; Liabilities-$15787; Personal; Individual; Discharged; Assets-$780

Satisfied Judgment Filed 07/99; Fulton CTY; Case or Other ID Number-898872; Defendant-Consumer; Amount-$8984; Plaintiff-ABC Real Estate; Satisfied 08/99; Verified 09/99

Collection Agency Account Information

Pro Coll (800) xxx-xxxx

Collection Reported 05/99; Assigned 09/98; to Pro Coll (800) XXX-XXXX Client - ABC Hospital; Amount-$978; Unpaid; Balance $978; Date of Last Activity 08/98; Individual Account; Account Number 787652JC

Credit Account Information

Company Name [1]	Account Number [2]	Whose Acct [3]	Date Opened [4]	Months Reviewed [5]	Date of Last Activity [6]	High Credit [7]	Terms [8]	Balance [9]	Past Due [10]	Status [11]	Date Reported [12]
Store	3251	J	10/96	36	9/99	$950		$0		R1	9/99
Bank	4735	A	11/95	24	5/99	$750		$0		I1	4/99
Gas	5411	A	6/96	12	3/99	$500		$0		O1	9/99
Auto	5297	I	5/95	48	12/99	$1100	$50	$300	$200	I5	4/99

Previous Payment History: 3 Times 30 days late; 4 Times 60 days late
Previous Status: 01/99 - I2; 02/99; - I3; 03/99; - I4

Companies that Requested your Credit File

06/06/98	Equifax - Disclosure	08/27/98	Department Store
07/29/98	PRM Bankcard	07/03/98	AM Bankcard
04/10/98	AR Department Store	12/31/97	Equifax - Update

Whose Account

Indicates who is responsible for the account and the type of participation you have with the account.

J = Joint
I = Individual
U = Undesignated
A = Authorized User
T = Terminated
M = Maker
C = Co-Maker/Co-Signer
B = On behalf of another person
S = Shared

Status   Type of Account

O = Open (entire balance due each month)
R = Revolving (payment amount variable)
I = Installment (fixed number of payments)

Timeliness of Payment

0 = Approved not used; too new to rate
1 = Paid as agreed
2 = 30+ days past due
3 = 60+ days past due
4 = 90+ days past due
5 = Pays or paid 120+ days past the due date; or collection account
7 = Making regular payments under wage earner plan or similar arrangement
8 = Repossession
9 = Charged off to bad debt

The following inquiries are NOT reported to businesses:

PRM– This type of inquiry means that only your name and address were given to a credit grantor so they could offer you an application for credit. (PRM inquiries remain for twelve months)

AM or AR– These inquiries indicate a periodic review of your credit history by one of your creditors. (AM and AR inquiries remain for twelve months)

Equifax, ACIS or Update– These inquiries inidicate Equifax's activity in response to your contact with us for either a copy of your credit file or a request for research.

PRM, AM, AR, Equifax, ACIS, Update and INQ– These inquiries do not appear on credit files businesses receive, only on copies provided to you.

Medical and Health inquiries are not displayed to the creditors, and are not used to calculate credit scores.

Reprinted with permission from Equifax.

Commonly Asked Questions About Credit Files

Q: *Why did you turn down my request for credit?*

A: Credit reporting agencies do not recommend that your credit application be accepted or rejected. Credit grantors make that decision based on your payment record and their own criteria.

Q: *Do credit reporting agencies rate my accounts?*

A: No. All we do is maintain records. Each creditor reports the status of your account according to your manner of payment.

Q: *How can I correct a mistake in my credit file?*

A: Complete the Research Request form and give details of the information you believe is incorrect. We will then check with the credit grantor, collection agency or public record source to see if any error has been reported. Information that cannot be verified will be removed from your file. If you and a credit grantor disagree on any information, you will need to resolve the dispute directly with the credit grantor who is the source of the information in question.

Q: *What is in my credit file that keeps me from obtaining credit?*

A: We do not know, since credit reporting agencies do not grant credit. Each credit grantor has established criteria for making credit decisions. Your credit may appear to be perfect, but having too much credit or too many outstanding balances are examples of why your request for credit might be declined. Sometimes the decision is not even based directly on the credit file; for instance, you may not have been at your current residence or in your present job long enough. If you have any questions about why you were not approved for credit, contact the credit grantor who turned you down for credit for an explanation.

Q: *Why is my last reported employment outdated?*

A: What is listed as your last reported employment is actually the last employment reported by credit grantors. Employment information is typically reported from applications for credit and therefore is not regularly updated. This information is not used by credit grantors or employers in making their decision, but is used for demographic purposes.

Q: *What is a credit score?*

A: A credit score is a composite that indicates how likely you are to pay on a loan or credit card as agreed. It is a predictor of future performance. It is one piece of information credit grantors use when evaluating your application for credit. Your credit score may be based solely on information in your credit file with the credit reporting agencies. Other scores may be based on a combination of credit information and other information you supply on your credit application. The way you have handled credit in the past may have a link as to how you will manage credit in the future. Credit scores cannot predict with certainty how you or anyone will manage credit. They do provide an objective estimate of how likely you are to repay on time and according to terms.

Q: *Is the credit score part of my credit file?*

A: The credit score is not part of your credit file. It is a process that assists the credit grantor during the credit application process. The score may change as your credit information changes.

Q: *If I do have credit problems, is there some place where I can get advice and assistance?*

A: Yes, there are several organizations that offer assistance. For example, the Consumer Credit Counseling Service (CCCS) is a non-profit organization that offers free or low-cost financial counseling to help people solve their financial problems. CCCS can help you analyze your situation and work with you to develop solutions. There are more than 600 CCCS offices throughout the country. Call 1-800-388-2227 for the telephone number of the office nearest you.

Q: *Should I use one of those companies that promise to help "fix" my credit?*

A: That is your choice. Remember, however, that these companies cannot have accurate information removed from your credit file. Much of what they do you can do for yourself at little or no cost.

Notice:

Upon receipt of your dispute, we first review and consider the relevant information you have submitted regarding the nature of your dispute. If that review does not resolve your dispute and further investigation is required, notification of your dispute, including the relevant information you submitted, is provided to the source that furnished the disputed information. The source reviews the information provided, conductds and investigation wit espect to the disputed information, and reports the results back to us. The credit reporting company then makes deletions or changes to your credit file as appropriate based on the results of the reinvestigation. The name and address and, if reasonably available, the phone number of the furnisher(s) of information contacted while processing your dispute(s) is shown under the Results of Your Investigation section on the cover letter that accompanies the copy of your revised credit file.

If you still disagree with an item after it has been verified, you may send to us a brief statement, not to exceed 100 words (200 words for Maine residents) explaining the nature of your disagreement. Your statement will become part of your credit file and will be disclosed each time your credit file is accessed.

If the reinvestigation results in a change to or deletion of the information you are concerned about, or you submit a statement in accordance with the preceding paragraph, you have the right to request that we send your revised credit file to any company that received your credit file in the past 6 months ofr any purpose (12 months for California, Colorado, Maryland, New Jersey and New York residents) or in the past two years for employment purposes.

If you order your Equifax report online, it will look like the sample on page 22.

✪ The report begins with your personal data, including address, Social Security number and date of birth. Previous addresses and employment history follows this.

✪ Public Records contains information about bankruptcies, liens, foreclosures as well as credit counseling services you have used.

✪ Collection Accounts lists any accounts that have been sent to collection agencies.

✪ Credit Information lists the creditor, account number, whether it is joint or individual, the date you opened the account and the last date of any reported activity. The type of account is described and a description of your status is included. The credit limit is listed. Then if there is a past due amount it is included, if not, that space is blank. The last column gives the date the information was last reported. Underneath all of this in the Prior Paying History section are some specific comments about the account, showing how often it has been past due.

✪ Credit Inquiries shows who has requested credit information about you and when the requests were made.

✪ Note there is a confirmation number on the online form that you can use in further correspondence.

Your Credit Report as of 04/09/2001

This Credit Report is available for you to view for 30 days. If you would like a current Credit Report, you may order another from MyEquifax.

Personal Data

John Q. Public
2351 N 85th Ave
Phoenix, AZ 85037

Social Security Number: 022-22-2222
Date of Birth: 1/11/1960

Previous Address(es):

133 Third Avenue
Phoenix, AZ 85037

Employment History

Cendant Hospitality FR

	Location: Phoenix,AZ	Employment Date: 2/1/1989	Verified Date: 1/3/2001

Previous Employment(s):

SOFTWARE Support Hospitality Franch

	Location: Atlanta, GA	Employment Date: 01/3/2001	Verified Date: 01/3/2001

Public Records

No bankruptcies on file
No liens on file
No judgements on file
No garnishments on file
No secured loans on file
No marital statuses on file
No financial counseling on file
No foreclosures on file
No non-responsibility entries on file

Collection Accounts

No collections on file.

Credit Information

Company Name	Account Number and Whose Acount	Date Opened	Last Activity	Type of Account and Status	High Credit	Items as of Date Reported Terms	Balance	Past Due	Date Reported
Americredit	40404XXXX			Installment					
Financial Services	JOINT ACCOUNT	03/1999	03/2000	REPOSSESION	$16933	$430	$9077	$128	2/2000

Prior Paying History

30 days past due 07 times; 60 days past due 05 times; 90+ days past due 03 times

INVOLUNTARY REPOSSESION AUTO

Company Name	Account Number and Whose Acount	Date Opened	Last Activity	Type of Account and Status	High Credit	Items as of Date Reported Terms	Balance	Past Due	Date Reported
Capital One	412174147128XXXX INDIVIDUAL ACCOUNT	10/1997	01/2001	Revolving PAYS AS AGREED	$777	15	$514		01/2001

Reprinted with permission from Equifax.

Prior Paying History

30 days past due 02 times; 60 days past due 1 times; 90+ days past due 00 times

CREDIT CARD

Desert Schools FCU	423325003406XXXX INDIVIDUAL ACCOUNT	07/1997 06/1998	Revolving PAYS AS AGREED	$500	$0		07/1999

Prior Paying History

30 days past due 02 times; 60 days past due 00 times; 90+ days past due 00 times

ACCOUNT PAID
CLOSED ACCOUNT

Heilig-Meyers Company	7360300XXXX INDIVIDUAL ACCOUNT	03/1998 07/1999	Revolving PAYS AS AGREED	$1000	$0		07/1999

Prior Paying History

30 days past due 02 times; 60 days past due 1 times; 90+ days past due 00 times

CREDIT CARD
AMOUNT IN H/C COLUMN IS CREDIT LIMIT

Sears	806050211XXXX INDIVIDUAL ACCOUNT	09/1998 07/1999	Revolving PAYS AS AGREED	$720	$0		07/1999

Prior Paying History

CHARGED
AMOUNT IN H/C COLUMN IS CREDIT LIMIT

Wells FARGO	503830276150XXXX INDIVIDUAL ACCOUNT	11/1996 12/2000	Installment PAYS AS AGREED	$17146	$401	$4058 12/2000	

Prior Paying History

AUTO

Credit Inquiries

Companies that Requested your Credit File

04/29/2001 EFX Credit Profile Online
06/30/2001 Automotive
06/16/2000 AR-Associates National Bank
01/18/2000 Desert Schools Federal C.U.
01/15/2000 Desert Schools Federal C.U.
07/02/1999 Time Life, Inc

THE FOLLOWING INQUIRIES ARE NOT REPORTED TO BUSINESSES:
PRM - This is a promotional inquiry in which only your name and address were given to a credit grantor so you could be solicited you with an offer such as a credit card. (PRM inquiries remain on file for 12 months.)
AM or AR - These inquiries indicate a periodic review of your credit history by one of your creditors (AM and AR inquiries remain on file for 12 months.)
EQUIFAX, ACIS or UPDATE - These inquiries indicate Equifax's activity in response to your contact with us for either a copy of your credit file or a request for research.
PRM, AM, AR, INQ, EQUIFAX, ACIS and UPDATE inquiries do not show on credit files that businesses receive, only on copies provided to you.

- Your confirmation number is **109933931**. **Please keep this number in your records for future communication with us.**

Equifax Consumer Services, Inc.

Experian   The Experian report is also very user-friendly. (see page 26.)

✪   The report starts with a list of negative items that are on your report, followed by positive items. Accounts without dashes are in good standing. Each account is listed by creditor name and the address is also given. Underneath the creditor's name and address and your account number, columns appear with these headings, which have the following meanings:

Status: This section shows the current status of the account and whether it is overdue, including the amount overdue and the date due.

Status Details: This section shows when (and if) the report will change to a positive status. It also can show how long the particular item will appear on the credit report.

Date opened/Reported since: These columns show the date the account was first opened and then give the date the last information about the account was reported.

Date of status/Last reported: These columns give the date the present status was reported and the last date any report was made.

Type/Terms/Monthly payment: These columns tell what kind of account it is. For *type* you will see installment or revolving. *Installment* means there are set monthly payments. *Revolving* means it is like a credit card where your amount due changes depending on how much you use it. For *terms*, the report will list how many months the loan is for. If it is revolving it will list "N/A." The monthly payment is the amount you are obligated to pay each month.

Responsibility: The next column indicates who is responsible for the account. If it just yours alone it is *individual.* If both you and your spouse are responsible it will say *joint.* Other possibilities include authorized user (if your spouse or someone else opens the account and authorizes you to have a credit card from it as well), cosigner, etc.

Credit limit/Original amount: Your *credit limit* is the total amount you are authorized to borrow at any given time. If this is a loan, it will instead list the original amount you borrowed.

High balance: The high balance shows the biggest amount you ever owed for one month.

Recent balance and Recent payment: The *recent balance* is the last amount reported that you owed. The *recent payment* indicates the last payment you made that was reported.

- ✪ The next section lists businesses who have requested information about you. The contact number for the business is given, as well as the date the request was made.

- ✪ You will next find a section that lists your personal information, name, current and past residences, Social Security number, date of birth, spouse's name, employer and other information. (page 7 of the samples.)

- ✪ The Personal Statements section displays any written statement you submitted. (See page 28 for information about doing this.)

- ✪ The report ends with contact information for Experian.

experían

Report Number

2818573907

Personal Credit Report from Experian for
John Q. Consumer

Report Date: 04/12/00

Index:
- <u>Potentially Negative Items</u>
- <u>Accounts in Good Standing</u>
- <u>Requests for Your Credit History</u>
- <u>Personal Information</u>
- <u>Your Personal Statement(s)</u>
- <u>Important Message Fom Experian</u>

Go Back

Potentially Negative Items   -   <u>back to top</u>

Credit Items

BNBUSA/COMPUSA

Address:	**Account Number:**
P O BOX 15519	7001306000461...
WILMINGTON, DE 19850	

Status:
open/past due 30 days. $20 past due as of 8-1998.

Status Details:
As of 6-2005, this account is scheduled to go to a positive status.

Date Opened:	**Type:**	**Credit Limit/Original Amount:**
10/1997	Revolving	$3000
Reported Since:	**Terms:**	**High Balance:**
10/1997	NA	$3193
Date of Status:	**Monthly Payment:**	**Recent Balance:**
08/1998	10	$0as of 08/30/1998
Last Reported:	**Responsibility:**	**Recent Payment:**
08/1998	Individual	3193

CHEVY CHASE FED SAV BANK

Address:	**Account Number:**
6202 PRESIDENTS COURT	5407301009607...
FREDERICK, MD 21701	

Status:
open/past due 60 days. $96 past due as of 8-1998.

Status Details:
As of 7-2005, this account is scheduled to go to a positive status.

Date Opened:	**Type:**	**Credit Limit/Original Amount:**
11/1995	Revolving	$1500
Reported Since:	**Terms:**	**High Balance:**
12/1995	NA	$1798
Date of Status:	**Monthly Payment:**	**Recent Balance:**
08/1998	131	$0 as of 08/15/1998
Last Reported:	**Responsibility:**	**Recent Payment:**
08/1998	Joint	1798

Reprinted with permission from Experian. This report format is subject to change.

CITIBANK PREFERRED VISA

Address:
P O BOX 6500
SIOUX FALLS, SD 57117

Account Number:
4271382104687...

Status:
account charged off/past due 150 days. $8,486 written off in 8-1998. $1,538 past due as of 8-1998.

Status Details:
This account is scheduled to continue on record until 1-2005.

Date Opened:
01/1997
Reported Since:
01/1997
Date of Status:
05/1998
Last Reported:
08/1998

Type:
Revolving
Terms:
NA
Monthly Payment:
0
Responsibility:
Individual

Credit Limit/Original Amount:
$8000
High Balance:
$8486
Recent Balance:
$0 as of 08/30/1998
Recent Payment:
8486

Account History:
Between 3-1998 and 4-1998, your credit limit/high balance was $8,000

Balance History:
$8337 04/1998
$8171 03/1998

Accounts in Good Standing   back to top

BB & B

Address:
2035 WEST 4TH STREET
TEMPE, AZ 85281

Account Number:
138300759...

Status:
open/never late.

Status Details:

Date Opened:
10/1997
Reported Since:
10/1997
Date of Status:
10/1997
Last Reported:
12/1997

Type:
Revolving
Terms:
NA
Monthly Payment:
0
Responsibility:
Individual

Credit Limit/Original Amount:
NA
High Balance:
$Unknown
Recent Balance:
$0/paid as of 12/1997
Recent Payment:
0

MACYS NJ NY

Address:
9111 DUKE BLVD
MASON, OH 45040

Account Number:
335646403...

Status:
closed/never late.

Status Details:
This account is scheduled to continue on record until 4-2005.

Date Opened:
09/1994
Reported Since:
02/1996
Date of Status:
04/1998
Last Reported:
04/1998

Type:
Revolving
Terms:
NA
Monthly Payment:
5
Responsibility:
Individual

Credit Limit/Original Amount:
$500
High Balance:
$75
Recent Balance:
$0 as of 04/1998
Recent Payment:
75

Creditor's statement regarding this item: Account closed at credit grantor's request.

Requests for Your Credit History   back to top

MBNA AMERICA/CREDIT

Address:
400 CHRISTIANA RD MS7009
NEWARK, DE 19713

Date of Request:
09/1998

CITIBANK

Address:
670 MASON RDGE CTR MS761
SAINT LOUIS, MO 63141

Date of Request:
03/1998

ADVANTA NATIONAL BANK
Address:
650 NAAMANS ROAD
CLAYMONT, DE 19703

Date of Request:
12/1997

PROVIDIAN BANCORP
Address:
PO BOX 9120
PLEASANTON, CA 94566

Date of Request:
05/1997

Personal Information   <u>back to top</u>

For your protection, the Social Security number you used to obtain this report is not displayed.

Names:
John Q. Consumer
Jonathon Q. Consumer
J.Q. Consumer

Social Security Number Variations:
999999999

Date of Birth:
09/03/1954

Spouse's First Name:
Jane

Employers:
DEBAJ ENGINEERING CORP

Address: 123 MAIN STREET
ANYTOWN, MD 90001-9999
Type of Residence: Multifamily
Geographical Code: 0-156510-31-8840

Address: 13415 BUCHANAN DR
FORT WASHINGTON, MD20744-2932
Type of Residence: Single family
Geographical Code: 0-176510-33-8840

Address: 8604 2ND AVE #163
SILVER SPRING, MD20910-3380
Type of Residence: Apartment complex
Geographical Code: 0-156510-31-8840

Notices:
This address is a non-residential address: 8604 2ND AVE SILVER SPRING MD 20910.
COMMERCIAL BUSINESS ADDRESS: 8604 2ND AVE, SILVER SPRING, MD, 20910.

Your Personal Statement(s)   <u>back to top</u>

There are no general personal statements currently displaying on your personal credit report

---

Important Message Fom Experian   <u>back to top</u>

Contacting Us   <u>back to top</u>

PO Box 9556
Allen, TX 75013
1-888-524-3390
Monday - Friday, 9:00am to 5:00pm in your time zone.

End of Report

Reprinted with permission from Experian. This report format is subject to change.

Trans Union　　The Trans Union report does not look very reader friendly at first glance. There are a lot of words and numbers crammed together on the pages. However, if you slow down and look at it carefully you will find that it really is fairly simple to read and understand.

- ✪　The beginning of the report lists your name and current address.

- ✪　Next it lists previous addresses and employment history.

- ✪　Under the line following these sections you will find public record information about yourself, which includes things like bankruptcies, judgments against you, tax liens and other recorded information. Each item listed contains a docket number, which refers to the case number the case was given in court. It indicates the court it is from and the type of recorded item. The plaintiff, or person who brought the case against you is listed, as well as his or her attorney. The date of the first entry of the judgment or record appears, followed by the total amount originally owed and if and when it was paid in full.

- ✪　The next section of the report deals with accounts that have negative information about you. The information that is considered negative is surrounded by brackets (><) so you can find it easily.

- ✪　Next you will see accounts you have with creditors. The accounts that are considered negative are listed first. All accounts are listed in the same way. The name of the creditor is set off to the left. Next to it is your account number and then a description of what kind of account it is. Negative accounts indicate what the status is with the account—whether it has gone to collection and what the payment status is. An account that is listed as "profit and loss writeoff" means that the creditor has stopped trying to collect the money and has written it off as a bad debt (giving them a tax deduction). The next line lists the date the account was last reported or updated and the balance on that date. To the right of this is the information as to who is responsible for the account, whether it is individual, joint, etc.

- ✪　The next line shows when the account was opened and the highest amount you ever owed at one time on the account. The payment terms are described next to this and a credit limit may be listed.

✪ The following line shows the status of the account on the last day it was reported. The following line gives some information about any late or overdue payments.

✪ After the listing of all of your accounts you will find a list of businesses who have received your report (including your request for a copy for yourself, indicated by "TU").

✪ The next section shows companies who received limited information about you to try to solicit you.

✪ The next section shows companies who obtained information to update your existing accounts or for other business transactions.

✪ The consumer statement section is the area where any statements you have submitted will appear. See page 33 for information about doing this.

✪ The special messages section includes information that verifies or comments on the items you submitted in your personal statement.

✪ The report ends with contact information for Trans Union.

✪ Following the report, you will find a page about your credit score. This page lists your credit score and shows the minimum and maximum possible. It lists some of the factors that have impacted your credit score.

✪ Next you will see a page with questions and answers about credit scores.

✪ The following two pages summarize the Fair Credit Reporting Act

✪ The last two pages of the report include the Request for Dispute Resolution. This is the form to use if you need to contact Trans Union about errors on your report. See page 37 for more information about reporting errors on your report.

If you are still unclear about anything on your own credit report, do not hesitate to call the company that prepared it. Credit reporting agencies are not your creditors and they will not harass you for money if you call them. Call and ask for an explanation of whatever you do not understand.

```
          P.O. BOX 99999                YOUR TRANS UNION FILE NUMBER: 999DE0062
          ANYTOWN, SD 88888             PAGE  1 OF  4
                                        DATE THIS REPORT PRINTED: 09/12/2001
          RETURN SERVICE REQUESTED
                                        SOCIAL SECURITY NUMBER: 987-65-4321
                                        BIRTH DATE:             12/1967
                                        YOU HAVE BEEN IN OUR FILES SINCE: 02/1980
                                        AKA: REPORT,MARY
                                        PHONE: 765-4321

CONSUMER REPORT FOR:


     ****
     REPORT, MARY, C
     1000 E NORTHFIELD AV APT 987
     STONY POINT, NY 10980


FORMER ADDRESSES REPORTED:

   6767 E HARRISON BLVD, SEATTLE, WA 98100
   1569 S FRANKLIN DR, OGUNQUIT, ME 03907

EMPLOYMENT DATA REPORTED:

   CNA INSURANCE                        BANK ONE
   DATE REPORTED: 05/1999               DATE VERIFIED: 10/1989
   POSITION: MANAGER


   STUDENT
   DATE REPORTED: 11/1978
```

YOUR CREDIT INFORMATION

THE FOLLOWING ITEMS OBTAINED FROM PUBLIC RECORDS APPEAR ON YOUR REPORT. YOU MAY
BE REQUIRED TO EXPLAIN PUBLIC RECORD ITEMS TO POTENTIAL CREDITORS. ANY BANK-
RUPTCY INFORMATION WILL REMAIN ON YOUR REPORT FOR 10 YEARS FROM THE DATE OF
FILING. UNPAID TAX LIENS MAY GENERALLY BE REPORTED FOR AN INDEFINITE PERIOD OF
TIME DEPENDING ON YOUR STATE OF RESIDENCE. PAID TAX LIENS MAY BE REPORTED FOR
7 YEARS FROM DATE OF PAYMENT. ALL OTHER PUBLIC RECORD INFORMATION, INCLUDING
DISCHARGED CHAPTER 13 BANKRUPTCY AND ANY ACCOUNTS CONTAINING ADVERSE
INFORMATION REMAIN FOR 7 YEARS. ALL OTHER PUBLIC RECORD INFORMATION INCLUDING
DISCHARGED CHAPTER 13 BANKRUPTCY, MAY BE REPORTED FOR 7 YEARS.

```
DOCKET #99922000250  DISTRICT COURT       PAID CIVIL JUDGMENT
PLAINTIFF:           KATE ASHLEY L MD PHD          ENTERED:  11/1996
PLAINTIFF ATTORNEY: HOWARD                         AMOUNT:       $873
                                                   PAID:     11/1999


DOCKET #99930900111  RECORDER OF DEEDS    RELEASE OF TAX LIEN
PLAINTIFF:           STATE OF CALIFORNIA           ENTERED:  08/1997
                                                   AMOUNT:      $5297
                                                   PAID:     05/2000
```

Reprinted with permission from Trans Union.

THE FOLLOWING ACCOUNTS CONTAIN INFORMATION WHICH SOME CREDITORS MAY CONSIDER TO
BE ADVERSE. ADVERSE ACCOUNT INFORMATION MAY GENERALLY BE REPORTED FOR 7 YEARS
FROM THE DATE OF THE FIRST DELINQUENCY, DEPENDING ON YOUR STATE OF RESIDENCE.
THE ADVERSE INFORMATION IN THESE ACCOUNTS HAS BEEN PRINTED IN >BRACKETS< FOR
YOUR CONVENIENCE, TO HELP YOU UNDERSTAND YOUR REPORT. THEY ARE NOT BRACKETED
THIS WAY FOR CREDITORS. (NOTE: THE ACCOUNT # MAY BE SCRAMBLED BY THE CREDITOR
FOR YOUR PROTECTION).

```
 CRSS CNTY BK              # 99911166622288800   REVOLVING ACCOUNT
>PROFIT AND LOSS WRITEOFF<                       CREDIT CARD
    VERIF'D  10/2000   BALANCE:      $2711       JOINT ACCOUNT
    OPENED   06/1996   MOST OWED:    $2711       CREDIT LIMIT:      $1500
    CLOSED   05/2000  >PAST DUE:      $586<
   >STATUS AS OF 05/2000: CHARGED OFF AS BAD DEBT<


>COLLECTION RECORD<
 SAVIT COLL               # 66633344400          COLLECTION ACCOUNT
>PAID COLLECTION<                                 COLLECTION AGENCY/ATTORNEY
    UPDATED  12/2000   BALANCE:        $0         INDIVIDUAL ACCOUNT
    PLACED   09/1998   MOST OWED:     $80         WESTFIELD ASSOC IN INT MED
    PAID OFF 12/2000
   >STATUS AS OF 12/2000: PAID COLLECTION<


 CRSS CNTY BK             # 67899933312398700    REVOLVING ACCOUNT
                                                 CREDIT CARD
    UPDATED  08/2001   BALANCE:       $575        JOINT ACCOUNT
    OPENED   03/1997   MOST OWED:     $948        PAY TERMS:  MINIMUM $35
                                                 CREDIT LIMIT:      $1200
   >STATUS AS OF 10/2000: 120 DAYS PAST DUE<
   >IN PRIOR 20 MONTHS FROM DATE PAID   1 TIME   90 DAYS,
      3 TIMES 60 DAYS,   4 TIMES 30 DAYS LATE<
   >MAXIMUM DELINQUENCY OF   90+ DAYS OCCURRED IN 10/2000<
```

THE FOLLOWING ACCOUNTS ARE REPORTED WITH NO ADVERSE INFORMATION

```
 CAPITAL 1 BK             # 12398725845644700    REVOLVING ACCOUNT
                                                 CREDIT CARD
    UPDATED  08/2001   BALANCE:       $102        INDIVIDUAL ACCOUNT
    OPENED   06/2001   MOST OWED:      $96        PAY TERMS:  MINIMUM $15
    STATUS AS OF 08/2001: PAID OR PAYING AS AGREED
    IN PRIOR  2 MONTHS FROM LAST UPDATE NEVER LATE

 MITSUBISHI               # 011155761200         INSTALLMENT ACCOUNT
                                                 AUTO LEASE
    UPDATED  08/2001   BALANCE:     $19352        JOINT ACCOUNT
    OPENED   09/2000   MOST OWED:   $25790        PAY TERMS: 48 MONTHLY $537
    STATUS AS OF 08/2001: PAID OR PAYING AS AGREED
    IN PRIOR 11 MONTHS FROM LAST UPDATE NEVER LATE
```

```
REPORT ON REPORT, MARY, C                                    PAGE  3 OF  4
SOCIAL SECURITY NUMBER: 987-65-4321   TRANS UNION FILE NUMBER: 999DE0062
```

THE FOLLOWING COMPANIES HAVE RECEIVED YOUR CREDIT REPORT. THEIR INQUIRIES
REMAIN ON YOUR CREDIT REPORT FOR TWO YEARS. (NOTE: "TU CONSUMER DISCLOSURE"
INQUIRIES ARE NOT VIEWED BY CREDITORS).

```
INQUIRY TYPE   DATE          SUBSCRIBER NAME
INDIVIDUAL     09/11/2001    F.MAC/COUNTRYWIDE FUND
PARTICIPANT    09/10/2001    COUNTRYWIDE VIA LANDSAFE CREDIT
   PERMISSIBLE PURPOSE = CREDIT TRANSACTION
INDIVIDUAL     08/03/2001    TU CONSUMER DISCLOSURE
JOINT          07/13/2001    224 FLEET MORTGAGE VIA CBC COMPANIES
   PERMISSIBLE PURPOSE = CREDIT TRANSACTION
INDIVIDUAL     06/20/2001    CAPITAL ONE BANK
INDIVIDUAL     06/12/2001    PLAZA ASSOCIATES
JOINT          03/05/2001    3103 PAYLESS MORTGAG VIA CREDIT LENDERS SVC AGEN
   PERMISSIBLE PURPOSE = CREDIT TRANSACTION
PARTICIPANT    01/16/2001    COLUMBIA EQUITIES  L VIA AUTOMATED INFORMATION S
   PERMISSIBLE PURPOSE = CREDIT TRANSACTION
```

THE COMPANIES LISTED BELOW RECEIVED YOUR NAME, ADDRESS AND OTHER LIMITED
INFORMATION ABOUT YOU SO THEY COULD MAKE A FIRM OFFER OF CREDIT OR INSURANCE.
THEY DID NOT RECEIVE YOUR FULL CREDIT REPORT, AND THESE INQUIRIES ARE NOT SEEN
BY ANYONE BUT YOU.

```
DATE       SUBSCRIBER NAME          DATE       SUBSCRIBER NAME
07/2001    UNITED READERS SERVICE   07/2001    FIRST CONSUMERS NATIONAL
06/2001    FULL SPECTRUM LENDING    04/2001    PROVIDIAN BANCORP
```

THE COMPANIES LISTED BELOW OBTAINED INFORMATION FROM YOUR CONSUMER REPORT FOR
THE PURPOSE OF AN ACCOUNT REVIEW OR OTHER BUSINESS TRANSACTION WITH YOU. THESE
INQUIRIES ARE NOT DISPLAYED TO ANYONE BUT YOU AND WILL NOT AFFECT ANY
CREDITOR'S DECISION OR ANY SCORE.

```
DATE       SUBSCRIBER NAME
02/2001    NTL CITY BK
11/2000    NTL CITY BK
09/1999    SEARS
```

CONSUMER STATEMENT:
     #HK# ID FRAUD VICTIM ALERT: FRAUDULENT APPLICATIONS MAY BE SUBMITTED
     IN MY NAME USING CORRECT PERSONAL INFORMATION. DO NOT EXTEND
     CREDIT WITHOUT FIRST CONTACTING ME PERSONALLY AND VERIFYING ALL
     APPLICATION INFORMATION AT HOME (555) 123-4567. DATE REPORTED
     02/01.

SPECIAL MESSAGES:
     CONSUMER STATEMENT ON FILE RELATES TO TRUE NAME FRAUD OR CREDIT FRAUD

IF YOU BELIEVE ANY OF THE INFORMATION IN YOUR CREDIT REPORT IS INCORRECT,
PLEASE LET US KNOW. FOR YOUR CONVENIENCE, AN INVESTIGATION FORM IS INCLUDED.
PLEASE COMPLETE IT AND MAIL TO:

TRANS UNION CONSUMER RELATIONS
P.O. BOX 99999
ANYTOWN, SD 88888

1-800-800-0000
OUR BUSINESS HOURS IN YOUR TIME ZONE ARE:
8:30 A.M. TO 4:30 P.M. EXCEPT MAJOR HOLIDAYS.
MONDAY THRU FRIDAY

FOR ADDITIONAL CONSUMER INFORMATION OR TO DISPUTE YOUR CREDIT REPORT ONLINE
VISIT THE PERSONAL SOLUTIONS PAGE AT WWW.TRANSUNION.COM

Trans Union
Consumer Credit Score

Name: REPORT, MARY, C
Address: 1000 E NORTHFIELD AV APT 987
STONY POINT, NY 10927

File Number: 999DE0062
Date of Credit Score: 09/12/2001

About your credit score:

A credit score is a computer generated mathematical calculation of the information which appears in a credit report. It represents your credit worthiness as a number or a numerical value. The credit score is based on data about your credit history and payment behavior. Credit scores are used to assist a lender in determining the level of risk associated with granting you a loan, credit limit, and / or rate of interest. Credit scores can change over time, depending on how your credit history and payment behavior changes and how well you manage your credit obligations.

Since, the credit score is based on information in your credit history, it is important that you review the credit report that is being furnished with this document to make sure it is complete and accurate.

The credit score, displayed below, is created by Trans Union. A higher credit score means a lower likelihood of delinquency in the next two years on a new account. The credit score is presented with up to four key factors. These factors will print in the order of importance as to the reasons your credit score is not higher.

Please note that this credit score may be different than a credit score used by a lending institution. The credit industry uses many different types of credit scores. For more information, visit www.transunion.com.

Your credit score: +559	Minimum possible score: +150	Maximum possible score: +934

Factor 1: Number of delinquent accounts is too high in proportion to total number of accounts:
Your credit report reflects too many accounts with delinquent payment history compared to the total number of accounts on your report.

Factor 2: Too many active accounts with a balance:
Your credit report reflects several accounts with balances, which has a negative impact on your credit score.

Factor 3: Too many derogatory accounts or public records:
Your credit report reflects one or more accounts with a derogatory payment rating or a public record such as a civil judgement, bankruptcy or tax lien.

Factor 4: Too many inquiries:
Excessive inquiries on the credit report have a negative impact on your credit score. Limiting the number of credit applications you complete may improve your credit score.

Credit Scoring Questions and Answers:

- **How are Credit Scores used?**

A Credit Score is one of the primary tools a lender uses when determining whether or not to grant you credit and if so, how much credit and at what interest rate. Lenders also typically consider other information in addition to your credit report, such as income, employment, or their previous credit experience with you. Taken together, this factual information provides credit grantors with a fair representation of the risk in lending money to you.

- **Does every consumer have a Credit Score?**

No. For a score to be calculated, your credit report must contain at least one account which is commonly referred to as a trade line. If this information is missing, then Trans Union cannot accurately report a score. In addition, a credit score will not be calculated if one or more of the following has occurred; a trade line has a notation which references a person associated with the account as deceased or the social security number on the credit report is a match on the Social Security Administration's "Death Claim Index".

- **How is my Credit Score calculated?**

The Trans Union credit scoring model is based on many interrelated characteristics of credit information. Numerical weights are placed on different aspects of your credit report and a mathematical formula is used to arrive at a final credit score. There are many different credit score models used in the credit industry which consider different variables for different types of credit. The credit score characteristics may be generally summarized in to six categories:

Maintaining Credit — considers how you are paying your accounts.
Total Balances — considers how much money you currently owe.
Credit Experience — considers how long your accounts have been open.
Credit Mix — considers the different types of credit you use.
Utilization of Credit — considers the amount of credit you use in relation to the amount you have available.
Credit Applications — considers how often and how recently you have applied for credit.

- **How often does my Credit Score change?**

Your credit file is continually updated with new information from your creditors. The Trans Union credit score is calculated based on the current information contained in the credit file at the time the credit score is requested. Therefore, every time a credit file is requested, the credit score may be different because the information in your credit report continually changes.

- **How do inquiries impact my Credit Score?**

A common misperception is that inquiries will always negatively impact a credit score. Typically, the presence of inquiries on the credit file has only a small impact on the credit score. Inquiries have less impact than delinquencies, balances owed, and the length of time you have used credit. Inquiries will usually have a larger impact on the credit score for consumers who have a limited credit history.

- **How can I improve my Credit Score?**

First, it is important to review your credit report for accuracy. In addition, maintaining a good credit standing and continuing to exhibit responsible credit behavior are the most effective means of presenting a positive picture of your credit worthiness. Improving one's credit standing or credit score is not a one time only fix, but more of a change in how you view and handle credit over time.

For more information on credit scoring, visit our website at www.transunion.com

Reprinted with permission from Trans Union.

A Summary of Your Rights Under the Fair Credit Reporting Act

The federal Fair Credit Reporting Act (FCRA) is designed to promote accuracy, fairness, and privacy of information in the files of every "consumer reporting agency" (CRA). Most CRAs are credit bureaus that gather and sell information about you -- such as if you pay your bills on time or have filed bankruptcy -- to creditors, employers, landlords, and other businesses. You can find the complete text of the FCRA, 15 U.S.C.§§1681-1681u, at the Federal Trade Commission's web site *(http://www.ftc.gov)* The FCRA gives you specific rights, as outlined below. You may have additional rights under state law. You may contact a state or local consumer protection agency or a state attorney general to learn those rights.

- ◆ **You must be told if information in your file has been used against you.** Anyone who uses information from a CRA to take action against you -- such as denying an application for credit, insurance, or employment -- must tell you, and give you the name, address, and phone number of the CRA that provided the consumer report.

- ◆ **You can find out what is in your file.** At your request, a CRA must give you the information in your file, and a list of everyone who has requested it recently. There is no charge for the report if a person has taken action against you because of information supplied by the CRA, if you request the report within 60 days of receiving notice of the action. You also are entitled to one free report every twelve months upon request if you certify that (1) you are unemployed and plan to seek employment within 60 days, (2) you are on welfare, or (3) your report is inaccurate due to fraud. Otherwise, a CRA may charge you up to eight dollars and fifty cents ($8.50).

- ◆ **You can dispute inaccurate information with the CRA.** If you tell a CRA that your file contains inaccurate information, the CRA must investigate the items (usually within 30 days) by presenting to its information source all relevant evidence you submit, unless your dispute is frivolous. The source must review your evidence and report its findings to the CRA. (The source also must advise national CRAs -- to which it has provided the data -- of any error.) The CRA must give you a written report of the investigation, and a copy of your report if the investigation results in any change. If the CRA's investigation does not resolve the dispute, you may add a brief statement to your file. The CRA must normally include a summary of your statement in future reports. If an item is deleted or a dispute statement is filed, you may ask that anyone who has recently received your report be notified of the change.

- ◆ **Inaccurate information must be corrected or deleted.** A CRA must remove or correct inaccurate or unverified information from its files, usually within 30 days after you dispute it. **However, the CRA is not required to remove accurate data from your file unless it is outdated (as described below) or cannot be verified.** If your dispute results in any change to your report, the CRA cannot reinsert into your file a disputed item unless the information source verifies its accuracy and completeness. In addition, the CRA must give you a written notice telling you it has reinserted the item. The notice must include the name, address and phone number of the information source.

- ◆ **You can dispute inaccurate items with the source of the information.** If you tell anyone -- such as a creditor who reports to a CRA -- that you dispute an item, they may not then report the information to a CRA without including a notice of your dispute. In addition, once you've notified the source of the error in writing, it may not continue to report the information if it is, in fact, an error.

- **Outdated information may not be reported.** In most cases, a CRA may not report negative information that is more than seven years old; ten years for bankruptcies.

- **Access to your file is limited.** A CRA may provide information about you only to people with a need recognized by the FCRA -- usually to consider an application with a creditor, insurer, employer, landlord, or other business.

- **Your consent is required for reports that are provided to employers, or reports that contain medical information.** A CRA may not give out information about you to your employer, or prospective employer, without your written consent. A CRA may not report medical information about you to creditors, insurers, or employers without your permission.

- **You may choose to exclude your name from CRA lists for unsolicited credit and insurance offers.** Creditors and insurers may use file information as the basis for sending you unsolicited offers of credit or insurance. Such offers must include a toll-free phone number for you to call if you want your name and address removed from future lists. If you call, you must be kept off the lists for two years. If you request, complete, and return the CRA form provided for this purpose, you must be taken off the lists indefinitely.

- **You may seek damages from violators.** If a CRA, a user or (in some cases) a provider of CRA data, violates the FCRA, you may sue them in state or federal court.

The FCRA gives several different federal agencies authority to enforce the FCRA:

FOR QUESTIONS OR CONCERNS REGARDING:	PLEASE CONTACT:
CRAs, creditors and others not listed below	Federal Trade Commission Consumer Response Center - FCRA Washington, DC 20580 *1-877-FTC-HELP
National banks, federal branches/agencies of foreign banks (word "National" or initials "N.A." appear in or after bank's name)	Office of the Comptroller of the Currency Compliance Management, Mail Stop 6-6 Washington, DC 20219 *800-613-6743
Federal Reserve System member banks (except national banks, and federal branches/agencies of foreign banks)	Federal Reserve Board Division of Consumer & Community Affairs Washington, DC 20551 *202-452-3693
Savings associations and federally chartered savings banks (word "Federal" or initials "F.S.B." appear in federal institution's name)	Office of Thrift Supervision Consumer Programs Washington, DC 20552 *800-842-6929
Federal credit unions (words "Federal Credit Union" appear in institution's name)	National Credit Union Administration 1775 Duke Street Alexandria, VA 22314 *703-518-6360
State-chartered banks that are not members of the Federal Reserve System	Federal Deposit Insurance Corporation Division of Compliance & Consumer Affairs Washington, DC 20429 *800-934-FDIC
Air, surface, or rail common carriers regulated by former Civil Aeronautics Board or Interstate Commerce Commission	Department of Transportation Office of Financial Management Washington, DC 20590 *202-366-1306
Activities subject to the Packers and Stockyards Act, 1921	Department of Agriculture Office of Deputy Administrator - GIPSA Washington, DC 20250 *202-720-7051

Reprinted with permission from Trans Union.

Request for Dispute Resolution

File Number: **99DE0062-001**

To dispute information on your credit report, **please complete this form and return it** to Trans Union Consumer Relations.

1 If any of this information in the box on the left is incorrect or incomplete, write the corrections in the boxes on the right.

Name: **REPORT, MARY, C** **Other Names(s):** **REPORT, MARY** **Address:** **1000 E NORTHFIELD AV APT 987** **STONY POINT, NY 10980** **Social Security Number:** **987-65-4321** **Date of Birth:** **12/1967** **Driver's License Number:** **Telephone Number(s):** **765-4321** **Employer:** **CNA INSURANCE**	**Name:** **Other Name(s):** **Address:** **Social Security Number:** **Date of Birth:** **Driver's License Number:** **Telephone Number(s):** **Employer:**

2 Tell us what you disagree with on your credit report. Use the additional space on the back of this form if necessary.

Company Name:		Company Name:	
Account #:		**Account #:**	

The reason I disagree:
- ▨ This is not my account
- ▨ I have never paid late
- ▨ This account is in bankruptcy
- ▨ This account is closed
- ▨ I have paid this account in full
- ▨ I paid this before it went to collection or before it was charged off
- ▨ Other

The reason I disagree:
- ▨ This is not my account
- ▨ I have never paid late
- ▨ This account is in bankruptcy
- ▨ This account is closed
- ▨ I have paid this account in full
- ▨ I paid this before it went to collection or before it was charged off
- ▨ Other

3 Return this form to:

> **TRANS UNION CONSUMER RELATIONS**
> **P.O. BOX 99999**
> **ANYTOWN, SD 88888**

Signature:

Upon receipt of your request for dispute resolution, an investigation will be initiated and completed within 30 days. Upon completion, you will receive written notice of the results of our investigation. We recommend that you do not apply for credit while your request for resolution is pending.

Reprinted with permission from Trans Union.

File Number: **99DE0062-001**

Additional space for 2 Tell us what you disagree with on your credit report.

Company Name:	

Account #:	

The reason I disagree:
☐ This is not my account
☐ I have never paid late
☐ This account is in bankruptcy
☐ This account is closed
☐ I have paid this account in full
☐ I paid this before it went to collection or before it was charged off
☐ Other

Company Name:	

Account #:	

The reason I disagree:
☐ This is not my account
☐ I have never paid late
☐ This account is in bankruptcy
☐ This account is closed
☐ I have paid this account in full
☐ I paid this before it went to collection or before it was charged off
☐ Other

Company Name:	

Account #:	

The reason I disagree:
☐ This is not my account
☐ I have never paid late
☐ This account is in bankruptcy
☐ This account is closed
☐ I have paid this account in full
☐ I paid this before it went to collection or before it was charged off
☐ Other

Company Name:	

Account #:	

The reason I disagree:
☐ This is not my account
☐ I have never paid late
☐ This account is in bankruptcy
☐ This account is closed
☐ I have paid this account in full
☐ I paid this before it went to collection or before it was charged off
☐ Other

4   Optional: Write any additional comments. For example, tell us if you have any corrections to your previous address or previous employer.

Additional Comments:
_____
_____
_____

To investigate your request, we will contact the source of the disputed inforatmion. Each source will be told the nature of your dispute and will be asked to verify the accuracy and/or completeness of the inforamtion they reported.

Side 2

Reprinted with permission from Trans Union.

Your Spouse and Your Report You and your spouse are considered to be two separate entities as far as credit goes. However, you have the right to have each other's credit information appear on each other's reports. This may be a good idea if one of you has poor credit and the other has terrific credit. Use **Letter Requesting Merger of Spouse's Report** to request that an agency do this. (see form 7, p.182.) You also have the right to have each other's negative reports removed from each other's files. If your spouse has terrible credit and it shows up on your report, you need to request that it be removed from yours. Then you can use your good credit to apply for loans and credit cards that can benefit you both. Use **Letter Requesting Individualization of Credit Report**. (see form 8, p.183.)

What Makes a Good Credit Report

In general, the following factors make for a good credit report:

- ✪ no more than eleven accounts, open or closed, on the report;

- ✪ no more than one change of address on the report;

- ✪ steady employment;

- ✪ regular payments;

- ✪ no overdue payments, no defaults, no foreclosure, no late fees;

- ✪ low balances; and,

- ✪ a credit score of at least 680.

The following things make financial sense, but in fact can look bad on a credit report.

- ✪ Opening accounts to get special offers (for example, 15% off your purchases with a new account) and then closing them after paying the balance. While this is a deal, it increases the number of accounts on your credit report and in fact looks bad for the consumer.

✪ Using a credit card for a lot of purchases to take advantage of convenience and the thrity day grace period and then paying off the balance each month. While this offers convenience and doesn't cost you any interest, future creditors who get your report will only see the current balance on the account and will not realize you pay it off each month. This will appear as a large balance.

✪ Consolidating student loans. While this may get you a better interest rate and offer the convenience of one payment per month, it increases the number of accounts on your report. The more accounts you have, the lower your credit score.

NOTE: *Taking special offers, paying your balance in full every month, and consolidating loans have advantages that more often outweigh the disadvantages. However, you should be aware of the effect they have on your credit report.*

3

CHANGING YOUR CREDIT REPORT

Now that you have learned what a credit report contains and how to obtain yours, read and understand it, you need to look yours over very closely. Organize all of your debt information that you used to complete the Debt Assessment worksheet in Chapter 1. (see form 1, p.176.) Compare your information to the information on your three separate credit reports. Check everything, from account numbers to high balances to payment dates. To compare some of this information you are going to have to sort through some of your old records. If the items on the report are favorable, do not worry too much about cross-checking them (unless they are accounts that are closed, but are not listed as closed). If they are negative, you should examine them very closely for errors.

Disputing Bills

While this chapter is primarily about how to change your credit report, it is important to understand how to deal with incorrect charges on credit cards and other bills. Resolving these problems before they affect your credit card is the simplest and best way to maintain good credit.

Credit Cards   If you find an error on a current credit card bill (not credit reports, but an actual bill from one of your credit cards), you need to:

- ✪ contact your credit card company directly. (Credit reporting agencies do not handle these disputes.) and

- ✪ send a **LETTER TO CREDITOR REGARDING BILLING ERROR**. (see form 9, p.184.)

A phone call is not the way to handle this. You need to put it in writing for the Fair Credit Billing Act to cover you on this situation. You must send the letter within *sixty (60) days of the date of the bill* and send it certified mail, return receipt requested. The creditor has thirty (30) days to acknowledge receipt of your letter.

You may withhold payment for a disputed item on the credit card bill (not the whole credit card bill—just the item you are disputing) if:

- ✪ the charge is over $50 and

- ✪ the store is within one hundred miles of your residence or is in your state.

Before you do so, you must:

- ✪ first attempt to resolve the billing dispute with the store the item is from and

- ✪ inform the credit card company in writing about the dispute.

The credit card company cannot report your account as delinquent while the dispute is being handled and they must resolve it within two billing cycles (or ninety days).

Other Bills   You should always check other bills for errors as well. Make sure you are being charged for services or goods you used or purchased. If you find an error on a bill, it is ok to call about it, but always follow this phone call up with a letter to document the problem and your telephone call that reported it.

NOTE: *Remember to send all correspondence to the address for customer service and not to the address for making payments—call and ask for this address if you cannot find it on your bill.*

Correcting Your Credit Report

After obtaining a copy of your credit report, as described in Chapter 2, you need to check it carefully for errors, out of date information, and items that are misleading. Errors are not at all uncommon on credit reports, so do not assume that yours is correct without completely checking it over.

If you have identified any items on your credit report that you believe are out of date or wrong, you have the right to dispute them under the Fair Credit Reporting Act. You are permitted to dispute any items you reasonably believe to be wrong or incomplete. To dispute an item, you need to send a letter to the credit agency, via certified mail.

NOTE: *Remember to keep a log of all correspondence and phone calls. (see form 6, p.181.)*

Often, credit reporting agencies enclose a form called a *Request for Reinvestigation* with your credit report. Trans Union uses a form called *Request for Dispute Resolution* (see page 37), which it encloses with its credit reports. To complete the Trans Union form, fill in the boxes next to your name and personal information only if the information listed is incorrect. Fill in part 2 with the name of the creditor, your account number and an indication of what is wrong in the report. You can fill in part 4 to further explain the problem. Note that this is NOT how to submit a personal statement (also called a 100 word statement). See page 193 for information about this.

You can use the provided form to list the items you are disputing or you can send a letter such as **LETTER DISPUTING CREDIT REPORT**. (see form 10, p.185.) It is best to not dispute more than three items in one letter. If you wish to dispute more then three items, use separate letters for each group of three. A long list of disputes can indicate to the agency that you are not serious and are disputing everything just to make trouble. Include copies of any documents that support your position, such as letters confirming an account has been paid off or closed.

Generally, the agency has thirty days to contact you after receiving your letter. When you send your letter or form, be sure to include any copies of documents that support your argument. There is no cost to you at all to dispute your credit report. This is your legal right, so do not be afraid to exercise it!

If you do not hear back from the agency within thirty days, send **SECOND REQUEST FOR REINVESTIGATION**. (see form 11, p.186.) Once the agency receives your request, it has thirty days to reinvestigate the items you are disputing. If you provide the agency with information about the item, then the agency has fifteen extra days to investigate, a total of forty-five days.

The agency is required to contact the creditor whose item you are disputing and consider information and documentation from you. Once all of the facts have been reviewed, the agency must:

✪ give you the results of the reinvestigation within five days of the completion;

✪ remove the item you are disputing if you are correct or if it is unverifiable (most creditors destroy records after twenty-five months, so it is very possible that the item you are disputing can no longer be verified);

✪ ensure that an item that was corrected does not incorrectly reappear on your report; and,

✪ provide you with a copy of your corrected report.

If the agency determines that the item you are disputing is correct and that you are wrong, then it will remain on the report.

If your report is corrected, the agency must send a copy of the corrected report to any creditors who have requested your report in the last year and to any employer who has requested it in the last two years.

Wait a few months after your credit report has been corrected and then request a copy of it. Verify that the error was corrected and has not reappeared. If it has reappeared (and this does happen), send a letter indicating this to the credit reporting agency and detail the history of the matter. Use **LETTER REQUESTING CORRECTION OF REAPPEARING INCORRECT ITEM**. (see form 12, p.187.)

Disputing after Reinvestigation

If the credit agency determines that it believes an item you are disputing is in fact correct, it will not remove the item. If you still believe that the item is wrong, there are further steps you can take to attempt to have it removed.

First, contact the creditor the item is from. Do so in writing, using **LETTER TO CREDITOR REGARDING INCORRECT CREDIT REPORT**. (see form 13, p.188.) Send this letter to the customer service department. You can also send this letter to the director of marketing and to the president or CEO of the company if you wish. Send a copy of the letter to the credit reporting agency as well. Follow your letter up with phone calls or in-person visits to the customer service office.

You are not asking a favor of the creditor, you are demanding that they follow the Fair Credit Reporting Act (FCRA), which requires them to provide credit reporting agencies with correct information when it is brought to their attention that they have reported incorrect information. Insist that the law be followed. (FCRA, Secs. 1681(c) and (n).)

Get any correction from the creditor in writing and send it yourself to the credit reporting agency. Do not rely on the creditor to send this information in. Send it with **LETTER SHOWING CREDITOR ERROR**. (see form 14, p.189.)

If the creditor is not willing to discuss or deal with your problem, then you should contact a credit reporting agency and ask that they handle this dispute. They have a customer service department that is paid to assist consumers in resolving disputes. If you still get nowhere, you need to hire an attorney to bring a lawsuit. You can also contact your state attorney general's office.

If you are disputing a listing on your credit report of a judgment against you that you have paid in full, you will need to obtain a discharge of the judgment from the creditor who sued you. Use the **LETTER REQUESTING DISCHARGE**, and mail it to the creditor. (see form 15, p.190.) Once you receive the discharge, file it with the court your case was decided in and also send a copy of it to each of the credit reporting agencies and request that they remove the judgment from your report.

Adding Accounts to Your Credit Report

When you reviewed your credit reports, you may have found that you have accounts that were not listed on the report. If you are trying to build a positive credit report, you may wish to ask the credit reporting agencies to include these accounts on your report. To do so, send **LETTER REQUESTING INCLUSION OF ACCOUNTS** to the credit reporting agency along with copies of recent statements of the accounts you want included. (see form 16, p.191.) You can be charged a fee for this and nothing requires the agencies to honor your request to include the accounts.

You may also wish to contact the creditor directly and ask that they report the information to the credit reporting agencies.

If your credit report is missing personal information about you, you should send **LETTER REQUESTING ADDITION OF INFORMATION**. (see form 17, p.192.) You may wish to ask that updated information about your employment, past and present residences, phone number, date of birth, Social Security number, bank accounts and investments be included. This type of information can show stability and improve your credit rating. The agencies are not required to add any of this information, but often will do so at your request. You should enclose something to verify the information you are giving, such as a copy of your driver's license, Social Security card, etc.

Adding a Statement to Your Credit Report

You have the right to add a 100 word statement to your credit report to explain something in your report or to point out an error the credit agency will not correct. Understand that although the agency must accept such a statement from you, it is not required to include the entire thing and may include only a summary of what you have written. It is important to understand that creditors often will ignore this type of statement and that the statement may end up remaining in your file even after the item you are explaining or disputing is removed.

This kind of statement can be useful if you have had temporary financial problems due to losing your job, being ill or caring for an ill family member. Make it short and sweet, and be sure to include good news—that your financial situation has improved because you found a job, recovered, or are no longer caring for the ill family member.

Use **LETTER WITH 100 WORD STATEMENT**, to submit this type of statement to the agency. (see form 18, p.193.) Be sure you only send it to the agency that is reporting the item you wish to explain or dispute.

Suing a Credit Agency

Sometimes you may request reinvestigation of an incorrect item and the credit agency fails to reinvestigate or leaves the incorrect item on your report despite a reinvestigation that showed it to be incorrect. If you are seriously harmed because of it (for example, you were denied a mortgage or were not hired for a job because of it), the Fair Credit Reporting Act gives you the right to sue the credit agency.

You have two years after you are harmed by a credit agency's willful or negligent failure to comply with the law to file a lawsuit against them. Your lawsuit can ask for expenses you have incurred because of the error, such as lost wages, attorney's fees, court costs, etc., as well as emotional distress you have suffered. You can also sue for punitive damages for malicious acts by the agency against you.

You may also sue a credit reporting agency that refuses to disclose your credit information to you or that gives false information about you. Another possible lawsuit can be based on a credit reporting agency breaking the rules about who they may give your credit report to. You may also sue a creditor who fails to correct billing errors. (FCRA, Sec. 1681(n).)

The laws we have been discussing are federal laws. Many states have their own laws about creditors and credit reporting agencies. You can also bring a lawsuit under your state law if you meet the requirements set forth in the law.

You will need to consult an attorney who is experienced in this area of law. Contact your local county, city, or state bar association for the name of an attorney experienced in these matters in your local area. Many attorneys will handle these types of cases with little or no cash up front and will take a percent of what you win (called a *contingency*).

Organizing Your Correspondence

It is important to keep copies of all of your correspondence and notes of all phone calls. Get an expandable divided file folder and keep a section for each creditor, credit agency, or collection agency you deal with. Place a copy of all correspondence you send and all correspondence you receive in the folder.

You also need to keep a **CORRESPONDENCE LOG**. (see form 6, p.181.) Fill out a section of this log each time you receive or send correspondence or have a phone call with a creditor, collection agency, credit reporting agency, attorney, etc. Recording this information makes it easy to determine the status of something and helps you follow up with creditors and credit reporting agencies.

4 REDUCING YOUR DEBT AND IMPROVING CASH FLOW

If you find yourself with more debt than you can handle, the simplest solution is to reduce the amount of debt you are facing. Easier said than done because you do not have enough money to pay your bills. However, there are steps you can take to reduce your debt load that you may not be aware of. Reducing your debt will not only get you out of financial trouble, but also will improve your credit report, particularly if it means you will be able to make payments on time for all or most of your obligations.

Prioritizing Your Debts

The first thing you need to do is get out your **DEBT ASSESSMENT** (form 1) and look closely at the obligations listed there. Fill out the **DEBT PRIORITIZATION**. (see form 19, p.194.) You need to list your debts in order of importance on this form. *Importance* is not determined by who is bothering you the most with calls or letters (and if this is a problem, read the section in Chapter 1 about your rights as a debtor). Importance is determined by what debt will most negatively impact your life the fastest. You need to think about what effect nonpayment will have on you and you also have to consider how easy it is for the creditor to stop its service or take back the property.

For example, if you are three months behind on your electric bill, it is likely that the electric company will soon turn off your power unless you get them some money. If you are two months behind on your mortgage, the bank's computers will not be happy with you, but because foreclosure is an expensive process, the bank is probably not ready to foreclose yet. If you do not pay your doctor, he or she will eventually refuse to see you and eventually may sue you, but you can find another doctor if necessary. Your credit cards are probably at the bottom of your list based on importance. Credit card companies make a lot of noise when they are not paid, but the only thing they can do to you is obtain a judgment in court. This is a process that takes time and is a hassle for them.

Dealing with Your Creditors

When you are dealing with creditors, you will need to keep very good records. Create a log and write in dates, times and contact people for phone calls, as well as the status and any details. Include any written correspondence in the log with the same information recorded. (see form 6, p.181.) This way you will have a record of what is going on and can easily find when your last contact was and what the result of it was.

Prioritize   Start at the top of your list of priorities on your **DEBT PRIORITIZATION** and list how much you have to pay the creditor to keep yourself out of immediate hot water. The electric company may be happy if you pay one month's bill. The bank may be willing to accept 60% of your monthly mortgage payment for a few months. You may not know how much is necessary until you begin to negotiate with the creditor.

Be Aggressive   Many people just want to run and hide from creditors and send in money when they can, hoping it will take care of the problem. The best solution is to be aggressive. If you are not going to be able to make a payment, call *before* it is due. If you are already past due, still call.

Call the creditor and tell the representative that you are having money problems. Give the real reason, such as you were laid off from work or are getting a divorce, etc. You should not give them the real reason if it is something like you went on a spending spree or you decided to just take the summer off. You want to appear like a reliable person who has fallen on hard times. Creditors are often sympathetic to consumers with real problems and you may be pleasantly surprised by the reaction you receive.

Arrange a Payment Plan

When you call, be polite, calm, and firm. Explain that you want to make a payment arrangement. Tell them what you can afford to pay this month and what you can afford to pay next month. Be clear that you intend to make payment in full eventually, even if this is not the case.

You can also consider extending your payment plan with smaller payments or arranging to defer payment for one month. Get all payment plans in writing. Use **LETTER REQUESTING PAYMENT PLAN** to request a payment plan in writing. (see form 25, p.204.)

Set Your Bottom Line

Before you call a creditor, you need to keep in mind exactly how much you can afford to pay. Do not agree to pay more than this amount no matter what. It may take you several phone calls to get the creditor to agree to a reduced payment. If you are told no, keep calling until you get a different answer. Ask to speak to a supervisor if you cannot make headway with the representative. Explain that you want to arrange a payment plan in exchange for the creditor removing negative references on your credit report. One such plan would be that you agree to a certain amount and if you make the payments for three months the creditor will change the account status to a neutral status and then if you continue to pay for another three months, to change it to a positive status.

Most creditors are going to agree to accept partial payments from you. Some money is better than no money in their eyes. But you have to be willing to go to them, ask for this type of arrangement, and stand your ground. Most creditors will find this type of arrangement easier and cheaper than repossessing the item or obtaining a judgment against you.

Negotiate

Here are some specific negotiation strategies to try with certain types of debts:

Rent. Negotiate with your landlord to miss a payment and make it up at the end of the lease. Consider asking for a reduction in your rent amount. Try offering to do repairs to the unit in exchange for a rent reduction. Consider taking on a roommate (you will need your landlord's permission for this) who will pay a portion of the rent. Consider subletting the unit and living in a less expensive one.

Mortgage. Explain that you will be paying late and ask to have late fees waived. Ask the lender about working out a financial hardship plan. There are programs in place to do this with federal Fannie Mae (202-752-7000) and Freddie Mac (800-FREDDIE) loans. One common plan is to pay interest only for a period of time. Realize that it takes between six and eighteen months for a foreclosure to actually happen, so you have time to negotiate on this type of loan. You may wish to refinance your loan and obtain a lower interest rate with lower payments. You could also refinance and get a loan with a longer lifetime.

Selling your home and paying off the loan is another option. You could rent the home out for the amount of the mortgage and make the payments using the rent and live somewhere cheaper yourself.

A last resort is to sign the home over to the bank with a quit claim deed so that you can avoid the costs of foreclosure. The debt is canceled and no negative remarks appear on your credit report. You could also get the bank to agree to a pre-foreclosure sale, where you sell the home yourself and give the bank the proceeds to cancel the mortgage.

Utilities. Consider switching to a budget plan. Under this kind of plan you pay a monthly average of your yearly charges, avoiding high payments in some months or you could set up a partial payment plan. As long as you are making some type of payment, the utility company will be unlikely to cut off your service.

Automobiles. You could sell your car and purchase a less expensive used one. Always notify the lender before you make a late payment. Cars can be quickly repossessed. Consider asking for an extension on the loan or permission to defer a payment. If you lease, terminate your lease early. Refuse to pay post-termination payments based on the Consumer Leasing Act. (United States Code (U.S.C.), Title 15, Section (Sec.) 1667-1667c.)

Student Loans. Contact your lender before you become delinquent on your loan.

Important Student Loan Payment Options:

Forbearance:	The lender allows you to postpone or make temporary reductions in your payments
Deferment:	The loan is essentially put on hold while you are enrolled in school, if you cannot find a job, if you have financial hardship, you are raising preschool children or you are temporarily or permanently disabled

Consolidation: You combine all of your loans into one and make one monthly payment that is lower

Cancellation: Certain federal loans can be completely canceled if you are disabled, are in the military, teach certain subjects or certain types of students, work in law enforcement, join the Peace Corps, etc.

Student loans can be a big problem if you've been a student for many years and are finding that your post-graduation employment choices aren't as good or as high paying as you had hoped. You will want to consider consolidating your loans down into one loan. Although this offers the benefit of reducing your monthly payment, it can stretch your repayment period to up to thirty years and can increase the interest you will be paying. The interest rate is a weighted average of all loans you consolidate. You need to weigh these facts when you make your decision. For more information see the Federal Student Loan Consolidation Program at **www.osfa.state.la.us/consold1.htm** .

The following loans are eligible for federal consolidation:

- Federal Stafford Loans;

- Federal Supplemental Loans for Students (SLS);

- Federal Perkins Loans (previously NDSL);

- Health Professions Student Loans (HPSL);

- Health Education Assistance Loans (HEAL);

- Federal PLUS Loans;

- Federal Nursing Loans (NSL);

- Federal Consolidation Loans; and,

- Federal Direct Student Loans.

When you consolidate you can choose various payment plans. Be sure to compare all of them—a low payment today may mean more interest in the long run.

The National Student Loan Clearinghouse can help you find all of your loans if you are unsure of what you owe. Contact them at:

The National Student Loan Clearinghouse
13454 Sunrise Valley Drive, Suite 300
Herndon, VA 20171
703-742-7791
www.studentclearinghouse.org/secure_area/loan_locator.asp

A federal consolidation loan application is available online at **www.slc.sc.edu /PDF/forms/consolidation/cons_appl.PDF** or at your school's financial aid office.

To qualify for consolidation you must be enrolled less than half time and be in your grace period or repayment period. Loans must be current (paid up to date) to qualify.

For more information, contact your private lender or the U.S. Department of Education at 800-621-3115. A pamphlet about student loans is available from this number as well.

Taxes. Contrary to popular belief, the Internal Revenue Service (IRS) is willing to help taxpayers who are unable to pay their tax obligations. If you are in this situation, contact your local IRS office for information about payment plans with the **COLLECTION INFORMATION STATEMENT FOR INDIVIDUALS** (IRS Form 433-A) and **OFFERS IN COMPROMISE** (IRS Form 656). There are instructions with the form 656 in Appendix B. (see form 30, p.209.) You fill out form 433-A as follows (see form 31, p.223):

◈   Complete your personal information in Items 1, 2, 3, 4a, and 4b.

◈   Fill in your employment information in Section I.

◈   Give the information requested in Section II. (Order of "kin" is your children, then parents, then siblings. List your oldest child. If no children, list one parent. If parents are deceased, list your oldest sibling.)

◈   List all of your bank accounts, retirement accounts, CDs, etc in number 13 in Section III.

◈   Credit cards and loan information should be filled in under number 14.

◈   List safe deposit box information in number 15.

◈   List real estate you own under number 16.

◈   Fill in life insurance information under number 17. (*Face amount* means the death benefit the policy will pay. The *loan value* is how much you can borrow against it.)

◈   Number 18 is where you list stocks and bonds and mutual funds.

◈   Complete number 19 if any items listed apply to you.

◈   Fill in the chart in Section IV. List what each item is currently worth (current market value), how much you owe on each (amount owed), your equity in the asset, the amount of your last monthly payment, the name and address of the creditor, the date the loan was signed (date pledged) and the date the final payment will be made.

◈   Do not complete the box after Section IV as it is for IRS use only.

◈   Give information about your monthly income in Section V and detail your living expenses. Total each column.

◈   Sign the form and have your spouse sign it as well. You may add any other information in the box under the signature area and attach anything you would like.

Credit Cards. Remember interest continues to accrue on credit cards. However, you can negotiate about future interest. Ask that it be reduced or eliminated for a certain period of time. If you have several credit cards, you can transfer the balances to a card with the lowest interest rate and save a lot of money in doing so. Credit card companies are often receptive to settlements where you pay 70% of the balance and they cancel the debt in return. Ask to have yearly fees waived.

Secured Goods. If you have purchased items for your home, such as furniture or appliances where the lender holds a security interest in the item, it is important to understand that the lender cannot enter your home to repossess the goods without a court order. Therefore, it takes time and money for the creditor to repossess them. This works in your favor because lenders like these are more likely to agree to a settlement than go to the expense of getting the item back.

Determine what the resale value of the item in dispute is. Offer the creditor a settlement offer. Use **Letter Offering to Return Secured Property**. (see form 24, p.203.) If the creditor has to hire an attorney, go to court, repossess the item, and then sell it, the company will net less money than what you are offering and your offer may thus seem like a good one. Be sure to get the agreement in writing and make sure that any negative entries on your credit report from this creditor will be removed as part of the agreement.

General Negotiating Tips

It is important to remember that you will almost always obtain a better outcome when you negotiate directly with a creditor rather than with a collection agency. The collection agency is authorized to make only certain concessions to debtors. If you speak directly to the creditor, you may be able to work out a better deal. If the creditor will not speak with you about your debt, ask how many payments you must make to the collection agency before they will agree to speak to you. Once you have demonstrated your willingness to pay, the creditor may be more willing to discuss the debt with you.

Some collection agencies buy debts from creditors and your original creditor may be out of the picture completely. If this is the case, the collection agency can then negotiate with you. If you are not sure who owns the debt, ask the collection agent, or call the original creditor.

If you disagree with an amount of a debt, you will need to discuss this with the creditor. The collection agency will not have any records beyond the current amount owed and is not able to deal with adjustments for errors made by the creditor.

Eliminating Debts You Do Not Owe

You may have debts attributed to you that you really are not legally responsible for. You may have entered into a contract that is not legal, or you may have contracts you can dispute, such a car you bought that is a Lemon Law car.

NOTE: *You will need to consult an attorney or read up on contract law to determine this—but in general look to see if there was any fraud involved or if the contract is grossly unfair.*

Look closely at your debts and see if there are any that you truly do not owe. It is also possible to cancel some orders or contracts so that you will no longer be responsible for them, such as canceling a contract to have your house re-roofed before the work is done.

Negotiating Settlements

Reducing monthly payments is at best a temporary measure in relieving debt and improving your credit. The interest on the debt is going to continue to pile up, especially when you are only making partial payments. To really reduce your debt, you need to work out settlements. A settlement is a legally binding agreement that ends your obligation to the creditor. These are some examples of settlements you may wish to consider:

Example: You owe $3000 on your Visa card. The original amount charged was $1900. The rest of the amount is from accumulated interest. You have been behind on your payments for six months and have only been able to pay portions of the monthly amounts. The company is becoming more insistent that you pay the full monthly payment. You call the company and explain that your financial situation has become difficult since you became ill.

Solution: Agree to pay them $2000 as a settlement in full of the amount due. They agree to report your account as current to the credit reporting agency.

Example: You lost your job and cannot make your mortgage payment. There is no job in sight and your wife is expecting a baby. You have not paid on your mortgage in four months. You contact the bank and explain your situation to them. There is simply no way you can get any money together to pay for the past or current mortgage payments. You know that if you fail to pay, the bank will eventually foreclose on the home. The bank will evict you, sell the home at auction and accept a price less than it is really worth. The amount you owe, as well as all the costs of the sale and legal work, will be deducted from the sale price. Any money left over is yours. You should not expect to see anything unless you have a large amount of equity.

Solution: You tell the bank you would like to deed the house back to them as payment in full on the mortgage. You will be out, with no payments due and no costs of the sale or foreclosure. This method keeps your credit history clean and makes it possible for you to purchase a smaller, less expensive home when you get back on your feet.

These basic strategies can be applied to any debt. Either offer the creditor less than the total amount due as payment in full or give back the security interest as payment in full. If you use one of these strategies you will get the creditor off your back and salvage your credit rating.

Make sure that part of the settlement is that the creditor agrees to report your account as paid in full with any negative indications removed from your credit report. Most creditors will require that you pay at least 70% of the debt before they will agree to remove negative references from your credit report.

When you negotiate a settlement you get the creditor to agree to take less than you owe in exchange for your paying it immediately. Creditors are more happy with cash in hand than with accounts they must continue to pursue for months or years. Finding the cash so you can live up to your settlement agreement is discussed in the next section.

NOTE: *If you need to skip a payment completely, use Letter Requesting No Payment. (see form 28, p.207.)*

Finding Cash

To use some of the debt reduction strategies described above, you need to find the money to make the settlement. Remember that there are ways to find large chunks of cash, but that it is also important to find ways to get together small amounts of cash or to save small amounts. If you can try a few of these strategies, the money you save will really add up. Follow some of these suggestions for raising or conserving cash:

✪ Sell your investments.

✪ Sell other assets, such as a boat, coin collection, second car, jewelry, etc.

✪ Seek a reduction in your child support obligations.

✪ Ask for a raise.

✪ Use your tax refund or alimony payment.

✪ Take a second job. Even small jobs like baby sitting or yard work can help you raise the money you need.

✪ Transfer your credit card balances to a card with a low interest rate.

✪ Ask your credit card companies to waive your annual fee. Most are willing to do this.

✪ Get a second mortgage or home equity loan. Use the money to pay for your settlements and pay the loan back over time. Just be certain that you will be able to handle the monthly payments.

✪ Borrow money from family or friends. (Be aware that an outstanding loan can drastically change a relationship.)

✪ Raise the deductible on your insurance or reduce the amount of coverage you have.

✪ Get rid of overdraft protection on your bank accounts. This just gives you an excuse to overdraw your account.

✪ Rip up any checks you are given by your credit card company. The interest rate on these will devastate you.

✪ Cancel any insurance you have purchased from your credit card companies. It is overpriced. If you feel you must have some life insurance, shop around with local agents.

✪ Take out a loan against life insurance or retirement accounts.

✪ Cancel any insurance against credit card theft or loss that you have purchased. You do not need this since you are only liable for the first $50 used on a card after you report it stolen or missing.

✪ Withdraw money from your bank accounts at the bank and not at ATMs where you may be charged a fee.

✪ Have a garage sale.

✪ Sell items to a pawn shop. Be aware that you will only receive about 50% of the value of the item this way.

✪ Sell items to a consignment shop.

✪ Barter. For example, fix your neighbor's car in exchange for haircuts.

✪ Cut coupons, shop sales and use rebates.

✪ Turn a hobby into a money-making venture. Sell homemade pies to local restaurants, sell birdhouses you make at a flea market, etc.

✪ Sell your car and buy a less expensive used one or take the subway or the bus until you can afford a new one.

✪ Do small home repairs yourself instead of paying someone.

✪ Sell your home and buy a smaller, less expensive one.

✪ Move in with family or friends for a short time to save on rent.

✪ Apply for public assistance if you are out of work or disabled. This money will not be enough to make even a medium sized settlement, but it will keep food on your table.

✪ Cancel your cable service.

✪ Cancel your cell phone service.

✪ Return things you have purchased and do not need. Get cash back if you have the receipt. If you do not, you can get a store credit to purchase things you DO need.

✪ Borrow books from the library instead of buying them.

✪ Rent videos instead of going to movies.

✪ Cook at home instead of getting take out.

✪ Go on a diet.

✪ Cancel your home phone and use only your cell phone.

✪ Do your own repairs, laundry or other services.

✪ Suggest that your teenage children get jobs and contribute to the household.

✪ Buy store brands instead of name brands.

✪ Plant a vegetable garden.

✪ Join a wholesale club and buy in bulk. Split large quantities with friends.

✪ Use a hose instead of the car wash.

✪ Carpool.

✪ Take the bus to work instead of driving.

✪ Ride a bike or walk places if possible.

✪ Cancel your long distance service.

✪ Turn off lights when you are not in the room.

✪ Lower the heat at night and when you are away.

✪ Open the window instead of turning on the air conditioning.

✪ Use birth control to avoid unplanned pregnancies.

✪ Keep your extra cash in a savings account where you can earn a few dollars on it.

✪ Buy nothing you do not need.

✪ Give up drinking or smoking.

✪ Take coffee and a brown bag lunch to work with you.

✪ Use free classifieds in local community newspapers to sell things.

✪ Put off giving to charity until you can afford to do so.

✪ Severely cut back your gift-giving.

✪ Try making some gifts yourself.

✪ Cancel your newspaper and magazine subscriptions.

✪ Shop at secondhand stores.

✪ Accept "hand-me-downs" for your children.

✪ Cancel your credit cards so you cannot charge more than you can afford.

✪ Increase the number of dependents you claim on your W-2 forms (but only if you can do so without owing taxes at the end of the year).

✪ Cancel your Internet account and sign up for a free service or a company that pays you to surf or get free access at your local library.

✪ Learn how to budget and stick to it (Chapter 9).

✪ Find out if you qualify for assistance from a local food pantry or other charity.

✪ Save money in a special account or in an envelope instead of using layaway for which there are fees.

✪ Bake and cook items yourself that you normally purchase prepared.

✪ Sell items on eBay.

✪ Use credit cards that offer incentives (such as money back) but only if you can control your credit card spending.

✪ Cancel any trips you have planned or substitute less expensive vacations, such as camping.

✪ Send e-cards instead of buying and mailing cards.

Dealing with Judgments and Liens

If you have been experiencing debt problems for some time, you may have a judgment against you. A *judgment* is a court order stating that you must pay the amount owed. A judgment gives a creditor the right to garnish your wages or seize your assets. A *lien* is a court order that gives the creditor an interest in some piece of real property you own. Should you ever sell the property, the creditor must be paid out of the sale money. You have the right to a trial to contest a judgment that is being sought against you.

NOTE: *If you cannot afford an attorney, contact your local Legal Aid Society for assistance. Many local bar associations have attorneys who provide legal help on a volunteer basis for people who cannot afford to pay for it. Call your local county or city bar association to inquire about this.*

It is important to understand that once a lien has been placed against your property, that the only way to get rid of it is to pay it or reach a settlement with the creditor for removing it.

Even if a court proceeding has begun, there is still time to settle. Approach the creditor's attorney (if you have an attorney, he or she will do this for you) and offer to settle the case for a certain amount of money. Start with 40% of the total amount owed. This will save the creditor time and money in legal bills.

If a court decides that you owe all or part of what the creditor is asking for, a judgment or lien will be entered against you. Once a judgment is entered, the creditor can begin to collect the money from you. This can include garnishing your wages (taking a portion out of your paycheck) and seizing your assets and bank accounts. Once a judgment or lien is entered you can still approach the creditor about a settlement. They may agree because seizing assets, waiting on a lien, and garnishing wages can be expensive and time consuming. Be sure that if you do settle the judgment in this way that the creditor files papers with the court indicating that the judgment has been satisfied. (This is often called a satisfaction of judgment or discharge.)

It is important to note that some people are *judgment proof*. This means they have little or no assets, no income (other than government assistance), and have basically nothing a creditor can take. If you are judgment proof, you may not wish to make any attempt to settle your account. However, you must realize that if you rack up many judgments against you it will be extremely difficult to obtain credit. Also, should your situation change in the future, you will have judgments and liens to pay off.

If you are judgment proof, you can use **Letter Explaining Judgment Proof Status** to let your creditors know this. (see form 26, p.205.) This will discourage many from pursuing the debt, since they will not be able to collect anything. If you are planning to file for bankruptcy, you should let your creditors know this as well, as it will keep them from pursuing you. Use **Letter Explaining Plan to Go Bankrupt.** (see form 27, p.206.)

Proof of Payment Whether you settle with your creditor before, during, or after a court case or if you pay a judgment in full, you must make certain that you receive proof of payment. When reaching a settlement, you should not send any funds until you have a legal document in your hands that indicates the terms of the settlement. Keep a copy of it for yourself. Make payment after you sign this and request a receipt or proof of payment from the creditor. Keep these documents.

Should you settle or pay a judgment, the creditor is responsible for filing a judgment discharge with the court, indicating that you have completely paid what you owe. If you do not receive a copy of this—request one. You may find it necessary to prod the creditor into filing this document since it often is not considered high priority.

If you owed taxes, the IRS may have filed a tax lien against you. Request a Certificate of Release of Federal Tax Lien from the IRS for each lien against you that you have paid in full. Have the credit reporting agencies contact the IRS to verify the release of the liens.

Closing Your Accounts

If you are deep in debt and many of your accounts are reporting you as delinquent to the credit reporting agencies, you may want to close all of your credit card accounts. When you close an account you still remain responsible for all the past charges and interest on the account, but you prevent yourself from adding more charges to the account and making your situation worse. Use **LETTER CLOSING ACCOUNT** to notify the creditor with which you wish to close an account. (see form 29, p.208.)

5 | GETTING HELP

There is nothing wrong with deciding you could use some assistance resolving your problems. When might you need help? You probably need help if you do not have enough money to pay even reduced payments on your accounts. You probably need some help if you just cannot work out a budget or if you can create a budget but cannot follow it no matter what you do. You need help if there are errors on your credit report and either you just cannot handle trying to get them fixed as discussed in Chapter 3, or if you have gone as far as you feel you can on your own in trying to get them fixed. If you are in danger of losing your home or you car and do not have enough money to survive on, you need to get some help.

Where to Turn

If you are in immediate danger of losing your home or some other emergency situation, consider seeing an attorney to discuss bankruptcy, as described below. If you are feeling deeply depressed or suicidal, you need to get help from a mental health professional. You should not feel embarrassed about these feelings. Considering the difficulties you have faced, they are a common reaction. If you are in a situation where you have no money and cannot afford basic necessities, you need to get assistance from your local social services department.

Agencies That Can Assist You

There are many different agencies that can provide various types of assistance, support, and information as you confront your debts.

Consumer Credit Counseling Agencies

Consumer Credit Counseling Service (CCCS) is the best known credit counseling agency. CCCS is a nonprofit corporation that is funded by creditors. CCCS can help you set up a payment plan to manage all of your debt. Basically, CCCS negotiates with the creditors on your behalf to reduce interest or lower payments. Your debt is organized into one monthly payment that is less than the total of your normal monthly obligations. The agency also tries to provide clients with credit and finance education to help avoid future problems. You pay a small monthly fee to CCCS for the service. You do need to be aware that CCCS cannot reduce your debt and it requires that you pay all of your debts in full. If you miss payments, collection actions can be pursued by your creditors. Be aware that there may be a waiting list at CCCS and also that the payment plan that is set up for you can last up to forty-two months.

Your credit report will reflect the fact that you used credit counseling services and some lenders may be hesitant to lend to you because of this since it is a clear sign you are having trouble managing your payments. It's also important to realize that using this service will freeze your accounts. You will be able to make payments towards them but not use them.

It is important to be careful when selecting a credit counseling agency. While CCCS is the best known, there are many others. Many charge a set up fee, as well as a monthly fee for their services, which consists mainly of consolidating a consumer's debt into one payment. Make sure you choose an agency that:

   ✪   provides you with a written statement of your rights;

   ✪   does not ask for cash before speaking with you;

   ✪   does not promise to eliminate, reduce or get rid of your debts;

✪ discloses all fees up front;

✪ makes payments to creditors on time;

✪ does not charge more than $50 for a set up or $25 for a monthly fee (although realize that if the agency provides extensive educational programs you may have to pay for these);

✪ employees work on commission;

✪ does not promise free services (in credit counseling as elsewhere there is no such thing as a free lunch); and,

✪ spends time with you (usually at least twenty minutes is recommended) before offering a debt management or consolidation plan that fits your needs.

Unfortunately the quality of many agencies is decreasing, so it is important to shop around. Over nine million Americans seek help from credit counseling services each year and this is often a last resort before bankruptcy for many people who are having debt problems.

The National Foundation for Credit Counseling is the national non-profit organization of consumer credit counseling agencies. The national office can direct you to a credit counseling office in your area and also can provide basic debt and budgeting information online. You can reach the National Foundation for Credit Counseling at 800-388-2227 or at **www.nfcc.org**.

Consumer Counseling Centers of America is an organization similar to CCCS and can be reached at 202-637-4851 or at **www.consumercounseling.org**.

Debtors Anonymous

Debtors Anonymous offers a twelve step program similar to Alcoholics Anonymous. The program helps people who have recurring debt problems face and overcome them. Contact them at 781-453-2743 or go to their website at **www.debtorsanonymous.org**.

Institute of Consumer Financial Education

Another organization to consider is the Institute of Consumer Financial Education. This is a nonprofit group that works with consumers to help them manage, invest, save, and spend money in an educated way. They have monthly newsletters and a packet about credit cards available. Contact them at 619-239-1401 or at **www.icfe.info**. The Institute also offers "credit card condoms," which are sleeves that fit over credit cards. They are supposed to act as a deterrence to using them, or at least get the user to think for a moment before using them.

National Consumer Law Center The National Consumer Law Center (NCLC) offers information for consumers about laws about credit and bankruptcy, as well as other topics. NCLC has recently published a report called *Credit Counseling in Crisis: The High Impact on Consumers of Funding Cuts, Higher Fees and Aggressive New Market Entrants*. You can read the report online at:

www.nclc.org/initiatives/content/creditcounselingreport.pdf

Better Business Bureau The Better Business Bureau can assist you with complaints against any business, credit repair, or credit reporting agency that is a member of the Bureau. Check your phone book for the local office. The national office address is:

4200 Wilson Blvd., Suite 800
Arlington, VA 22203-1838

National Internet Fraud Watch Information Center This non-profit organization is designed to help consumers detect and avoid telemarketing and internet fraud. You can call them or email them with a report of suspicious activity or you can call to get advice. For information and advice, call 800-876-7060. To report fraud, call 800-876-7060. For more information, visit their website at **www.fraud.org**.

National Fraud Information Center The National Fraud Information Center can provide assistance to consumers who have been defrauded by credit repair organizations. Reach them at 800-876-7060, or at **www.fraud.com**.

State Banking Authorities State Banking Authorities regulate and supervise state-chartered banks. Many also handle problems with other financial institutions. These agencies can answer questions about credit and also about banking. Contact your state agency to find out exactly what services they can provide. A list of State Banking Authorities can be found in Appendix A.

Other Assistance You can also obtain information from the federal government about programs and services they offer at **www.pueblo.gsa.gov**.

The Federal Trade Commission (FTC) provides information designed to help consumers spot fraud in the marketplace. You can contact them at 877-FTC-HELP (877-382-4357) or at **www.ftc.gov**.

Consumer Sentinel is run by the FTC and offers information on fraud and scams. You can find them online at **www.consumer.gov/sentinel**.

A website that has a wealth of information about credit and debt is: **www.creditpage.com.**

If you are looking to get some legal information beyond that which is offered in this book or in the statutes provided in Appendix B, go to **www.findlaw.com**. All federal and state statutes can be accessed there as well as many court decisions.

If you need legal assistance but cannot afford an attorney, you may qualify for a free attorney. Contact Legal Services Corporation (202-336-8800 or 202-336-8959, **www.lsc.gov**) or National Legal Aid and Defender Association (202-452-0620, **www.nlada.org**).

www.creditguide.com offers a section on building good credit.

www.debtwizards.com/consolidate.html gives information about how to consolidate your debts.

www.freecreditanalyzer.com offers a credit analysis.

www.quicken.com/shopping/parenting has a debt reduction planner and other calculating tools.

Other Credit Repair Agencies

There are many companies that advertise that they can help you reduce or eliminate your debt and quickly and easily repair your credit problems. Because many of these companies have proven to be less than honest, the Credit Repair Organizations Act was passed by Congress to try to control some of the problems that have happened with these types of companies. Under this act, it is illegal for such an agency to advise a consumer to alter identification (such as using a different name to get credit) or to hide accurate information in a credit report.

Credit repair agencies cannot accept any payment before performing work for a consumer and must also give each client a statement of their rights. You have the right to cancel any contract you agree to with a credit repair agency within three days of signing it. Should any agency request that you pay them before they do any work for you, fail to give you a statement of your rights, or suggest you use a different name or identity to obtain credit, you need to refuse their services and report them to your local authorities. If you participate in any illegal activity with a credit repair agency, even if it is their idea and they provide the paperwork, you can be criminally prosecuted and face jail time.

In general, you need to be wary of anyone who promises you quick and easy fixes for your credit problems. There is nothing that a credit repair agency can do for you that you cannot do yourself. There is no magic involved in credit repair and there is nothing so highly technical that the average consumer cannot handle. Do not let anyone pressure you into doing things you feel are dishonest or potentially illegal. If it sounds too good to be true, it probably is.

Government Agencies

Government agencies such as the Federal Trade Commission (FTC), or your state attorney general's office (in the government guide section of your phone book) can be of assistance to you if you need information about laws on credit or if you are experiencing difficulty dealing with a creditor or credit reporting agency. The FTC keeps records about credit reporting agencies and can prosecute them if they break the law. If you have a complaint against a credit reporting agency, you should always let the FTC know. It is unlikely they will become involved in your particular situation, but the information you provide can assist them if it appears there is an ongoing pattern of problems with one agency. The FTC can be reached at:

Federal Trade Commission
6th and Pennsylvania Avenue NW
Washington, D.C. 20580
www.FTC.gov

When to Get a Lawyer

Just because you are experiencing credit or debt problems, you do not automatically need a lawyer. You can negotiate arrangements with creditors yourself without an attorney. You can get changes made to a credit report on your own.

You have probably seen ads for attorneys who advertise that they can reduce your debt and help you avoid bankruptcy. Most of what they offer, you can do yourself, by following the procedures and suggestions in this book.

There are times, however, when an attorney may be helpful. If you are dealing with credit reporting agencies about an incorrect entry on your report and you have sent letters and made phone calls for several months with little progress, it may be a good idea to get an attorney.

This does not mean you must pay a retainer fee and then be billed by the hour. Start by hiring an attorney only to write a simple letter on your behalf to the credit agency. An attorney's letterhead will garner much more attention than yet another letter from you and may be just the thing to push things into motion. You can negotiate with the attorney about how much you will be charged should other services like phone calls or more correspondence be required.

If you have been served with court papers, you may wish to consult an attorney to at least have him or her look them over and help you understand them completely. If you are being sued for nonpayment of a debt you owe and have no defense, you will most likely be throwing good money after bad if you hire a lawyer to defend you in the case. If you are uncomfortable or unable to try to reach a settlement with the creditor's attorney yourself, you can hire an attorney for the specific purpose of working out a settlement.

If you believe that you need to at least consider bankruptcy, you should contact an attorney for a free consultation. To find a bankruptcy attorney, contact attorneys you have had contact with in the past for a referral, or call your state, county, or city bar association for a referral to an attorney in your area who practices bankruptcy law.

Bankruptcy

Bankruptcy is a procedure you can go through in a federal bankruptcy court that allows you to *discharge* (or get rid of) all or a portion of your debt. One of the most important and beneficial things about bankruptcy is that the minute you file your petition with the court stating that you are asking to be declared bankrupt, all of your creditors are stopped from any collection attempts. This is called an *automatic stay* and can do a lot to relieve the tension and mounting panic you feel.

This means creditors cannot take your car, garnish your wages, call you about your debt or try to collect in any way. When a bankruptcy is filed, a *trustee* is appointed to handle the case. The trustee divides up your assets among your creditors.

There are two types of bankruptcies available to consumers: *Chapter 7* and *Chapter 13*. You must reside in a state for 90 days prior to filing for bankruptcy in that state. To file for bankruptcy, you will probably need an attorney, who will require that you pay him or her. You must also pay a filing fee with the court. The attorney will complete a Petition for Bankruptcy, which is a very long document that lists your personal information as well as details all of your assets and your debts. If you do attempt to file bankruptcy without an attorney, bankruptcy forms are available online at **http://forms.lp.findlaw.com/federal/fjnbf_1/html**.

When you go bankrupt, all of your assets and debts come under the control of the court. It is important to understand that there are some assets that are called *exempt assets*. Things such as your clothing, food, books, personal belongings, furniture, some cash, and wedding ring cannot be taken away from you. Other things such as your car and some real estate, especially your home, have additional protections. The law about what is considered exempt differs by state, but in general you are permitted to keep things you require for daily living. Your *non-exempt* assets are those that the court can divide up among your creditors. These include investments, large amounts of cash, and valuable items you own.

It is important to note that recently there has been an effort by bankruptcy judges to be harder on people who are going bankrupt since in the recent past there have been many abuses of the system. It is also important to know that if you believe you are going to go bankrupt you should NOT go and max out all of your credit cards right before you do so. The court will see this as an abuse and may not allow you to include those debts in your bankruptcy.

At the time this book was published, discussion had continued in both the House and Senate that would revise the current U.S. bankruptcy laws. If passed (and it is quite likely it will pass), the new law will make it more difficult to qualify for bankruptcy. There will be a means test, which means the filer's income and records will be closely scrutinized to ensure he or she in fact truly needs bankruptcy relief. Before filing, most filers must receive credit counseling. Most filers will also be required to attend budgeting classes. Additionally the law will try to funnel more filers through *Chapter 13* as opposed to *Chapter 7* (see discussion in the following section).

The two types of consumer bankruptcies are explained in detail below:

Chapter 7   A *Chapter 7* bankruptcy lets the debtor discharge (or wipe out) all of his or her debts and is also called *liquidation* bankruptcy. This may sound like a pretty good deal, but it's not quite that simple. When a debtor goes into a *Chapter 7* bankruptcy, the trustee takes possession (legally) of all of the debtors possessions that are not exempt under state or federal law. The trustee *liquidates* or sells all of your non-exempt assets and uses the cash to pay your creditors. (Most only get a small percentage, if that, of the total amount of the debt.) All debts are *discharged*, or forgiven, and completely wiped off the slate. Even if this sounds like a good deal, you must know that not all debts can be discharged in a bankruptcy. Taxes, child support, alimony, student loans, as well as some other specialized items can never be discharged in bankruptcy. You will be responsible for repaying these types of debt no matter what.

You may only file for a *Chapter 7* bankruptcy every six years and you should be aware that bankruptcy courts in some areas are cracking down on what they see as consumer misuse of bankruptcies. Some *Chapter 7* bankruptcies have been denied when it appears the debtor piled up debt without any plans to be able to pay it off. *Chapter 7* bankruptcies appear on credit reports for ten years after the discharge.

A *Chapter 7* bankruptcy can be a lifesaver for people who are overcome with debt and have no hope of reaching settlements or being able to make negotiated payments to creditors. They can also hurt your credit for a long time.

Chapter 13   *Chapter 13* bankruptcies are also called *reorganizations*. A *Chapter 13* bankruptcy allows the debtor to keep most assets and arranges for partial or full payment of the debts owed over three to five years. Creditors must be paid at least as much as they would have received in a *Chapter 7* situation. The debtor must pay all *disposable* (not necessary for living essentials) income into the plan. Money is paid to the trustee who then pays the creditors. The major benefit of a *Chapter 13* plan is that it allows the debtor to keep assets that would have to be liquidated in a *Chapter 7* plan. However, a *Chapter 13* bankruptcy will also stay on your credit report for ten years. If you are having problems making mortgage payments or some other similar situation, you would be better off to work with your creditor independently and find a way to catch up, so that the late or missed payments only haunt your credit report for seven years. Creditors are more afraid of bankruptcies on a credit report than they are of late payments. Creditors usually do not receive full payment in a bankruptcy, but if the debtor merely falls behind, a profit can still be made.

Other benefits of *Chapter 13* plans are that they do include taxes into the plan and that the plan is like a consolidation loan. However, no interest is charged. Interest on your debts stops accumulating on the day you file for bankruptcy. The amount you owe does not continue to grow through accumulating interest.

In general you are better off trying to make your own settlements or payment plans with your creditors than going into a *Chapter 13* bankruptcy. Keep it as a last resort.

If you have already filed for bankruptcy before reading this book and feel you may have made a mistake in doing so, you may be able to withdraw your bankruptcy petition, depending on where your case is at. You will need to consult with your attorney about this.

Reaffirmation Agreements

If you do file for bankruptcy, you will be surprised to find that often as you literally walk out the courtroom door, you will be stopped by a representative from one of your creditors. This representative will offer you new credit if you agree to "reaffirm" your debt with the company, in other words, agree to owe them the money which your bankruptcy just wiped out. Many consumers have fallen into this trap and have found themselves deep in debt almost immediately after a bankruptcy. Don't agree to anything to right away. Take some time to reassess your financial situation. Read Chapter 8 about how to re-establish credit. Remember that reaffirming a debt you've just wiped out can be a foolish move. On the other hand, if it is a small amount, it might serve your purposes to agree to reaffirm it so that you can have immediate credit with that company.

Other Assistance

There are many agencies and organizations available to assist you. Check Appendix A at the back of the book for listings of state banking authorities, consumer protection agencies and state attorneys general who can assist consumers with financial and debt problems and questions.

Coping With Bankruptcy

Many people feel embarrassed when bankruptcy becomes an option or a choice for them. It is important to remember that bankruptcy was invented to help people, and that it is ok to find yourself in a situation where you need help. Bankruptcy can relieve a lot of stress in a much faster way than most other options. Think for a minute about the many celebrities or famous people who have gone through bankruptcy—Larry King, Anna Nicole Smith, Kim Basinger, Burt Reynolds, Henry Ford, Jerry Lee Lewis, and even President Ulysses S. Grant.

Try to think of it as a reorganization of your finances and as a way to get your debt (and stress) under control. Bankruptcy gives you a fresh start. Resolve to use that new start wisely. Do not let yourself fall into the same traps again after your bankruptcy. Above all do not feel embarrassed or demeaned about going through bankruptcy.

6 COPING WITH MARRIAGE, DIVORCE, AND DEBT

Marriage does have an impact on credit and debt and it is important to be aware of the implications. It is important to discuss divorce and debt together because many people who are experiencing debt or credit problems are either divorcing, recently divorced or having marital difficulties and contemplating divorce. Because serious debt problems cause stress, and stress can lead to marital problems, this is not surprising. It can also work in the opposite direction as well—marital problems can or divorce can be a direct cause of financial problems.

Divorce can certainly complicate financial problems, but you should never stay in a marriage just to avoid these problems. Your problems can be worked out no matter how difficult they may seem. This chapter will also address your credit rights during marriage.

Your Credit Rights During Marriage

Women, and sometimes men, change their names when they marry. This happens when you take your spouse's last name, hyphenate the two names, or create a new surname to use together. When you do this, you risk losing your old credit history. If you change your name due to marriage (or for any other reason), be sure to have your accounts changed to your new name and ask that this change be reported on your credit report.

If joint accounts are opened during marriage, be sure that they are reported to both spouse's credit reports. If a woman changes her name due to marriage, she has the right to apply for and hold credit in her birth name, married name or both. It is not so clear cut for men who change their names during marriage. The rules should apply to men as well, but our society does not take for granted that men may want to take on a marital name, and men may find there to be obstacles in the way.

There is no requirement to tell a creditor if you should be addressed as Miss, Ms., or Mrs. The *Equal Credit Opportunity Act* states that no one may be denied credit because of marital status. Creditors also may not ask about a person's desire to have children or his or her use of birth control. When a married person applies for credit, the creditor may not ask for information about the person's spouse unless his or her individual income is not high enough alone, they are in a community property state, or the spouse will be a joint holder or a user on the account.

Divorce Is Not a Debt Solution

Some people believe that if they could just get away from their spouse, they could get out of debt, or at least stop building up debt. While you are married, creditors can pursue you for your spouse's debts that were incurred without your knowledge on a joint account. If you live in a community property state then you are both responsible for each other's individual debts incurred during marriage as well. Once you are divorced, a court rules who will be responsible for each debt, but until then, expect to hear from your spouse's creditors. If you are separated, you can simply tell them that you are divorcing and ask not to be contacted again.

Divorce usually makes financial troubles worse. Think about it. When a couple is married they have a certain combined income and pay for one residence, and one set of furniture. They have one set of utility bills. After the divorce, they still have the same combined income, but must now pay for two residences, two sets of bills, and buy duplicate furnishings and household items. The expenses are doubled but the income stays the same. Divorce can cause tremendous debt problems for any couple.

Dividing Debt   When you divorce, part of what happens is that the court takes a look at all of your assets and debts and distributes them according to the laws of your state. You will need to consult an attorney or read a book to learn about the specific laws in your state that govern debt division. Once the judge divides these debts, you will only be responsible for the debts the judge assigns to you.

Before you divorce, you should try to work out a division of debts with your spouse, either on your own or with help from a mediator or attorney. If you are able to do this, you can divide your debts in a way that both of you can manage, rather than end up with a plan made by a judge who will not have the same insight into your situation.

Mortgages. Often in a divorce, one spouse ends up keeping the house. Usually this means that the person who keeps the house assumes responsibility for the mortgage. What about the other spouse? When you bought the house, you did it together and you both signed the mortgage papers, making both of you responsible to the bank for the payments. When the judge awards the house to one spouse and makes that spouse responsible for the mortgage, the divorce decree often says that the other spouse is to be "held harmless" for the mortgage, meaning he or she is not to be responsible for the debt. This spouse sometimes thinks he or she is off the hook. However, the judge's ruling does not affect the bank at all. The judge's ruling means that the spouse keeping the house is supposed to make mortgage payments. If he or she does not and the bank comes after the other spouse, the spouse who is keeping the house can be sued by the other one.

As far as the bank is concerned, you are both still responsible for the mortgage. The only way to get around this is for the spouse who is keeping the house to refinance the mortgage, thereby removing the other spouse from the mortgage. It is sometimes possible to work with a bank and convince it to remove one person from the mortgage, though this is not a very common occurrence because the bank has little incentive to do so.

Joint Accounts. Most married couples have joint checking and savings accounts. This means that both people entirely own the total amount of money in the accounts. The wife can remove all of the money and so can the husband. If you are divorcing and you have joint accounts, the best course of action is to divide them yourselves. If this is not possible, you can ask the court to freeze the account until it can be divided. If you empty out the accounts yourself, you may be held liable to the other spouse for the amount you took, so do not do this without consulting an attorney or reaching an agreement with your spouse.

Most couples also have joint credit card accounts. You are both completely responsible for the total amount of the debt on these accounts. When it becomes clear that a divorce is imminent, it is best to close all joint credit cards and open individual accounts. You can pay off the balance on the joint account together if possible, or you can each transfer a portion of it to your own individual accounts. If you cannot agree, open individual accounts, cut up the joint cards and each pay half of the monthly payment on the joint account until you can reach an agreement on how to divide it.

Child Support and Alimony

When you divorce, the court not only divides up your possessions but must make sure that every member of the family will be financially cared for after the divorce. This includes both spouses as well as the children. *Child support* is usually ordered by the judge in a divorce when there are children. Usually the *non-custodial parent* (the one who does not live with the children) pays a certain amount on a weekly or monthly basis to the other parent. The amount is determined using the non-custodial parents' income and a percentage based on the number of children. Child support is supposed to be used to pay for the children's expenses.

Alimony (also called maintenance or spousal support in some states) is an amount of money paid by one spouse to the other. It is often thought of as a way to help the non-moneyed spouse get back on his or her feet financially after the divorce.

Divorce and Bankruptcy

Bankruptcy can be a solution to your financial problems. Be aware that you cannot discharge child support or alimony in bankruptcy.

If your spouse or ex-spouse goes through a bankruptcy, he or she will get all of the debt in his or her name discharged or forgiven. Be aware that if you still have joint debts and your spouse includes them in the bankruptcy, that you then end up being solely responsible for them.

The bankruptcy court may not always release a debtor from a property settlement agreement or hold harmless agreement on a mortgage. If the court thinks that the debtor cannot meet basic living expenses, then these debts can be forgiven in bankruptcy. If your spouse files for bankruptcy and seeks to have these debts discharged, you need to hire an attorney and file an adversary proceeding with the bankruptcy court within 60 days of the creditors meeting (you will be notified by the court of this date). (See Chapter 5 for more on bankruptcy.)

After Divorce   After a divorce, a creditor may not inquire as to your marital status. If you apply for credit, all of your income, including child support and alimony must be considered. You can no longer include your spouse's income when applying for loans or credit.

Death of a Spouse

If your spouse dies, creditors may not close or change the terms of joint accounts you held together. You would, however, be wise to open an account in your own name before notifying creditors of the death of your spouse so you have some credit should you have problems with the joint accounts. It is also important to understand that even if your spouse held debts in his or her name alone, the creditors can file claims against the deceased's estate to be paid. In essence this will come out of your and your children's inheritance.

7 IDENTITY THEFT

Identity theft occurs when someone else uses your personal information, such as date of birth, name or Social Security number as their own. Identity thieves use this information to obtain new credit or use your existing credit and make purchases leaving you responsible for them. They sometimes open new credit or phone accounts or take out loans using your name and Social Security number. Identity thieves sometimes complete change of address forms to divert your mail to them. They also have been known to file for bankruptcy in your name to avoid creditors or eviction. It can be hard to immediately recognize when identity theft is happening to you, so it is important to learn to spot the signals. Identity theft is a federal crime, under the *Federal Identity Theft and Assumption Deterrence Act* of 1998.

Preventing Identity Theft

To prevent identity theft, you need to pay attention to how you give out your personal information and how you dispose of garbage that contains your personal information. Before giving out any personal information ask why it is needed and how it will be used.

**Social
Security
Number**

Avoid giving out your Social Security number. There are times when it is necessary—when applying for a loan, opening a bank account and so on. However, there is no reason to give out this information if you are making a purchase or filling out a background information form for a dentist. Your best line of defense is to keep this information to yourself except when it is absolutely necessary. Always ask why it is being requested and do not give it out unless there is a valid reason. Do not carry your Social Security card in your wallet or purse. You will hardly ever need it, so keep it in a safe place at home. Never give out your Social Security number using email.

**Passwords
and Account
Numbers**

Do not give your passwords or account numbers to anyone. Use different passwords for different accounts. Choose passwords and PINs that are not easy to guess—avoid your birth date, anniversary or middle name. Do not write your passwords down or carry them in your purse or wallet. If you find you need to keep a written record of them, keep it at home and don't label it clearly as such. Keep it in a hard to find place.

**Credit and
ATM cards**

Carry only those cards that you use on a regular basis. Leave the rest at home in a secure location. Close accounts that you don't use. Before discarding credit card receipts, make sure you tear them up so the account number and expiration date is not readable. Cut up credit cards you are discarding.

Some credit cards offer you the option of including a small photo of yourself on the card. This can help reduce identity theft, or at least prevent that particular card from being used.

Know when to expect your credit card bill in the mail and if it doesn't arrive when you expect it, call the credit card company. Your bill could have been stolen.

**Online
Purchases or
Loan
Applications**

When you make online purchases or apply for loans online, make sure the site you are dealing with is using a secure server. Never give out account numbers or Social Security numbers via email since it could possibly be intercepted. If you must give an account number or Social Security number to a merchant who does not use a secure server, fax the information to them.

Be aware that one scam identity thieves use is sending you email pretending to be from your internet service provider telling you that you need to update your account information or re-verify your credit card information.

Telephone Sales

Never give out your account numbers, Social Security information or other personal information to a person over the phone. If someone contacts you by phone with a special offer or service for sale, ask for the information in writing.

Garbage Disposal

You also need to be careful about how you dispose of garbage that contains account numbers or other personal information. Buy a shredder or rip things up before throwing them out. Cut up old credit cards before discarding them. Rip or shred credit card convenience checks before throwing them out. Shred account statements, deposit receipts, withdrawal receipts and other documents with numbers on them that could be copied.

Home Security

Consider purchasing a small fireproof safe to keep at home. Some of these are the size of a shoebox and cost under $40. Keep birth certificates, Social Security cards, marriage licenses, bonds and other valuable items in it. It is also a good idea to maintain a list of your credit cards, account numbers and contact information here so that if your purse or wallet is stolen, you can easily contact the credit card companies about the theft.

Protecting Your Mail

If your mail box is a roadside box (or a box attached to the house when no one is home all day), make sure that you remove mail as soon as it is delivered. If you are unable to do so, consider using a post office box for all mail. If you are concerned about your mail sitting in the box all day, consider renting a P.O. box. Do not leave outgoing mail sitting in a roadside box. Deposit it in a post office drop box. Mail that sits in boxes is easily stolen. Do not take your personal mail to work to be sent out with your employer's mail. Someone else in the office could open it and obtain your account numbers.

If you notice that some of your mail has been opened or tampered with, report it to your local post office.

Prevent identity theft with these important steps:

- ✪ shred all credit card receipts, application copies or bills you are disposing;

- ✪ never give out account numbers or Social Security numbers by email;

- ✪ only use secure servers when buying online;

- ✪ do not leave outgoing or incoming mail sitting in a roadside mailbox;

✪ consider using a post office box;

✪ take all outgoing mail to a post office or drop box;

✪ shred all credit card offers you are discarding;

✪ avoid giving your Social Security number unless absolutely required;

✪ obtain your credit report every year to check for accounts you did not open or balances you did not create;

✪ never carry your Social Security card in your wallet or purse;

✪ do not write down your pin numbers and especially do not write it on the card or carry it on a piece of paper in your wallet or purse;

✪ do not give your pin number to anyone, even close friends or family;

✪ pick pin numbers that are random and do not stand for your birth date, anniversary, middle name or anything of significance; and,

✪ always check credit cards bills and bank statements for transactions or charges you did not incur. This can be your first clue to an identity theft problem.

Recognizing Identity Theft

When identity theft happens you may not be aware of it. Many people find out when they receive a call from a creditor about a charge or balance they did not create. You might also notice unknown charges on a credit card bill. Getting your credit report every year will help make sure no one is using your identity or accounts.

Dealing With Identity Theft

Should identity theft happen to you, there are several steps you need to take. First make sure it is identity theft. If there is a charge on your credit card statement that you do not recognize, call the credit card company and get more information about it. You may have charged this item yourself and either do not recognize the name or the vendor holds its credit card accounts in a different name than the one you are familiar with. If there is a charge for a vendor or merchant you have charged other items with, this may be a duplicate charge made in error and not the result of identity theft. In this case, dispute the charge with the credit card company. If a vendor is listed in a city you have never visited, you can't assume it is identity theft. Often vendors list their corporate or central offices on credit cards. If you are unsure, call the credit card company and ask where the charge was originated. Credit card companies can also tell you if the actual card was presented at the time of purchase or if just the number was supplied, such as for a phone or online order. If other charges appear with other vendors that you did not authorize, it is likely there has been identity theft.

Once you are certain that you did not incur the charges, contact the police immediately and complete a report. Give a copy of the report to creditors.

Creditors Contact the creditor or loan company which was used by the thief. Notify them in writing that you did not incur the charges and that your information was used illegally. Immediately close the account and open a new one with a PIN or security code attached to it. Ask that PIN numbers be verified before changing the address on the accounts.

Credit Reporting Agencies Contact all three credit reporting agencies and alert them that your identity has been stolen. Obtain current copies of your credit reports to check for other instances of identity theft. Ask that a "security alert" be placed on your file as well as a victim's statement asking that creditors call you before opening an account in your name. Request that inquiries made on behalf of the thief be removed from your file.

Here are important numbers to call to alert credit reporting agencies of fraud and/or identity theft:

Equifax: 800-766-0008

Experian: 888-397-3742

Trans Union: 800-680-7289

Employer Notify your employer of the identity theft and make sure the HR department will not give out information from your personnel file without your permission.

Banks   Alert your bank that your identity has been stolen so that signatures for your accounts will be carefully verified. Close your accounts and open new PIN verified accounts if your bank accounts have been accessed. If checks have been stolen or used by the thief, stop payment on them. The following check verification companies can provide services (for a fee) to help you track down the checks:

- ✪ **SCAN:** 800-262-7771

- ✪ **TeleCheck:** 800-710-9898 or 927-0188

- ✪ **CrossCheck:** 707-586-0431

- ✪ **Equifax Check Systems:** 800-437-5120

- ✪ **International Check Services:** 800-526-5380

Cancel your ATM or debit card and get a new one. You are liable only for the first $50 withdrawn on your debit or ATM card by ID thieves, if you report it within two days (the liability goes up to $500 after this. After 60 days the consumer becomes responsible for the entire amount). However, if your card has not actually been stolen (and this is possible with new technology that allows thieves to gather the information directly from the card-swiping machines), your bank may not believe you. You may need to be insistent and make several phone calls and send letters. Eventually most banks want to keep customers happy though. This kind of fraud most commonly occurs at gas stations (pay at the pump), convenience stores and other non-bank ATMs locations.

Investments   If investments have been accessed by the thief, contact the SEC at 202-942-7040 or **www.sec.gov/complaint.shtml**

Phone Accounts   If the thief used your phone account (land line or cell phone) contact your state Public Utility Commission for local service providers or the Federal Communications Commission for long-distance service providers and cellular providers at **www.fcc.gov/ccb/enforce/complaints.html** or 888-CALL-FCC.

Driver's License   If your driver's license was used, contact your state DMV. If your Social Security number is your DMV number, ask that a new number be issued by the DMV.

Mail   If your mail has been stolen or tampered with, contact your local post office.

Attorney	If the perpetrator has been caught, talk to an attorney about a lawsuit to compensate you for the costs and problems you have faced.
New Accounts	If one of your accounts has been used, you need to contact the security department of the credit card company. Close the account and open a new one with a new number. Request that a password be required on the new account. File a police report and get copies of it. You may need these copies to prove you have been a victim of identity theft when dealing with credit reporting agencies or other creditors.

Make sure you notify the creditor and the credit reporting agencies in writing that you are a victim of identity theft. Include copies of all supporting documents.

If your wallet or purse was stolen, you must close every single account for which you had a card in your wallet, and have new cards issued with new account numbers.

ID Theft Affidavit The FTC has created an ID Theft Affidavit, a form you can complete and submit to everyone you need to contact about the theft of your identity. This form is accepted by many banks, credit card companies and other lenders and reduces the amount of paperwork you need to complete to report identity theft. A copy of the form with instructions can be found at: **www.consumer.gov/idtheft/affidavit.htm**.

Obtaining a New Social Security Number If your Social Security number was used by the thief, contact the Social Security Administration's Fraud Hotline at 800-269-0271. It is possible to obtain a new one. Contact:

> Social Security Fraud Hotline
> P.O. Box 17768
> Baltimore, Maryland 21235
> Fax# 410-597-0118
> www.ssa.gov/oig/when.htm

You will be required to prove that your Social Security number has been stolen before a new one will be issued.

Your Liability If your credit card is stolen or used without your permission, you are only liable for the first $50 charged if you report the theft within two business days. This also applies to ATM cards. If you wait more than two days, your liability increases, so it is important to report this kind of theft immediately. If your identity is stolen and someone applies for loans or credit cards using your information it can be very difficult to prove that you are not liable, however you cannot be held responsible if you can prove you were not the person incurring the debt. Should you learn that someone has used your identity, it's important to get your credit report immediately to find out if the thief has opened other accounts or tapped into other accounts of yours. Ask your credit reporting agency to assist you in contacting all of your creditors about the situation. If there are creditors who insist you are responsible for the debts, you will need to hire an attorney.

Looking at the Risk Realistically

While identity theft is a problem many people face, you can protect yourself by being careful about how you give out information and how you get rid of your garbage. Unless you have an ongoing problem with recurring identity theft, there is no reason to cancel all your credit cards, close your bank accounts and stop making online purchases.

Coping with Identity Theft Emotionally

Having your identity stolen or your personal information accessed and used by someone else is a terrible feeling. You may feel violated, frightened, nervous, depressed and very angry. The best way to deal with these feelings is to take active steps to deal with the theft. Keep good records, protect your information from future would-be thieves and always remember that it is not your fault. You didn't bring this on yourself, you didn't do anything wrong and you aren't the criminal. If you find you are having a hard time coping with the aftermath of identity theft, think about talking with a counselor or therapist. It is not uncommon to experience depression or anxiety after being the victim of a crime like this.

Other Resources to Assist You:

Here are some additional resources to assist you if you have been a victim of identity theft.

Identity Theft Clearinghouse
Federal Trade Commission
600 Pennsylvania Avenue, NW
Washington, DC 20580
FTC Identity Theft Hotline
877-IDTHEFT (438-4338)
www.consumer.gov/idtheft

Privacy Rights Clearinghouse
3100 5th Ave., Suite B
San Diego, CA 92103
619-298-3396
www.privacyrights.org

Identity Theft Resource Center
PO Box 26833
San Diego CA 92196
858-693-7935
www.idtheftcenter.org

Call for Action, Inc.
(provides phone counseling for identity theft victims)
866-ID-HOTLINE
(866-434-6854)
www.callforaction.org

8 CREATING A GOOD CREDIT RECORD

Now that you have begun to work on your credit record and have started to get your debts in hand, you should consider what you can proactively do to purposefully create a good credit record for yourself. It is important to remember that just as it took time to build up debt and poor credit, it takes a long time to create a credit record that will benefit you. Even if you have fairly good credit, it is important that you learn how to protect and maintain it.

Understanding Credit Terms

There are some basic terms to understand when you are working with credit.

- *Finance Charges.* There are two types of finance charges. APR (annual percentage rate) is the amount of interest you will pay each year on your balance, such as 19%. Monthly Periodic Rate is simply the APR divided by 12 months.

  To understand how much you are paying in interest, multiply the amount of your monthly payment by the number of months you will pay on the loan. This shows the total amount you will pay. Subtract the amount you borrowed from this number and it will show you how much you will be paying in interest alone over the life of the loan.

To understand how interest on your credit cards is calculated, contact the customer service department and they can give you a computer generated calculation of how interest will accrue and be paid on your credit card debt.

✪ *Annual Fees.* Some credit cards charge you a yearly fee just to use the card. The fee appears on your statement once a year and can range from $30 and up. Many companies will waive this fee if you ask. There are cards that do not charge this type of fee, so shop around.

✪ *Grace Period.* Some credit cards offer a grace period. This is the time between when the billing cycle closes and the date you have to pay the balance to avoid any finance charges.

✪ *Fees.* There are a myriad of fees you can encounter with credit cards. There are late payment fees, cash advance fees, fees for checks that bounce, fees for exceeding your credit limit, etc. One type of fee to avoid is a transaction fee. If your card has a transaction fee you will be charged a small amount each time you use the card. This can really add up so avoid it whenever possible.

Obtaining New Credit

If you have a bankruptcy or other poor credit entries on your record, you need to understand that you cannot walk out tomorrow and easily get a new credit card. Most creditors are going to turn you down. Even though you have now turned over a new leaf and have your financial situation under control, credit card companies are going to see you as a bad risk. Even if you have good credit, it is important to understand how to maintain your good credit standing.

Credit Agreements

There are some credit card companies who will eventually give you credit. You can often get a credit card within two years of bankruptcy. When you do apply for credit, read the agreements carefully and be sure to notice the interest rate and monthly fees proposed. Find out if there is a fee for cash advances, how the interest is calculated and how often credit limits are reviewed. If you are offered a terrific deal—such as no payments for six months, be sure to find out if interest accrues during this period.

Merchant Accounts

If you find that you are having difficulty being approved for new credit, try applying for credit with a local merchant, such as a department store. These types of cards are much easier to qualify for and can help you begin to build a good history so that you can then apply for a major credit card. Do not bother with catalog company credit cards. These cards have high interest rates and are not usually reported to credit reporting agencies and thus do nothing to improve your credit rating.

Debit Cards

Debit cards are a great substitute for credit cards. A debit card appears on its face like a credit card. When you make a purchase with a debit card, the amount of the purchase is automatically deducted from your bank account and paid to the debit card company. Any purchase over the amount of funds in the account is denied. This type of card limits you to money you actually have, but can still be abused when it is used to withdraw the money you are supposed to be saving for rent or utilities.

Secured Cards

A *secured card* is similar to a debit card, however the money you deposit remains untouched, earning interest. Your credit limit equals the amount you deposit with the bank. You are billed for your purchases and charged interest on them. If you fail to pay, the money you have deposited is kept by the bank. Make sure that the bank you deposit the money in is a federally insured bank and that the card can be converted to an unsecured card after eighteen months. Be sure you know the finance rate. Confirm that the company will report your account to credit reporting agencies. Also be sure that if there is an application fee for this type of card that it is refundable if your application is denied.

Co-Signers

If you cannot qualify for a credit card on your own and do not have the cash to set up a debit or secured card, you may wish to ask a family member or friend to co-sign for you on a credit card or loan. The other person promises to pay the lender if you cannot and gives the lender the extra protection desired.

User Accounts

Another alternative is to have a friend or relative set up a credit card in his or her own name and then request that a card be issued to you. You can use the card, but the other person will be responsible for payment. Request that the bank report the card on your credit report. This will not have much impact on your credit rating, but it will get you access to credit.

Credit Report References
When you apply for credit, if you know that one of your credit reports from one of the big three reporting agencies appears more favorable than the others, ask the potential creditor to use that report. Attach anything to your credit application that may be favorable, such as tax returns or information about your assets. Be sure to completely fill in applications—you can be denied for failing to complete the application.

Frequent Application
Do not apply for credit too often. Every time you apply, an inquiry is made on your credit report and the inquiry is recorded on your report. Reports that have too many inquiries are not regarded favorably. Future creditors will feel you have been turned down frequently, or that you are seeking too much credit.

Re-Application
If you apply for credit and your application is denied, ask that it be sent to the re-applications department. Most major creditors have such departments where they will seriously re-evaluate an application.

Fine Print
When you apply for credit be sure to carefully read all the fine print. Some cards charge many different fees that will add up substantially when using the card. You would also be wise to shop around for a low finance rate on the card if you plan to carry a balance.

Bank Listing
If you are having difficulty finding a bank that will give you credit, contact the Bankcard Holders of America (540-389-5445). This organization can provide you with a list of banks that offer both secured and unsecured credit cards.

Equal Credit Opportunity Act
The *Equal Credit Opportunity Act* protects consumers from discrimination when they apply for credit. Consumers may not be denied credit because of age, race, religion, national origin, religion, or because they receive public assistance, alimony or child support, or if they work part-time. Under this law creditors have thirty days from the date of receiving all of your information to notify you if you have been accepted or rejected. You must be notified in writing if you are rejected. You are entitled to a reason why you have been rejected (this may be in the letter or they may give you a phone number to call to get the information) as well the name and address of the credit reporting bureau from which your report was obtained.

The Internet can be a fast, convenient way to obtain information about the true costs of credit and to find credit cards. For example, you can use an online calculator to help you understand the true costs of any credit card offer (or other loans you are considering). One is available at **www.bankrate.com/brm/rate /calc_home.asp**. Other sites available to find credit cards include:

- ✪ www.americaslowestrates.com/creditcards /lowest-credit-card-rates-index.shtml

- ✪ www.bankrate.com/brm/rate/brm_ccsearch.ASP

- ✪ www.credit-land.com

- ✪ www.lowcards.com

Improving Current Credit

If you have current credit cards, there are steps you can take to improve your credit with them. To increase your line of credit, maintain a good payment history for a minimum of three months and then ask for an increase in your limit. Paying more than the minimum each month will also improve your chances of getting an increase. Avoid going over your credit limit, as this will count against you. Paying on time is important but you should know that most credit cards do not report delinquencies until they are at least two payments behind.

Statement of Circumstances

If you know you have some items on your credit report that are negative and you have been denied credit because of them, you may need to start submitting a Statement of Circumstances along with your application. (see form 20, p.195.) This statement offers an explanation for what happened. For example, you have been ill and unable to work and overcome with medical bills. Explain this to the creditor in writing and explain how your situation has changed and the steps you have taken.

Account Closings

If you have many credit cards, you should close the ones you do not use regularly and leave yourself no more then two or three cards. A long list of open accounts makes many lenders nervous, even if the accounts are inactive. At any time, you could decide to use them and charge more than you can pay.

How to Use Your New Credit Cards

If you have been able to obtain new credit cards, or if you still have your old cards, you must develop a new attitude about them. You need to think of the credit cards as a convenience and not as an extension of your spending capabilities. You should definitely use your credit cards, but you should be certain to pay the entire balance off each month and not let interest accrue on the account. Using the cards and paying them off responsibly will help improve your credit rating. The creditors will report that you are paying as agreed and on time. You should never use your credit card unless you have cash in the bank or in your possession to pay for it at the time of purchase. A credit card should be a convenience, not a necessity. Pay careful attention to the due date on each bill and pay it on time.

Payments   Most credit cards offer a thirty-day grace period on purchases. Purchases made on June 1 will not incur interest until July 1. This means you can *borrow* money from your credit card company interest free each month for thirty days. Grace periods only apply if you have no outstanding balance. If you are carrying a balance on your card, interest will be charged on new purchases as well the old balance. Mail it at least one week before the due date to be sure it will arrive on time.

It is to your advantage to pay off your credit card balances each month. If you already have an outstanding balance, you should attempt to spend some money each month toward the principal that you owe so that you can gradually eliminate the balance.

Maintaining   Avoid obtaining too many credit cards. One or two really should be more than
Accounts   enough. It can be tempting to open more when you receive an offer in the mail for a card with an initial low interest rate, but remember these initial rates always go up. Often these cards do not offer the best terms or interest rates available. If you do receive them, cut them up and send a letter to the bank rejecting them.

The more accounts you have open, the more you can charge and end up owing. Remember also that the more open accounts you have on your credit report, the less likely you are to be able to obtain new credit.

Choosing a Card

If you are trying to choose which accounts to keep and which accounts to close, consider the interest rates as well as any cash back or special discount programs the cards offer. Some cards offer a rebate (usually 1%) on purchases made with the card. Other cards allow you to accumulate frequent flyer miles or other special discounts. You also should avoid cards that require an annual fee, although often you can convince the company to waive the fee.

Cash Advances

Be aware that cash advances are not *free* money. Most credit cards charge transaction fees and interest begins accumulating immediately on these transactions. You are better off to charge something than to take a cash advance and pay cash.

Tracking Your Cards

Keep a list of all of your credit cards, including account numbers and phone numbers for customer service so that you know at all times what credit you have available and also so that you can easily make a report if your cards are stolen. It is also helpful to keep track of your credit limits so you do not exceed them.

Obtaining Loans

After you have had debt problems or after your credit report has had negative information that cannot be removed placed on it, you may despair over not being able to get a car loan or a mortgage, let alone a personal loan. There are in fact ways to get loans after experiencing these difficulties. One strategy is to make a large down payment on the car or home and pay a higher interest rate. When you put cash down for a car, the lender already holds a substantial amount in its hand and may be willing to lend you money. When you put a large down payment on a home, the bank can see that there will be plenty of equity in the home should a foreclosure happen and that the bank will certainly get its money out.

Be willing to accept loans with higher than average interest rates. Everything has a price. Lending money to someone who is a credit risk has a higher price than lending it to someone with a spotless report.

Use a *co-signer*. When you take out the loan or mortgage, someone else (perhaps a friend or relative) agrees to sign the loan and accept financial responsibility for it if you are ever unable to pay. The creditor now has someone else they can count on to get their money from, and may be willing to give you a chance.

Some other strategies that may allow you to purchase a home include rent-to-own leases, owner financed mortgages, and purchasing a HUD (U.S. Department of Housing and Urban Development) home.

If you already own a home, a home equity loan gives you an available credit line by giving the bank a security interest in your home. You can only get a home equity loan if you have enough equity in your home. This means that you must have either put down a large deposit or that you have paid off a portion of the original mortgage. A second mortgage is usually more difficult to get than a home equity loan because they are generally for larger amounts.

Remember that when you use a home equity loan you are taking value away from what you own in your home. Home equity loans are a great way to finance remodeling projects and can also be useful for paying off high interest credit card loans. But you are putting your home at risk, so it only makes sense if you are going to be able to pay it back.

Bank Accounts

To develop good credit, it is important to have stable bank accounts. You should have a savings and a checking account. Shop around for the bank that will offer you the best package—low fees, free checks, etc. Also check with any credit unions you belong to or are eligible to join because your parent or spouse is a member.

Use your savings account as a place to really save money, even if it is only a small amount. Use your checking account as the central organizing point for your monthly income and debts. Deposit your income, with deductions for savings, in the checking account. Write checks to pay bills from the account. Never write a check if you do not have the funds to cover it in the account. Sending a check to a creditor that will bounce as a way to delay payment or to temporarily get the creditor off of your back is never a good idea. It will only cost you more money and add negative ratings to your credit report.

When using a bank account, consider using one of the computer software programs available to help you manage your account. These types of programs will automatically balance your account for you, so you do not have to worry about making math errors.

You may also want to find out information about the online banking services offered by your bank. With these services you can transfer money between accounts and pay bills online. You may also be able to set up automatic transfers, so bills, like your mortgage payment, will always be on time, since it will be automatically deducted from your account on a specific date each month. You have to be careful to make sure you have the needed funds in the account though.

Another important tool is automatic deposit. Find out if your employer offers this. Automatic deposit often gets your earned wages in the account a day or two sooner than it would if you had to physically deposit the check yourself. Having automatic deposit often makes you eligible for perks on your account, such as no fees. If you have your bank accounts and mortgage with one bank and have automatic deposit, you are in an even better position to negotiate rates and fees.

Maintaining bank accounts will demonstrate to creditors that you are able to manage money and that you are able to save funds.

Name and Address Changes

When you are trying to improve your credit rating, you want to appear as stable as possible. Moving often will make you appear unstable. Try to maintain your residence at one address for at least a year if you can. If you do move, be sure to notify all creditors of your new address. It is important to remember that your credit report is linked to you by your Social Security number and that it will follow you wherever you move.

Changing your name for reasons other than marriage or divorce is also not recommended while you are trying to build a good credit history. While you might have a legitimate reason for doing so, creditors will not know what that reason is and become suspicious.

Negotiation with Past Creditors

If you have negative entries on your credit report, there are things you can do about it. Contact the creditor and offer to pay a sum of money in exchange for having the negative entry removed. You can still do this even if you have had a judgment obtained against you. See Chapter 8 for more information.

Marriage and Credit

The most important thing to understand about marriage and credit is that what happens to one, happens to both. If your spouse has a judgment against him or her, this will be noted on your report. You are both liable for debts incurred during the marriage on joint accounts, even if only one of you knew about them.

If you are in a situation where your credit has been impaired because of your spouse, you need to take steps to separate yourself from him or her and improve your credit rating. Obtain credit in your own name. Many women never do this and never develop an independent credit rating based on their own payment abilities. Upon divorce or the death of their spouse, they find themselves unable to get credit, even though they, as a marital unit, may have had a perfect credit rating.

Scams to Avoid

There is no quick fix to credit and debt problems. Anyone who promises you that there is one is either lying or is offering an illegal plan. There are attorneys who advertise that they can cut your debts in half without bankruptcy. You may find yourself paying a large amount of money for an attorney to do just what you can do yourself—negotiate with creditors.

There are also scams that tell you to obtain a federal employer identification number and use it as a "new" Social Security number, so that you can apply for credit and not be linked to your old credit report. Other scams involve transposing the numbers in your Social Security number, or applying for credit using someone else's name.

Do not try any of these plans. They are illegal and will make you liable for fraud and criminal prosecution. You should also remember that if you follow one of these illegal plans, you cheat yourself out of Social Security benefits.

You also cannot buy a clean credit report. The only report you are entitled to is your own, so anyone offering to sell you a clean credit report is offering you something illegal.

Avoid anyone who requires payment before providing any services, who does not tell you your rights, nor point out what you can do yourself for free. A scam is brewing if you are told not to contact credit reporting agencies yourself or if you are told that you should dispute all the information in your credit report. The *Credit Repair Organizations Act* sets rules for credit repair agencies. Report any suspicious agency to your local attorney general and to the Federal Trade Commission.

Reducing Unsolicited Offers for Credit

It is likely that you receive many unsolicited offers for credit in the mail. Most of these companies get your name and basic information from the credit reporting agencies. They contact the agencies and are given non-confidential information about you. It can be very tempting to overspend if you constantly receive offers of credit in the mail and it can also be annoying. Many people feel it violates their privacy when credit reporting agencies give out information about them. You can contact the credit reporting agencies and indicate that you wish to "opt out" of these offers and not have any of your information disclosed. To do so you need to send a letter, **REQUEST TO OPT OUT** (see form 21, p.196), to one or all of the credit reporting agencies at a special address designated for this purpose. They are as follows:

Equifax Options
Marketing Decisions System
PO Box 740123
Atlanta, GA 30374-0123

Trans Union LLC
Name Removal Option
PO Box 97328
Jackson, MS 39288-7328

Experian Consumer Opt Out
701 Experian Parkway
Allen, TX 75002

To further reduce unsolicited offers by mail or phone, you can also contact:

Direct Marketing Association
Mail Preference Association
PO Box 9008
Farmington, NY 11735

Direct Marketing Association
Telephone Preference Service
PO Box 9014
Farmington, NY 11735
Understanding Credit Terms

Direct Mail Marketing Association
11 W. 42nd St.
PO Box 3861
New York, NY 10163-3861,

National Fraud Information Center
www.fraud.org

Additionally, credit reporting agencies can give some of your information out to *prescreened offers*. Call 888-567-8688 to take your name off the list for all three major credit reporting agencies.

To remove your name from many email offers, contact **www.e-mps.org**.

9	**BUDGETING**

A *budget* is a way to organize your expenses and income so that you can anticipate the amount of funds you will have coming in and the funds you will have to pay out. If you find that you are having trouble seeing where all of your money goes, you will want to track your actual expenditures.

A budget is the most important tool you can have if you are trying to improve your finances. Using a budget will help you completely understand where all of your money goes and help you find ways to control your cash flow.

Why You Should Have a Budget

A budget is your most essential financial tool. It helps you pinpoint how much you have to spend all together, how much you can spend on non-essentials and anticipate when you will receive money. A budget gives you a plan and a visual mapping of how you will use your money. A budget gives you little room to make impulse buys and helps you keep your finances on target. A budget is a way to make a financial contract with yourself.

Creating a Budget

Use the **Budget** at the back of this book. (see form 22, p.197.) Make several copies of it since you will be making estimated and actual budgets for each month.

◈ Fill in all of your regular unchanging expenses, such as rent or mortgage, electric, water, phone, cable, etc.

◈ Next estimate your average monthly costs for essentials like food, gas, clothing, etc.

◈ Next estimate the non-essential expenses, such as entertainment, eating out, gifts, decorative home items, etc.

◈ Fill in the monthly amounts for loans and credit cards.

◈ Note how much you saved and how much you spent on education expenses.

◈ Fill in the yearly expenses. First you need to total what the yearly cost of these items are, then divide by 12 so you can estimate accurately.

◈ Total your expenses.

◈ Complete the monthly income section of the budget and total that.

◈ Compare the two figures. If your expenses are greater than your income, you need to make some adjustments.

◈ Eliminate some of those non-essential expenses. These are the ones that often wind up on credit cards.

◈ Look at the rest of your expenses to see what can be trimmed. (Refer to the list in Chapter 4 about increasing your cash for some ideas.)

Estimated Budget
Once you have completed the form, you will have what is your estimated budget. This is your best guess as to what your expenses are. It is important to create this form so that you can look at how you think you spend your money.

Actual Budget Now that you have estimated your budget, you need to find out what your actual expenses are. Starting on the first day of the month, use the **Spending Log** to record every penny you spend, whether you do so with cash, check, credit, debit, and so on. (see form 23, p.201.) Make sure to record those small expenditures like coffee, newspapers, fast food, and so on. You will be surprised at how quickly these add up.

Use a new **Spending Log** for each week in the month. When the month is over, sit down with your **Spending Logs** and tally them up and use them to complete a new budget form. This will be your actual budget and will show, on a monthly basis, how your money is spent.

Making Changes to Your Budget

Now that you know exactly where your money is going, look back at your estimated monthly budget. There are probably areas you underestimated and a few you over-estimated. Look closely at your actual spending and think about ways you can reduce or eliminate expenses. (See Chapter 4 with ideas for saving money.) You may be surprised at how much you find you can cut from your spending.

Keep **Spending Logs** each week and at the end of every month, tally them up and write out a budget for where your money went for that month. Be sure to write the month on the top of the form so you can easily refer to it.

It is important to remember that budgets are always in flux. Your electric bill may be higher in the summer because you ran a fan or air conditioning. Your food expenses may be less over the holidays if you go and stay with your family. Despite these fluctuations, it is essential that you plan out where your money is going to go, while leaving enough money in your miscellaneous expenses or by putting money into a savings account to cover these unexpected fluctuations.

When budgeting, it is a good idea to sit down at the beginning of each year and think about your plans for the year. If your car is in bad shape, anticipate a lot of repairs or even the expense of having to purchase another car. If you are starting a class in August, save up for tuition and books. The farther ahead you can foresee these things, the better you can plan for, and save money to cover them.

If you are having difficulty completing the **BUDGET** or **SPENDING LOG** forms or you find that your expenses consistently exceed your income, contact Consumer Credit Counseling (see Chapter 5) for assistance in creating a workable budget.

Getting Organized

In order to be able to budget well and be in control of your finances, you need to get all of your information organized.

- ✪ Locate all of your bills, financial statements and pay stubs.

- ✪ Create a separate file for each account, credit card, loan, utility and other expense (such as medical bills or child care bills). Create a separate file for pay stubs, and each bank account, CD or other investment or asset you own.

- ✪ Use individual file folders or one big expandable file folder that is divided into sections.

- ✪ File items as soon as you are done with them. When you pay a bill, file the bill. When you cash your pay check, file the pay stub.

- ✪ Create a separate folder to hold your yearly taxes as well as one to store product/manufacturer warranties.

- ✪ Store important items, such as bonds, birth certificates, Social Security cards, real estate titles, marriage licenses, cash and other valuable items in a fireproof safe (small household safe boxes can be purchased at discount and office supply stores for under $40). Keep this locked at all times and place the key somewhere where you will not lose it.

Paying Your Bills

If you toss all of your bills on your kitchen counter or desk when they arrive, it is unlikely that you are going to remember to pay them on time. You need to devise a system that will help you pay your bills on time. Late payments mean late fees— something you want to avoid at all cost because they are expensive and because they adversely affect your credit rating.

✪ Purchase a monthly folder or box. These have pockets or slots for each day of the month in numerical order.

✪ When you receive a bill, place it in the pocket for the date it is due.

✪ Sit down with your weekly organizer on a set day each week and check to see what is due and when.

✪ It is important to get your payments in the mail at least three to five days before the due date. It can take up to seven days for your payment to arrive, so be sure to allow adequate time.

✪ If you have payments automatically deducted from your bank account, write the date and amount of the deduction on a piece of paper and place it in the slot for the appropriate date so that you will be sure to have enough money in your account to cover it.

✪ Keep a supply of stamps in the folder or box, or nearby.

✪ File the bill in the appropriate spot after you have paid it.

Following Your Budget

You have created a budget that allows you to pay all of your bills using your current income. Now you have to stick to it. This is the hard part. Next week you may see a sweater you have to have. Your friends may want you to go to a concert with them. You might become sick and have to pay for a doctor and medication even though you do not have medical insurance. If you are able to place some money each month in your emergency fund, you will be able to handle expenses like these occasionally. This takes willpower and self-deprivation. Remind yourself that if you exceed your budget you are not going to be able to pay your rent or that awful things like repossession can occur.

Living on a Budget and Using Credit

Some financial advisors recommend not using credit at all if you are having trouble living on a budget. If a credit card in your pocket is like a license to spend and you cannot stop yourself, you should not have credit cards.

It is possible to live on a budget and use credit responsibly.

- ✪ Consider using your credit card only for true emergencies, such as car repairs, medical bills or other unexpected and necessary items. This will limit unnecessary expenses.

- ✪ To control your credit card spending, use the card only to buy things that you have the money to pay for. This way, the card gives you the convenience of being able to avoid carrying large amounts of cash while preventing you from overspending. If you have to, write down your bank account balance every day on a sticky note and attach it to your credit card so you know exactly how much money you have each day.

- ✪ Pay your account balance each month in full. Interest charges are the problem with carrying a balance and it accrues quickly.

- ✪ Pay your credit card bills on time. Late fees add up quickly and can throw off a careful budget.

- ✪ Think of your credit card as a convenience you must be careful with, not as an excuse to go into debt.

- ✪ Cancel all but one or two credit card accounts. It is difficult to keep a handle on the balances if you have too many cards.

- ✪ Cancel all your merchant accounts. Store-specific credit cards are never a good deal, even if they offer you a reward for signing up. The interest rates are higher and they do not carry as much weight on your credit report as big bank cards.

- ✪ Switch to a debit card if you find that you cannot use credit responsibly. A debit card gives you the freedom and convenience of a credit card but the same sense of responsibility as using a check or cash.

10 FACING THE FUTURE

This book has helped you deal with your debt problems, understand and improve your credit rating and manage your money more effectively. However there is still some work left to do.

Changing Your Outlook and Mindset About Money

You have experienced some difficulties with handling debt or in keeping a clean credit report. Now that those problems are cleared up, you need to think about how you can avoid repeating them in the future. Many of the solutions offered in this book will only work once. For example, you can only get a second mortgage on your home once.

You have to be very careful to follow your budget. Keep it on your refrigerator or in your wallet if it will help you stay on track. You need to change the way you deal with money. Become a *penny-pincher*. Keep track of where every cent goes. Use credit cards cautiously. Do not allow yourself to use a credit card without first understanding how and where you are going to get the money to pay for the purchase.

Give yourself a break occasionally. You are going to go off your budget just as when you diet you go off your diet occasionally. But just as with a diet, you have got to make up the difference somewhere else or you are going to be in trouble. Be aware of how you allow yourself to be lenient. It is one thing to spend a little extra to buy yourself an espresso on the way to work but quite another to splurge on a new couch. Each of these will have to be compensated for in a completely different way.

Dealing with Changes

You have a budget that works for you given your current expenses and income. However, it is unlikely that all of these are going to remain the same in your life forever. You might get a lower or higher paying job. Gas prices could go up or down. You might need to buy a newer car, or rent a different apartment with a different rent amount.

If your income and/or expenses change, you will need to adjust your budget accordingly. If your income goes down, you are going to need to find some way to cut your expenses or you will end up over your head in debt. If your income goes up, you might want to consider leaving your expenses at the level they are now and save the extra income. Place it in a bank account, CD, or even an investment account. Watch your money grow so that you can buy a house, take a vacation, or have a safety net for the future.

Keep in mind that if you do change jobs you are under no obligation to notify your creditors. If you want a higher credit limit and your income is higher, you may wish to notify them. However if you take a pay cut, they do not need to know as long as you adjust your expenses so that you can pay all your bills. Remember to notify creditors if you move so that you can continue to get your statements on time and pay your bills on time.

Dealing with Self-Esteem and Compulsion Issues

Many, many people have difficulty handling debt at one point or another in their lives. You are not alone. You may have ended up in this situation because of unexpected misfortune, like divorce, illness, or lay offs. Accept that some things in life just happen and that the best you can do is deal with the repercussions. Look to the future. Make plans for how you are going to get ahead and pursue them.

If you have ended up in this situation because of your own mistakes, look at what happened, find out how to change yourself or your habits and follow through. You may find you have a spending compulsion. If this is the case, seek assistance from a mental health professional or debt professional. Perhaps you are simply terrible with numbers. Have your spouse or a good friend help you follow a budget. Do not be afraid to look around you for help.

As you look to the future, think of money as an important but dangerous tool that you must use carefully.

Educating Children About Debt

Although debt is one of the biggest problems Americans face, very little is done to educate children and teens about money management. While some schools offer classes and instruction about avoiding pregnancy, parenting and other life skills, very few take the time to teach budgeting or to explain credit, loans, bank accounts, interest and other financial matters.

If you have children, take the time to talk to them about money and debt. Giving an allowance is a good way to help children learn to manage money. Setting up a savings account for your child is an important way to encourage saving and to teach the basics of account balancing.

If you have a teen, take the time to talk to him or her about credit cards. Many young adults head off to college and are bombarded with credit card offers. This *free money* can seem like a bonanza to a young adult who is on his or her own for the first time. Work with your college student so he or she learns to manage money and expenses.

Be honest with your kids about the mistakes you have made and involve them in the changes you are making to get on the right track. Setting a good example and teaching kids essential money management skills will ensure that debt problems do not spread to the next generation.

Move Forward

Whatever problems you had with debt or bankruptcy are in the past. You must always be careful to make sure you do not end up in a similar situation again, but you need to let go of those past problems. Stop blaming yourself and feeling guilty or inadequate. Remind yourself that you have developed a new plan to manage your finances and that you will control the future.

GLOSSARY

A

alimony. Money paid to an ex-spouse on a regular basis after a divorce as ordered by the court.

annual fee. A yearly amount charged by credit card companies for the privilege of holding the card.

APR (annual percentage rate). The amount of interest you will pay each year on your balance.

asset. Property or money you own.

B

balance. The total amount owed on an account.

bankruptcy. A legal process that freezes all actions by creditors against a debtor. If the petition for bankruptcy is approved, all of the debt will be discharged, or excused.

budget. A way to organize expenses and income so that you can control your spending.

C

cancellation. When a loan is forgiven.

child support. An amount of money paid by one parent to another under court order to assist in financially supporting a child.

co-signer. Someone who agrees to be responsible for a debt if the debtor does not make payments.

collection agency. A company that collects debts on behalf of creditors.

consolidation. Combining several loans into one with a lower monthly payment. Most often used with student loans.

Consumer Credit Counseling. A service that will assist you in combining your debts into one monthly payment.

contingency. A form of payment to an attorney. The attorney agrees to accept a percent of your winnings instead of a fee you pay up front.

correspondence. Any letters or items that you have sent or received through the mail, email or fax.

credit card. A card that allows you to charge items to your account. Interest is charged on balances not paid off during the billing cycle.

credit history. Your past credit reports that indicate how much of a risk you are to loan money to.

credit limit. The total amount you are authorized to charge on a credit card.

credit report. A document that lists all of your debts and their statuses.

credit reporting agencies. Companies that create credit reports by gathering information from creditors.

creditor. Person loaning money.

D

debit card. A type of credit card where the user deposits a certain amount of money with the bank and then charges against it, using that money to pay the items charged.

debt. An amount of money owed.

debt collector. Person whose job it is to collect money owed on debts.

debtor. The person who owes money.

deferment. Occurs when a loan is put on hold without payments becoming due. Usually only applies to student loans.

delinquent. Late or overdue.

E

eviction. When you are forced to move out of your residence by a landlord.

F

finance charge. Fees charged for borrowing money, often stated as a percentage.

forbearance. Occurs when the lender allows you to postpone or make temporary reductions in your payments.

foreclosure. Occurs when you fail to make mortgage payments on your home and the bank takes the property and sells it, forcing you to move out.

G

garnishment. Occurs when a court orders that money be deducted from your wages to pay a debt.

grace period. The time between when the billing cycle closes and the date you have to pay the balance by to avoid any finance charges.

I

identity theft. Problem that occurs when someone else uses your accounts or opens new accounts using your personal information.

income. Money you earn from a job or as interest on money you have saved.

interest. A percentage of the balance that is charged by the creditor as a fee for borrowing the money or a percentage you earn on money you have saved.

J

joint account. An account that is equally owned by two people.

judgment. A court order.

judgment proof. Someone who has little or no assets so that a judgment against them has no effect upon them since there is nothing that can be taken.

L

lien. A formal judgment of debt that is entered into court and county records indicating that you owe a creditor a certain amount and attaching the debt to a piece of real property so that if it is ever sold the debt must be paid.

M

minimum payment. The least amount you can pay to keep an account current.

monthly periodic rate. The APR divided by 12 months.

mortgage. A loan that allows you to purchase real estate and gives the bank a security interest in the property.

N

negotiation. The process of resolving a dispute to a mutually acceptable solution.

P

postdated check. A check dated with a future date.

prioritizing. Placing things in order of importance.

R

repossession. Occurs when a creditor seizes a piece of personal property to pay off a loan secured by the property.

S

secured credit card. A credit card where the debtor gives a certain amount of money to the bank to be used as a security. The debtor charges items and repays them and the security interest is held in case there is a failure to pay.

secured loan. A loan where you borrow money or buy a certain item and give the creditor a security interest or collateral in an item. For example, a car loan.

secured property. Items purchased or financed through a loan that gives the creditor a security interest in them.

security interest. The right maintained by a creditor to repossess or take back an item you borrowed money to buy if you fail to make payments.

settlement. An agreement that is reached between a debtor and creditor that solves or eliminates the dispute.

State Banking Authority. An agency that governs the banks and financial institutions within a state.

student loan. An unsecured loan that is usually offered through a bank or loan agency and backed by the government in order to pay for college. Student loans cannot be discharged in bankruptcy and are often a source of credit problems.

U

unsecured loan. A loan where the creditor does not hold a security interest in an item you own. Most credit cards are unsecured.

user accounts. A credit card account set up in one person's name that has a card issued to another person so that he or she may charge against the account. The person who holds the account is ultimately responsible for payments.

APPENDIX A: STATE-BY-STATE RESOURCES

This appendix contains a state-by-state listing of Attorneys General, Banking Authorities and Consumer Protection Agencies. These are state agencies that can answer questions, help you solve problems and provide assistance for problems involving discrimination, credit concerns, hate crimes, and housing problems. (The names of the officials are not included since these change often.)

Alabama

Attorney General:
11 South Union St.
Montgomery, AL 36103

Banking Authority:
Superintendent of Banks
Center for Commerce
401 Adams Avenue, #680
Montgomery, AL 36130-1201
334-242-3452
website: www.legislature.state.al.us

Consumer Protection Agency:
Office of the Attorney General
Consumer Affairs Section
11 South Union St.
Montgomery, AL 36130
334-242-7335
website: www.ago.state.al.us

Alaska

Attorney General:
State Capitol
PO Box 110300
Juneau, AK 99811-0300

Banking Authority:
Director of Banking
Securities and Corporations
Department of Commerce
150 Third St., Rm 217
Juneau, AK 99811-0807
907-465-2521
website: www.dced.state.ak.us

Consumer Protection Agency:
Consumer Protection Unit
Office of the Attorney General
1031 West 4th Avenue
Ste. 200
Anchorage, AK 99501-5903
907-269-5100
website: www.law.state.ak.us

Arizona

Attorney General:
1275 W Washington St.
Phoenix, AZ 85007

Banking Authority:
Superintendent of Banks
Arizona State Banking Department
2910 N. 44th St., Ste. 300
Phoenix, AZ 85018
602-255-4421
website: www.azbanking.com

Consumer Protection Agency:
Chief Counsel
Consumer Protection and Advocacy Section
Office of the Attorney General
1275 West Washington St.
Phoenix, AZ 85007
602-542-3702
website: www.ag.state.az.us

Office of the Attorney General
Consumer Protection
400 West Congress South Bldg., Ste. 315
Tucson, AZ 85701
520-628-6504
website: www.ag.state.az.us

Arkansas

Attorney General:
Tower Building
323 Center St.
Little Rock, AR 72201-2610

Banking Authority:
Bank Commissioner
Arkansas State Bank Department
Tower Building
323 Center St., Ste. 500
Little Rock, AR 72201-2613
501-324-9019
website: www.state.ar.us/bank

Consumer Protection Agency:
Consumer Protection Division
Office of the Attorney General
323 Center St., Ste. 200
Little Rock, AR 72201
501-682-2007
website: www.ag.state.ar.us

California

Attorney General:
1515 K St.
Sacramento, CA 95814

Banking Authority:
Commissioner
Department of Financial Institutions
State of California
111 Pine St., Ste. 1100
San Francisco, CA 94111-5613
415-263-8507
website: www.dfi.ca.gov

Consumer Protection Agency:
Acting Chief
Bureau of Automotive Repair
California Department of Consumer Affairs
10240 Systems Parkway
Sacramento, CA 95827
916-255-4300
website: www.autorepair.ca.gov

Director
California Department of Consumer Affairs
400 R St., Ste. 3000
Sacramento, CA 95814
916-445-4465
website: www.dca.ca.gov

Office of the Attorney General
Public Inquiry Unit
P.O. Box 944255
Sacramento, CA 94244-2550
916-322-3360
website: www.caag.state.ca.us

Colorado

Attorney General:
Department of Law
1525 Sherman St.
Denver, CO 80203

Banking Authority:
State Bank Commissioner
Department of Regulatory Agencies
Division of Banking
1560 Broadway
Ste. 1175
Denver, CO 80202
303-894-7575
website: www.dora.state.co.us/banking

Consumer Protection Agency:
Consumer Protection Division
Colorado Attorney General's Office
1525 Sherman St., 5th Floor
Denver, CO 80203-1760
303-866-5079

Connecticut

Attorney General:
55 Elm St.
Hartford, CT 06106

Banking Authority:
Banking Commissioner
Connecticut Department of Banking
260 Constitution Plaza
Hartford, CT 06103
860-240-8200
website: www.state.ct.us/dob

Consumer Protection Agency:
Commissioner
Department of Consumer Protection
165 Capitol Avenue
Hartford, CT 06106
860-713-6300
website: www.state.ct.us/dcp

Delaware

Attorney General:
Carvel State Office Building
820 N. French St.
Wilmington, DE 19801

Banking Authority:
State Bank Commissioner
555 East Lockerman St., Ste. 210
Dover, DE 19901
302-739-4235
website: www.state.de.us/bank

Consumer Protection Agency:
Director
Consumer Protection Unit
Office of Attorney General
820 N. French St., 5th Floor
Wilmington, DE 19801
302-577-8600
website: www.state.de.us/attgen/consumer.htm

Director
Fraud and Consumer Protection Division
Office of the Attorney General
820 N. French St., 5th Floor
Wilmington, DE 19801
302-577-8600
website: www.state.de.us/attgen/consumer.htm

District of Columbia

Office of the Corporation Counsel
414 4th St. NW
Washington, D.C. 20001

Banking Authority:
Commissioner of Banking and Financial Institutions
Office of Banking & Finance
1400 L St. NW
Washington, D.C. 20005
202-727-1563
website: www.obfi.dcgov.org

Consumer Protection Agency:
Senior Counsel
Office of the Corporation Counsel
441 4th St. NW
Ste. 450-N
Washington, D.C. 20001
202-442-9828

Florida

Attorney General:
The Capitol, PL 01
Tallahassee, FL 32399-1050

Banking Authority:
State Comptroller
Department of Banking and Finance
101 E. Gaines St.
Tallahassee, FL 32399-0350
850-410-9370
website: www.dbf.state.fl.us

Consumer Protection Agency:
Economic Crimes Division
Office of the Attorney General
110 SE 6th St., 10th Floor
Fort Lauderdale, FL 33301
954-712-4600
Fax: 954-712-4700
website: www.legal.firn.edu

Chief of Multi-State Litigation
Consumer Litigation Section
110 SE 6th St.
Fort Lauderdale, FL 33301
954-712-4600

Economic Crimes Division
Office of the Attorney General
135 West Central Blvd., 10th Floor
Century Plaza, Ste. 1000
Orlando, FL 32801
407-999-5588

Economic Crimes Division
Office of the Attorney General
The Capitol, Ste. PL01
Tallahassee, FL 32399-1050
850-414-3300

Director of Division Consumer Services
Department of Agriculture & Consumer Services
Terry L. Rhoads Building
2005 Apalachee
Tallahassee, FL 32399
850-922-2966
website: www.800helpfla.com

Georgia

Attorney General:
40 Capitol Square SW
Atlanta, GA 30334-1300

Banking Authority:
Legal & Consumer Affairs Specialist
State of Georgia (Dept of Banking & Finance)
2990 Brandywine Road, Ste. 200
Atlanta, GA 30341-5565
770-986-1633

Consumer Protection Agency:
Administrator
Governor's Office of Consumer Affairs
2 Martin Luther King, Jr. Drive
Ste. 356
Atlanta, GA 30334
404-656-3790
website: www2.state.ga.us/gaoca

Hawaii

Attorney General:
425 Queen St.
Honolulu, HI 96813

Banking Authority:
Commissioner
Financial Institutions
State of Hawaii
1010 Richards St., Rm. 602A
Honolulu, HI 96805
808-586-2820

Consumer Protection Agency:
Investigator
Office of Consumer Protection
Department of Commerce and Consumer Affairs
345 Kekuanaoa St. Room 12
Hilo, HI 96720
808-933-0910

Acting Executive Director
Office of Consumer Protection
Department of Commerce and Consumer Affairs
235 S. Beretania St., Room 801
Honolulu, HI 96813
808-586-2636

Investigator
Office of Consumer Protection
Dept of Commerce and Consumer Affairs
1063 L Main St., Ste C-216
Wailuku, HI 96793
808-984-8244
website: www.state.hi.us/dcca/

Idaho

Attorney General:
PO Box 83720
Boise, ID 83720-0010

Banking Authority:
Director
State of Idaho Department of Finance
700 W. State St., 2nd Floor
Boise, ID 83720-0031
208-332-8000
website: www.state.id.us/finance/dof.htm

Consumer Protection Agency:
Consumer Protection Unit
Idaho Attorney General's Office
650 West State St.
Boise, ID 83720-0010
208-334-2424
website: www.state.id.us/ag

Illinois

Attorney General:
J.R. Thompson Center
100 W Randolph St.
Chicago, IL 60601

Banking Authority:
Commissioner of Banks and Real Estate
Illinois Office of Banks and Real Estate
310 South Michigan Avenue, Ste. 230
Chicago, IL 60604-4278
312-793-3000
website: www.state.il.us/obr

Illinois Office of Banks and Real Estate
Springfield Office
500 East Monroe St.
Springfield, IL 62701-1509
217-782-3000
website: www.state.il.us/obr

Consumer Protection Agency:
Office of the Attorney General
1001 East Main St.
Carbondale, IL 62901
618-529-6400

Bureau Chief
Consumer Fraud Bureau
100 West Randolph
12th Floor
Chicago, IL 60601
312-814-3580
website: www.ag.state.il.us

Chief
Consumer Protection Division of the
Attorney General Office
100 West Randolph
12th Floor
Chicago, IL 60601
312-814-3000

Governor's Office of Citizens Assistance
222 South College, Room 106
Springfield, IL 62706
217-782-0244

Indiana

Attorney General:
219 State House
Indianapolis, IN 46204

Banking Authority:
Director
Department of Financial Institutions
402 W. Washington St., Room W-066
Indianapolis, IN 46204-2759
317-232-3955
website: www.dfi.state.in.us

Consumer Protection Agency:
Chief Counsel and Director
Consumer Protection Division
Office of the Attorney General
Indiana Government Center South
402 West Washington St., 5th Floor
Indianapolis, IN 46204
317-232-6201
website: www.in.gov/attorneygeneral

Iowa

Attorney General:
Hoover State Office Building
Des Moines, IA 50319

Banking Authority:
Superintendent of Banking
Iowa Division of Banking
200 East Grand, Ste. 300
Des Moines, IA 50309
515-281-4014
website: www.idob.state.ia.us

Consumer Protection Agency:
Consumer Protection Division
Office of the Attorney General
Director of Consumer Protection Division
1300 East Walnut St., 2nd Floor
Des Moines, IA 50319
515-281-5926
website: www.IowaAttorneyGeneral.org

Kansas

Attorney General:
Judicial Building
301 W 10th St.
Topeka, KS 66612-1597

Banking Authority:
State Bank Commissioner
Office of the State Bank Commissioner
700 Jackson St., Ste. 300
Topeka, KS 66603-3714
785-296-2266
website: www.ink.org/public/osbc

Consumer Protection Agency:
Consumer Protection Division
Office of the Attorney General
120 SW 10th, 4th Floor
Topeka, KS 66612-1597
785-296-3751
website: www.ink.org/public/ksag

Kentucky

Attorney General:
State Capitol, Room 116
Frankfort, KY 40601

Banking Authority:
Commissioner
Department of Financial Institutions
1025 Capitol Center Dr., Ste. 200
Frankfort, KY 40601
502-573-3390
website: www.dfi.state.ky.us

Consumer Protection Agency:
Director
Consumer Protection Division
Office of the Attorney General
1024 Capital Center Drive
Frankfort, KY 40601
502-696-5389
website: www.kyattorneygeneral.com/cp

Consumer Protection Division
Office of the Attorney General
9001 Shelbyville Rd., Ste. 3
Louisville, KY 40222
502-425-4825

Louisiana

Attorney General:
Department of Justice
PO Box 94005
Baton Rouge, LA 70804-4095

Banking Authority:
Acting Commissioner
LA Office of Financial Institutions
P.O. Box 94095
Baton Rouge, LA 70804-9095
225-925-4660
website: www.ofi.state.la.us

Consumer Protection Agency:
Chief
Consumer Protection Section
Office of the Attorney General
301 Main St., Ste. 1250
Baton Rouge, LA 70801
800-351-4889
website: www.ag.state.la.us

Maine

Attorney General:
State House Building
Augusta ME 04333

Banking Authority:
Superintendent of Banking
36 State House Station
Augusta, ME 04333-0036
207-624-8570
website: www.mainebankingreg.org

Consumer Protection Agency:
Director
Office of Consumer Credit Regulation
35 State House Station
Augusta, ME 04333-0035
207-624-8527
website: www.mainecreditreg.org

Maine Attorney General's
Consumer Mediation Service
6 State House Station
Augusta, ME 04333
207-626-8849
website: www.state.me.us/ag

Division Chief
Public Protection Division
Office of the Attorney General
6 State House Station
Augusta, ME 04333
207-626-8800

Maryland

Attorney General:
200 Saint Paul Place
Baltimore, MD 21202-2202

Banking Authority:
Commissioner of Financial Regulation Division
500 North Calvert St.
Baltimore, MD 21202
410-333-6808
website: www.dllr.state.md.us/finance

Consumer Protection Agency:
Chief
Consumer Protection Division
Office of the Attorney General
200 Saint Paul Pl., 16th Floor
Baltimore, MD 21202-2021
410-528-8662
website: www.oag.state.md.us/consumer

Manager
Business Licensing & Consumer Service
Motor Vehicle Administration
6601 Ritchie Highway, NE
Glen Burnie, MD 21062
410-768-7248

Massachusetts

Attorney General:
1 Ashburton Place
Boston, MA 02108-1698

Banking Authority:
Commissioner of Banks
MA Division of Banks
One South Station
Boston, MA 02110
617-956-1500
website: www.state.ma.us/dob

Consumer Protection Agency:
Director
Executive Office of Consumer Affairs
and Business Regulation
10 Park Plaza, Room 5170
Boston, MA 02116
617-973-8700
website: www.state.ma.us/consumer

Consumer Protection and Antitrust Division
Office of the Attorney General
200 Portland St.
Boston, MA 02114
617-727-8400
website: www.ago.state.ma.us

Consumer Protection and Antitrust Division
Office of the Attorney General - Springfield
436 Dwight St.
Springfield, MA 01103
413-784-1240

Michigan

Attorney General:
525 W Ottawa St.
Lansing, MI 48909-0212

Banking Authority:
Commissioner
Office of Financial and Insurance Services
Office of the Commissioner
333 S. Capitol Avenue, Ste. A
Lansing, MI 48933
517-373-3460
website: www.cis.state.mi.us/fib

Consumer Protection Agency:
Director
Bureau of Automotive Regulation
Michigan Department of State
Lansing, MI 48918-1200
517-373-4777

Assistant in Charge
Consumer Protection Division
Office of Attorney General
P.O. Box 30213
Lansing, MI 48909
517-373-1140

Minnesota

Attorney General:
State Capitol
Ste. 102
St. Paul, MN 55155

Banking Authority:
Assistant Commissioner
Minnesota Department of Commerce
Financial Exams
133 East Seventh St.
St. Paul, MN 55101
651-296-2751
website: www.commerce.state.mn.us

Consumer Protection Agency:
Manager
Consumer Services Division
Minnesota Attorney General's Office
1400 NCL Tower
445 Minnesota St.
St. Paul, MN 55101
612-296-3353
website: www.ag.state.mn.us/consumer

Mississippi

Attorney General:
Department of Justice
PO Box 220
Jackson, MS 39205-0220

Banking Authority:
Director Consumer Finance Division
Department of Banking and Consumer Finance
Consumer Finance
Walter Sillers Building
550 High St., Ste. 304
Jackson, MS 39205-3729
601-359-1031
website: www.dbcf.state.ms.us

Consumer Protection Agency:
Director
Consumer Protection Division of the
Mississippi Attorney General's Office
P.O. Box 22947
Jackson, MS 39225-2947
601-359-4230
website: www.ago.state.ms.us

Director
Bureau of Regulatory Services
Department of Agriculture and Commerce
121 North Jefferson St.
Jackson, MS 39201
601-359-1111
website: www.mdac.state.ms.us

Missouri

Attorney General:
Supreme Court Building
207 W High St.
Jefferson City, MO 65102

Banking Authority:
Acting Commissioner of Finance
Department of Finance
P.O. Box 716
Jefferson City, MO 65102
573-751-3242
website: www.ecodev.state.mo.us/finance

Consumer Protection Agency:
Deputy Chief Counsel
Consumer Protection and Trade Offense Division
1530 Rax Court
Jefferson City, MO 65102
573-751-6887
website: www.ago.state.mo.us

Montana

Attorney General:
Justice Building
215 N. Sanders
Helena, MT 59620-1401

Banking Authority:
Commissioner
Division of Banking & Financial Institutions
846 Front St.
Helena, MT 59620-0546
406-444-2091
website:
www.commerce.state.mt.us/finance/index.html

Consumer Protection Agency:
Chief Legal Counsel
Consumer Affairs Unit
Department of Administration
1424 Ninth Avenue
Box 200501
Helena, MT 59620-0501
406-444-4312

Nebraska

Attorney General:
State Capitol
PO Box 98920
Lincoln, NE 68509

Banking Authority:
Director
Department of Banking & Finance
1200 N. St., Ste. 311
Lincoln, NE 68509
402-471-2171
website: www.ndbf.org

Consumer Protection Agency:
Department of Justice
2115 State Capitol
Lincoln, NE 68509
402-471-2682
website: www.nol.org/home/ago

Nevada

Attorney General:
198 S. Carson
Capitol Complex
Carson City, NV 89710

Banking Authority:
Commissioner
Department of Business & Industry
Financial Institutions Division
406 E. Second St., Ste. 3
Carson City, NV 89701-4758
775-687-4259
website: www.state.nv.us/b&i

Consumer Protection Agency:
Commissioner
Nevada Consumer Affairs Division
1850 E. Sahara, Ste. 101
Las Vegas, NV 89104
702-486-7355
website: www.fyiconsumer.org

Bureau of Consumer Protection
555 E. Washington Ave, Ste. 3900
Las Vegas, NV 89101
702-486-3420

Deputy Chief Investigator
Consumer Affairs Division
Department of Business and Industry
4600 Kietzke Lane, Building B, Ste. 113
Reno, NV 89502
775-688-1800

New Hampshire

Attorney General:
State House Annex
25 Capitol St.
Concord, NH 03301-6397

Banking Authority:
State of New Hampshire Banking Department
Consumer Credit
56 Old Suncook Road
Concord, NH 03301
603-271-3561
website: www.state.nh.us/banking

Consumer Protection Agency:
Consumer Protection and Antitrust Bureau
New Hampshire Attorney General's Office
33 Capitol St.
Concord, NH 03301
603-271-3641
website: www.state.nh.us/nhdoj/Consumer/cpb.html

New Jersey

Attorney General:
Richard J. Hughes Justice Complex
25 Market St., CN 080
Trenton, NJ 08625

Banking Authority:
Acting Commissioner
Department of Banking and Insurance
20 West State St.
Trenton, NJ 08625
609-292-3420
website: states.naic.org/nj/njhomepg.html

Consumer Protection Agency:
Department of Law and Public Safety
Division of Consumer Affairs
PO Box 45025
Newark, NJ 07101
973-504-6200
website: www.state.nj.us/lps/ca/home.htm

New Mexico

Attorney General:
PO Drawer 1508
Santa Fe, NM 87504-1508

Banking Authority:
Financial Institutions Division
Regulation and Licensing Dept
725 St Michaels Drive
Santa Fe, NM 87501
505-827-7100
website: www.state.nm.us

Consumer Protection Agency:
Director
Consumer Protection Division
Office of the Attorney General
407 Galisteo
Santa Fe, NM 87504-1508
505-827-6060
website: www.ago.state.nm.us

New York

Attorney General:
120 Broadway
New York, NY 10271

Banking Authority:
Acting Superintendent of Banking
New York State Banking Department
Two Rector St.
New York, NY 10006-1894
212-618-6553
website: www.banking.state.ny.us

Consumer Protection Agency:
Bureau Chief
Bureau of Consumer Frauds and Protection
Office of the Attorney General
State Capitol
Albany, NY 12224
518-474-5481
website: www.oag.state.ny.us

Chairwoman and Executive Director
New York State Consumer Protection Board
5 Empire State Plaza, Ste. 2101
Albany, NY 12223-1556
518-474-3514
website: www.consumer.state.ny.us

Deputy Bureau Chief
Consumer Frauds and Protection Bureau
Office of the Attorney General
120 Broadway, 3rd FL
New York, NY 10271
212-416-8300

Assistant Attorney General in Charge
Consumer Fraud and Protection Bureau
New York State Office of the Attorney General
Harlem Regional Office
163 West 125th St.
New York, NY 10027-8201
212-961-4475

Assistant Attorney General in Charge
Plattsburgh Regional Office
Office of Attorney General
70 Clinton St.
Plattsburgh, NY 12901
518-562-3282

Assistant Attorney General in Charge
Consumer Fraud and Protection Bureau
New York State Office of the Attorney General
Westchester Regional Office
101 East Post Road
White Plains, NY 10601-5008
914-422-8755

North Carolina

Attorney General:
Department of Justice
PO Box 629
Raleigh, NC 27602-0629

Banking Authority:
North Carolina Commissioner of Banks
4309 Mail Service Center
Raleigh, NC 27699-4309
919-733-3016
website: www.banking.state.nc.us

Consumer Protection Agency:
Senior Deputy Attorney General
Consumer Protection Division
Office of the Attorney General
P.O. Box 629
Raleigh, NC 27602
919-716-6000
website: www.jus.state.nc.us/cpframe.htm

North Dakota

Attorney General:
State Capitol
600 East Boulevard Ave.
Bismarck, ND 58505-0040

Banking Authority:
Commissioner
ND Department of Banking and Financial Institutions
2000 Schafer St., Ste. G
Bismarck, ND 58501-1204
701-328-9933
website: www.state.nd.us/bank

Consumer Protection Agency:
Director
Consumer Protection and Antitrust Division
Office of the Attorney General
600 East Boulevard Avenue
Department 125
Bismarck, ND 58505-0040
701-328-3404
website: www.ag.state.nd.us/ndag/cpat/cpat.html

Office of the Attorney General
600 East Boulevard Avenue
Department 125
Bismarck, ND 58505-0040
701-328-2210
website: www.ag.state.nd.us

Ohio

Attorney General:
State Office Tower
30 East Broad St.
Columbus, OH 43266-0410

Banking Authority:
Training and Communications Manager
Department of Commerce - State of Ohio
Financial Institutions Division
77 S. High St., 21st Floor
Columbus, OH 43266-0121
614-728-8400
website: www.som.state.oh.us/dfi

Consumer Protection Agency:
Ohio Consumers' Counsel
77 S. High St., 15th Floor
Columbus, OH 43266-0550
614-466-8574
website: www.state.oh.us/cons/

Ohio Attorney General's Office
30 E. Broad St., 25th Floor
Columbus, OH 43215-3428
614-466-8831
website: www.ag.state.oh.us

Oklahoma

Attorney General:
State Capitol
2300 N Lincoln Blvd., Room 112
Oklahoma City, OK 73105

Banking Authority:
Bank Commissioner
OK State Banking Department
4545 North Lincoln Blvd., Ste. 164
Oklahoma City, OK 73105
405-521-2782
website: www.state.ok.us/~osbd

Consumer Protection Agency:
Administrator
Department of Consumer Credit
4545 North Lincoln Blvd., #104
Oklahoma City, OK 73105
405-521-3653

Oklahoma Attorney General
Consumer Protection Unit
4545 N. Lincoln Avenue
Ste. 260
Oklahoma City, OK 73105
405-521-2029
website: www.oag.state.ok.us

Consumer Protection Division
Office of the Attorney General
440 South Houston, Ste. 505
Tulsa, OK 74127-8913
918-581-2885
website: www.oag.state.ok.us

Oregon

Attorney General:
Justice Building
1162 Court St. NE
Salem OR 97310

Banking Authority:
Administrator
Department of Consumer & Business Services
Division of Finance & Corporate
350 Winter St., NE
Room 410
Salem, OR 97310-3881
503-378-4140
website: www.cbs.state.or.us/external/dfcs

Consumer Protection Agency:
Attorney in Charge
Financial Fraud/ Consumer Protection Section
Department of Justice
1162 Court St., NE
Salem, OR 97310
503-378-4732
website: www.doj.state.or.us

Pennsylvania

Attorney General:
Strawberry Square
Harrisburg, PA 17120

Banking Authority:
Secretary of Banking Department
333 Market St., 16th Floor
Harrisburg, PA 17101-2290
717-787-6991
website: www.banking.state.pa.us

Consumer Protection Agency:
Director
Bureau of Consumer Protection
Office of Attorney General
14th Floor, Strawberry Square
Harrisburg, PA 17120
717-787-9707
website: www.attorneygeneral.gov

Senior Deputy Attorney General
Health Care Unit
Bureau of Consumer Protection
Office of the Attorney General
14th Floor Strawberry Square
Harrisburg, PA 17120
717-705-6938

Consumer Advocate
Office of the Consumer Advocate
Office of the Attorney General
Forum Place, 5th Floor
Harrisburg, PA 17101-1921
717-783-5048
website: www.oca.state.pa.us

Rhode Island

Attorney General:
72 Pine St.
Providence, RI 02903

Banking Authority:
Associate Director and Superintendent
Banking
233 Richmond St., Ste. 231
Providence, RI 02903-4231
401-222-2405

Consumer Protection Agency:
Director
Consumer Unit
Consumer Protection Unit
Department of Attorney General
150 South Main St.
Providence, RI 02903
401-274-4400

Consumer Credit Couseling Services
535 Centerville Rd., Ste. 103
Warwick, RI 02886
website: www.creditcounseling.org

South Carolina

Attorney General:
Rembert C. Dennis Office Building
P.O. Box 11549
Columbia, SC 29211-1549

Banking Authority:
Commissioner of Banking
State Board of Financial Institutions
1015 Sumter St., Room 309
Columbia, SC 29201
803-734-2001

Consumer Protection Agency:
Senior Assistant Attorney General
Office of the Attorney General
P.O. Box 11549
Columbia, SC 29211
803-734-3970
website: www.scattorneygeneral.org

Administrator/Consumer Avocate
SC Department of Consumer Affairs
2801 Devine St.
Columbia, SC 29205-5757
803-734-4200
website: www.state.sc.us/consumer

State Ombudsman
Office of Executive Policy and Program
1205 Pendleton St., Room 308
Columbia, SC 29201
803-734-0457
website: www.myscgov.com

South Dakota

Attorney General:
500 E Capitol
Pierre, SD 57501-5070

Banking Authority:
Director
SD Division of Banking
217 1/2 W. Missouri Avenue
Pierre, SD 57501-4590
605-773-3421
website: www.state.sd.us/banking

Consumer Protection Agency:
Director of Consumer Affairs
Office of the Attorney General
500 East Capitol
State Capitol Building
Pierre, SD 57501-5070
605-773-4400

Tennessee

Attorney General:
450 James Robertson Parkway
Nashville, TN 37243-0495

Banking Authority:
Commissioner
Tennessee Department of Financial Institutions
John Sevier Building
500 Charlotte Ave., 4th Floor
Nashville, TN 37243-0705
615-741-2236
website: www.state.tn.us/financialinst/

Consumer Protection Agency:
Director
Division of Consumer Affairs
500 James Robertson Parkway
5th Floor
Nashville, TN 37243-0600
615-741-4737
website: www.state.tn.us/consumer

Deputy Attorney General
Division of Consumer Protection
Consumer Advocate and Protection
Tennessee Attorney General's Office
P.O. Box 20207
Nashville, TN 37243-0491
615-741-1671
Fax: 615-532-2910

Texas

Attorney General:
Capitol Station
PO Box 12548
Austin, TX 78711-2548

Banking Authority:
Banking Commissioner
Texas Department of Banking
2601 North Lamar
Austin, TX 78705
512-475-1300
website: www.banking.state.tx.us

Consumer Protection Agency:
Consumer Protection/ Austin Regional Office
P.O. Box 12548
Austin, TX 78711-2548
512-463-2185
Fax: 512-463-8301
website: www.oag.state.tx.us

Consumer Protection Division
Office of Attorney General
P.O. Box 12548
Austin, TX 78711-2548
512-463-2070

Public Counsel
Office of Public Insurance Counsel
333 Guadalupe, Ste. 3-120
Austin, TX 78701
512-322-4143
website: www.opic.state.tx.us

Consumer Protection/Houston Regional Office
Office of the Attorney General
808 Travis, Ste. 812
Houston, TX 77002
713-223-5886, ext. 118

Utah

Attorney General:
State Office Building
Salt Lake City, UT 84114

Banking Authority:
Commissioner
Department of Financial Institutions
P.O. Box 89
Salt Lake City, UT 84110-0089
801-538-8854
website: www.dfi.state.ut.us

Consumer Protection Agency:
Director
Division of Consumer Protection
Department of Commerce
160 East 300 South
Box 146704
Salt Lake City, UT 84114-6704
801-530-6601
website: www.commerce.state.ut.us

Vermont

Attorney General:
109 State St.
Montpelier, VT 05609-1001

Banking Authority:
Information Policy & Program Chief
State of Vermont
Banking, Insurance, Securities and Health Care
Administration
89 Main St.
Drawer 20
Montpelier, VT 05620-3101
802-828-4872
website: www.state.vt.us/bis

Consumer Protection Agency:
Consumer Assistance Program
For Consumer Complaints & Questions
104 Morrill Hall
UVM
Burlington, VT 05405
800-549-2424
website: www.state.vt.us/atg

Chief
Public Protection Division
Office of the Attorney General
109 State St.
Montpelier, VT 05609-1001
802-828-5507
website: www.state.vt.us/atg

Supervisor
Consumer Assurance Section
Food and Market
Department of Agriculture
116 State St.
Montpelier, VT 05602
802-828-3456

Virginia

Attorney General:
Supreme Court Building
101 North Eighth St., 5th Floor
Richmond, VA 23219

Banking Authority:
Commissioner
Bureau of Financial Institutions
1300 E. Main St., Ste. 800
Richmond, VA 23218-0640
804-371-9657
website: www.state.va.us/scc

Consumer Protection Agency:
Senior Assistant Attorney General and Chief
Office of the Attorney General
Antitrust and Consumer Litigation Section
900 East Main St.
Richmond, VA 23219
804-786-2116
website: www.oag.state.va.us

Program Manager
Office of Consumer Affairs
Department of Agriculture and Consumer Services
Washington Building, Ste. 100
P.O. Box 1163
Richmond, VA 23219
804-786-2042
website: www.vdacs.state.va.us

Washington

Attorney General:
PO Box 40100
905 Plum St., Building 3
Olympia, WA 98504-0100

Banking Authority:
Director
Department of Financial Institutions
P.O. Box 41200
Olympia, WA 98504-1200
360-902-8707
website: www.wa.gov/dfi

Consumer Protection Agency:

Consumer Resource Center
Office of the Attorney General
103 E. Holly St., Ste. 308
Bellingham, WA 98225-4728
360-738-6185

Consumer Resource Center
Office of the Attorney General
500 N. Morain St., Ste. 1250
Kennewick, WA 99336-2607
509-734-2967

Consumer Resource Center
Office of the Attorney General
905 Plum St. Bldg 3
Olympia, WA 98504-0118
360-753-6210

Consumer Resource Center
Office of the Attorney General
900 Fourth Avenue, Ste. 2000
Seattle, WA 98164-1012
206-464-6684
website: www.wa.gov/ago

Consumer Resource Center
Office of the Attorney General
1116 West Riverside Avenue
Spokane, WA 99201-1194
509-456-3123

Program Manager
Consumer Resource Center
Office of the Attorney General
Consumer Protection Division
1019 Pacific Avenue, 3rd Floor
Tacoma, WA 98402-4411
253-593-2904
website: www.wa.gov/ago

Consumer Resource Center
Office of the Attorney General
1220 Main St., Ste. 510
Vancouver, WA 98660
360-759-2150

West Virginia

Attorney General:

State Capitol
Charleston, WV 25305-0070

Banking Authority:

Commissioner
State Capitol Complex
Division of Banking
Building 3, Room 311
1900 Kanawha Blvd. East
Charleston, WV 25305-0240
304-558-2294
website: www.wvdob.org

Consumer Protection Agency:

Consumer Protection Division
Office of the Attorney General
812 Quarrier St., 6th Floor
Charleston, WV 25326-1789
304-558-8986
website: www.state.wv.us/wvag

Director
Division of Weights and Measures Section
570 MacCorkle Avenue
St. Albans, WV 25177
304-722-0602

Wisconsin

Attorney General:

State Capitol
PO Box 7857
Madison, WI 53707-7857

Banking Authority:

Secretary
Department of Financial Institutions
345 West Washington Avenue, 5th Floor
Madison, WI 53708-8861
608-261-1622
website: www.wdfi.org

Consumer Protection Agency:

Regional Supervisor
Division of Trade and Consumer Protection
Department of Agriculture
Trade and Consumer Protection
3610 Oakwood Hills Parkway
Eau Claire, WI 54701-7754
715-839-3848

Regional Supervisor
Department of Agriculture Trade & Consumer
Protection
Division of Trade and Consumer Protection
200 N. Jefferson St., Ste.146A
Green Bay, WI 54301
920-448-5110
website: datcp.state.wi.us

Administrator
Division of Trade and Consumer Protection
Department of Agriculture
2811 Agriculture Dr.
Madison, WI 53708
608-224-4953
website: www.datcp.state.wi.us

Wyoming

Attorney General:

State Capitol Building
Cheyenne, WY 82002

Banking Authority:

Commissioner
Division of Banking
Herschler Building
3rd Floor, East
Cheyenne, WY 82002
307-777-7797
website: audit.state.wy.us/banking/default.htm

Consumer Protection Agency:

Office of the Attorney General
Consumer Protection Unit
123 State Capitol Building
Cheyenne, WY 82002
307-777-7874
website: attorneygeneral.state.wy.us

APPENDIX B: STATUTES

FAIR CREDIT REPORTING ACT
UNITED STATES CODE
TITLE 15
CHAPTER 41
SUBCHAPTER III

Section 1681. Congressional findings and statement of purpose

(a) Accuracy and fairness of credit reporting

The Congress makes the following findings:

(1) The banking system is dependent upon fair and accurate credit reporting. Inaccurate credit reports directly impair the efficiency of the banking system, and unfair credit reporting methods undermine the public confidence which is essential to the continued functioning of the banking system.

(2) An elaborate mechanism has been developed for investigating and evaluating the credit worthiness, credit standing, credit capacity, character, and general reputation of consumers.

(3) Consumer reporting agencies have assumed a vital role in assembling and evaluating consumer credit and other information on consumers.

(4) There is a need to insure that consumer reporting agencies exercise their grave responsibilities with fairness, impartiality, and a respect for the consumer's right to privacy.

(b) Reasonable procedures

It is the purpose of this subchapter to require that consumer reporting agencies adopt reasonable procedures for meeting the needs of commerce for consumer credit, personnel, insurance, and other information in a manner which is fair and equitable to the consumer, with regard to the confidentiality, accuracy, relevancy, and proper utilization of such information in accordance with the requirements of this subchapter.

Section 1681a. Definitions; rules of construction

(a) Definitions and rules of construction set forth in this section are applicable for the purposes of this subchapter.

(b) The term "person" means any individual, partnership, corporation, trust, estate, cooperative, association, government or governmental subdivision or agency, or other entity.

(c) The term "consumer" means an individual.

(d) Consumer Report. –

(1) In general. - The term "consumer report" means any written, oral, or other communication of any information by a consumer reporting agency bearing on a consumer's credit worthiness, credit standing, credit capacity, character, general reputation, personal characteristics, or mode of living which is used or expected to be used or collected in whole or in part for the purpose of serving as a factor in establishing the consumer's eligibility for -

(A) credit or insurance to be used primarily for personal, family, or household purposes;

(B) employment purposes; or

(C) any other purpose authorized under section 1681b of this title.

(2) Exclusions. - The term "consumer report" does not include-

(A) any -

(i) report containing information solely as to transactions or experiences between the consumer and the person making the report;

(ii) communication of that information among persons related by common ownership or affiliated by corporate control; or

(iii) communication of other information among persons related by common ownership or affiliated by corporate control, if it is clearly and conspicuously disclosed to the consumer that the information may be communicated among such persons and the consumer is given the opportunity, before the time that the information is initially communicated, to direct that such information not be communicated among such persons;

(B) any authorization or approval of a specific extension of credit directly or indirectly by the issuer of a credit card or similar device;

(C) any report in which a person who has been requested by a third party to make a specific extension of credit directly or indirectly to a consumer conveys his or her decision with respect to such request, if the third party advises the consumer of the name and address of the person to whom the request was made, and such person makes the disclosures to the consumer required under section 1681m of this title; or

(D) a communication described in subsection (o) of this section.

(e) The term "investigative consumer report" means a consumer report or portion thereof in which information on a consumer's character, general reputation, personal characteristics, or mode of living is obtained through personal interviews with neighbors, friends, or associates of the consumer reported on or with others with whom he is acquainted or who may have knowledge concerning any such items of information. However, such information shall not include specific factual information on a consumer's credit record obtained directly from a creditor of the consumer or from a consumer reporting agency when such information was obtained directly from a creditor of the consumer or from the consumer.

(f) The term "consumer reporting agency" means any person which, for monetary fees, dues, or on a cooperative nonprofit basis, regularly engages in whole or in part in the practice of assembling or evaluating consumer credit information or other information on consumers for the purpose of furnishing consumer reports to third parties, and which uses any means or facility of interstate commerce for the purpose of preparing or furnishing consumer reports.

(g) The term "file", when used in connection with information on any consumer, means all of the information on that consumer recorded and retained by a consumer reporting agency regardless of how the information is stored.

(h) The term "employment purposes" when used in connection with a consumer report means a report used for the purpose of evaluating a consumer for employment, promotion, reassignment or retention as an employee.

(i) The term "medical information" means information or records obtained, with the consent of the individual to whom it relates, from licensed physicians or medical practitioners, hospitals, clinics, or other medical or medically related facilities.

(j) Definitions Relating to Child Support Obligations. –

(1) Overdue support. - The term "overdue support" has the meaning given to such term in section 666(e) of title 42.

(2) State or local child support enforcement agency. - The term "State or local child support enforcement agency" means a State or local agency which administers a State or local program for establishing and enforcing child support obligations.

(k) Adverse Action. -

Actions included. - The term "adverse action" –

(A) has the same meaning as in section 1691(d)(6) of this title; and

(B) means—

(i) a denial or cancellation of, an increase in any charge for, or a reduction or other adverse or unfavorable change in the terms of coverage or amount of, any insurance, existing or applied for, in connection with the underwriting of insurance;

(ii) a denial of employment or any other decision for employment purposes that adversely affects any current or prospective employee;

(iii) a denial or cancellation of, an increase in any charge for, or any other adverse or unfavorable change in the terms of, any license or benefit described in section 1681b(a)(3)(D) of this title; and

(iv) an action taken or determination that is—

(I) made in connection with an application that was made by, or a transaction that was initiated by, any consumer, or in connection with a review of an account under section 1681b(a)(3)(F)(ii) of this title; and

(II) adverse to the interests of the consumer.

(2) Applicable findings, decisions, commentary, and orders. - For purposes of any determination of whether an action is an adverse action under paragraph (1)(A), all appropriate final findings, decisions, commentary, and orders issued under section 1691(d)(6) of this title by the Board of Governors of the Federal Reserve System or any court shall apply.

(l) Firm Offer of Credit or Insurance. - The term "firm offer of credit or insurance" means any offer of credit or insurance to a consumer that will be honored if the consumer is determined, based on information in a consumer report on the consumer, to meet the specific criteria used to select the consumer for the offer, except that the offer may be further conditioned on one or more of the following:

(1) The consumer being determined, based on information in the consumer's application for the credit or insurance, to meet specific criteria bearing on credit worthiness or insurability, as applicable, that are established -

(A) before selection of the consumer for the offer; and

(B) for the purpose of determining whether to extend credit or insurance pursuant to the offer.

(2) Verification—

(A) that the consumer continues to meet the specific criteria used to select the consumer for the offer, by using information in a consumer report on the consumer, information in the consumer's application for the credit or insurance, or other information bearing on the credit worthiness.

(B) of the information in the consumer's application for the credit or insurance, to determine that the consumer meets the specific criteria bearing on credit worthiness.

(3) The consumer furnishing any collateral that is a requirement for the extension of the credit or insurance that was-

(A) established before selection of the consumer for the offer of credit or insurance; and

(B) disclosed to the consumer in the offer of credit or insurance.

(m) Credit or Insurance Transaction That Is Not Initiated by the Consumer. - The term "credit or insurance transaction that is not initiated by the consumer" does not include the use of a consumer report by a person with which the consumer has an account or insurance policy, for purposes of -

(1) reviewing the account or insurance policy; or

(2) collecting the account.

(n) State. - The term "State" means any State, the Commonwealth of Puerto Rico, the District of Columbia, and any territory or possession of the United States.

(o) Excluded Communications. - A communication is described in this subsection if it is a communication -

(1) that, but for subsection (d)(2)(D) of this section, would be an investigative consumer report;

(2) that is made to a prospective employer for the purpose of -

(A) procuring an employee for the employer; or

(B) procuring an opportunity for a natural person to work for the employer;

(3) that is made by a person who regularly performs such procurement;

(4) that is not used by any person for any purpose other than a purpose described in subparagraph (A) or (B) of paragraph (2); and

(5) with respect to which –

(A) the consumer who is the subject of the communication -

(i) consents orally or in writing to the nature and scope of the communication, before the collection of any information for the purpose of making the communication;

(ii) consents orally or in writing to the making of the communication to a prospective employer, before the making of the communication; and

(iii) in the case of consent under clause (i) or (ii) given orally, is provided written confirmation of that consent by the person making the communication, not later than 3 business days after the receipt of the consent by that person;

(B) the person who makes the communication does not, for the purpose of making the communication, make any inquiry that if made by a prospective employer of the consumer who is the subject of the communication would violate any applicable Federal or State equal employment opportunity law or regulation; and

(C) the person who makes the communication -

(i) discloses in writing to the consumer who is the subject of the communication, not later than 5 business days after receiving any request from the consumer for such disclosure, the nature and substance of all information in the consumer's file at the time of the request, except that the sources of any information that is acquired solely for use in making the communication and is actually used for no other purpose, need not be disclosed other than under appropriate discovery procedures in any court of competent jurisdiction in which an action is brought; and

(ii) notifies the consumer who is the subject of the communication, in writing, of the consumer's right to request the information described in clause (i).

(p) Consumer Reporting Agency That Compiles and Maintains Files on Consumers on a Nationwide Basis. - The term "consumer reporting agency that compiles and maintains files on consumers on a nationwide basis" means a consumer reporting agency that regularly engages in the practice of assembling or evaluating, and maintaining, for the purpose of furnishing consumer reports to third parties bearing on a consumer's credit worthiness, credit standing, or credit capacity, each of the following regarding consumers residing nationwide:

(1) Public record information.

(2) Credit account information from persons who furnish that information regularly and in the ordinary course of business.

Section 1681b.

(a) In general

Subject to subsection (c) of this section, any consumer reporting agency may furnish a consumer report under the following circumstances and no other:

(1) In response to the order of a court having jurisdiction to issue such an order, or a subpoena issued in connection with proceedings before a Federal grand jury.

(2) In accordance with the written instructions of the consumer to whom it relates.

(3) To a person which it has reason to believe -

(A) intends to use the information in connection with a credit transaction involving the consumer on whom the information is to be furnished and involving the extension of credit to, or review or collection of an account of, the consumer; or

(B) intends to use the information for employment purposes; or

(C) intends to use the information in connection with the underwriting of insurance involving the consumer; or

(D) intends to use the information in connection with a determination of the consumer's eligibility for a license or other benefit granted by a governmental instrumentality required by law to consider an applicant's financial responsibility or status; or

(E) intends to use the information, as a potential investor or servicer, or current insurer, in connection with a valuation of, or an assessment of the credit or prepayment risks associated with, an existing credit obligation; or

(F) otherwise has a legitimate business need for the information -

(i) in connection with a business transaction that is initiated by the consumer; or

(ii) to review an account to determine whether the consumer continues to meet the terms of the account.

(4) In response to a request by the head of a State or local child support enforcement agency (or a State or local government official authorized by the head of such an agency), if the person making the request certifies to the consumer reporting agency that—

(A) the consumer report is needed for the purpose of establishing an individual's capacity to make child support payments or determining the appropriate level of such payments;

(B) the paternity of the consumer for the child to which the obligation relates has been established or acknowledged by the consumer in accordance with State laws under which the obligation arises (if required by those laws);

(C) the person has provided at least 10 days' prior notice to the consumer whose report is requested, by certified or registered mail to the last known address of the consumer, that the report will be requested; and

(D) the consumer report will be kept confidential, will be used solely for a purpose described in subparagraph (A), and will not be used in connection with any other civil, administrative, or criminal proceeding, or for any other purpose.

(5) To an agency administering a State plan under section 654 of title 42 for use to set an initial or modified child support award.

(b) Conditions for furnishing and using consumer reports for employment purposes

(1) Certification from user

A consumer reporting agency may furnish a consumer report for employment purposes only if -

(A) the person who obtains such report from the agency certifies to the agency that -

(i) the person has complied with paragraph (2) with respect to the consumer report, and the person will comply with paragraph (3) with respect to the consumer report if paragraph (3) becomes applicable; and

(ii) information from the consumer report will not be used in violation of any applicable Federal or State equal employment opportunity law or regulation; and

(B) the consumer reporting agency provides with the report, or has previously provided, a summary of the consumer's rights under this subchapter, as prescribed by the Federal Trade Commission under section 1681g(c)(3) of this title.

(2) Disclosure to consumer

(A) In general

Except as provided in subparagraph (B), a person may not procure a consumer report, or cause a consumer report to be procured, for employment purposes with respect to any consumer, unless -

(i) a clear and conspicuous disclosure has been made in writing to the consumer at any time before the report is procured or caused to be procured, in a document that consists solely of the disclosure, that a consumer report may be obtained for employment purposes; and

(ii) the consumer has authorized in writing (which authorization may be made on the document referred to in clause (i)) the procurement of the report by that person.

(B) Application by mail, telephone, computer, or other similar means If a consumer described in subparagraph (C) applies for employment by mail, telephone, computer, or other similar means, at any time before a consumer report is procured or caused to be procured in connection with that application -

(i) the person who procures the consumer report on the consumer for employment purposes shall provide to the consumer, by oral, written, or electronic means, notice that a consumer report may be obtained for employment purposes, and a summary of the consumer's rights under section 1681m(a)(3) of this title; and

(ii) the consumer shall have consented, orally, in writing, or electronically to the procurement of the report by that person.

(C) Scope

Subparagraph (B) shall apply to a person procuring a consumer report on a consumer in connection with the consumer's application for employment only if -

(i) the consumer is applying for a position over which the Secretary of Transportation has the power to establish qualifications and maximum hours of service pursuant to the provisions of section 31502 of title 49, or a position subject to safety regulation by a State transportation agency; and

(ii) as of the time at which the person procures the report or causes the report to be procured the only interaction between the consumer and the person in connection with that employment application has been by mail, telephone, computer, or other similar means.

(3) Conditions on use for adverse actions

(A) In general

Except as provided in subparagraph (B), in using a consumer report for employment purposes, before taking any adverse action based in whole or in part on the report, the person intending to take such adverse action shall provide to the consumer to whom the report relates -

(i) a copy of the report; and

(ii) a description in writing of the rights of the consumer under this subchapter, as prescribed by the Federal Trade Commission under section 1681g(c)(3) of this title.

(B) Application by mail, telephone, computer, or other similar means

(i) If a consumer described in subparagraph (C) applies for employment by mail, telephone, computer, or other similar means, and if a person who has procured a consumer report on the consumer for employment purposes takes adverse action on the employment application based in whole or in part on the report, then the person must provide to the consumer to whom the report relates, in lieu of the notices required under subparagraph (A) of this section and under section 1681m(a) of this title, within 3 business days of taking such action, an oral, written or electronic notification -

(I) that adverse action has been taken based in whole or in part on a consumer report received from a consumer reporting agency;

(II) of the name, address and telephone number of the consumer reporting agency that furnished the consumer report (including a toll-free telephone number established by the agency if the agency compiles and maintains files on consumers on a nationwide basis);

(III) that the consumer reporting agency did not make the decision to take the adverse action and is unable to provide to the consumer the specific reasons why the adverse action was taken; and

(IV) that the consumer may, upon providing proper identification, request a free copy of a report and may dispute with the consumer reporting agency the accuracy or completeness of any information in a report.

(ii) If, under clause (B)(i)(IV), the consumer requests a copy of a consumer report from the person who procured the report, then, within 3 business days of receiving the consumer's request, together with proper identification, the person must send or provide to the consumer a copy of a report and a copy of the consumer's rights as prescribed by the Federal Trade Commission under section 1681g(c)(3) of this title.

(C) Scope

Subparagraph (B) shall apply to a person procuring a consumer report on a consumer in connection with the consumer's application for employment only if -

(i) the consumer is applying for a position over which the Secretary of Transportation has the power to establish qualifications and maximum hours of service pursuant to the provisions of section 31502 of title 49, or a position subject to safety regulation by a State transportation agency; and

(ii) as of the time at which the person procures the report or causes the report to be procured the only interaction between the consumer and the person in connection with that employment application has been by mail, telephone, computer, or other similar means.

(4) Exception for national security investigations

(A) In general

In the case of an agency or department of the United States Government which seeks to obtain and use a consumer report for employment purposes, paragraph (3) shall not apply to any adverse action by such agency or department which is based in part on such consumer report, if the head of such agency or department makes a written finding that -

(i) the consumer report is relevant to a national security investigation of such agency or department;

(ii) the investigation is within the jurisdiction of such agency or department;

(iii) there is reason to believe that compliance with paragraph (3) will -

(I) endanger the life or physical safety of any person;

(II) result in flight from prosecution;

(III) result in the destruction of, or tampering with, evidence relevant to the investigation;

(IV) result in the intimidation of a potential witness relevant to the investigation;

(V) result in the compromise of classified information; or

(VI) otherwise seriously jeopardize or unduly delay the investigation or another official proceeding.

(B) Notification of consumer upon conclusion of investigation

Upon the conclusion of a national security investigation described in subparagraph (A), or upon the determination that the exception under subparagraph (A) is no longer required for the reasons set forth in such subparagraph, the official exercising the authority in such subparagraph shall provide to the consumer who is the subject of the consumer report with regard to which such finding was made -

(i) a copy of such consumer report with any classified information redacted as necessary;

(ii) notice of any adverse action which is based, in part, on the consumer report; and

(iii) the identification with reasonable specificity of the nature of the investigation for which the consumer report was sought.

(C) Delegation by head of agency or department

For purposes of subparagraphs (A) and (B), the head of any agency or department of the United States Government may delegate his or her authorities under this paragraph to an official of such agency or department who has personnel security responsibilities and is a member of the Senior Executive Service or equivalent civilian or military rank.

(D) Report to the Congress

Not later than January 31 of each year, the head of each agency and department of the United States Government that exercised authority under this paragraph during the preceding year shall submit a report to the Congress on the number of times the department or agency exercised such authority during the year.

(E) Definitions

For purposes of this paragraph, the following definitions shall apply:

(i) Classified information

The term "classified information" means information that is protected from unauthorized disclosure under Executive Order No. 12958 or successor orders.

(ii) National security investigation

The term "national security investigation" means any official inquiry by an agency or department of the United States Government to determine the eligibility of a consumer to receive access or continued access to classified information or to determine whether classified information has been lost or compromised.

(c) Furnishing reports in connection with credit or insurance transactions that are not initiated by consumer

(1) In general

A consumer reporting agency may furnish a consumer report relating to any consumer pursuant to subparagraph (A) or (C) of subsection (a)(3) of this section in connection with any credit or insurance transaction that is not initiated by the consumer only if -

(A) the consumer authorizes the agency to provide such report to such person; or

(B) (i) the transaction consists of a firm offer of credit or insurance;

(ii) the consumer reporting agency has complied with subsection (e) of this section; and

(iii) there is not in effect an election by the consumer, made in accordance with subsection (e) of this section, to have the consumer's name and address excluded from lists of names provided by the agency pursuant to this paragraph.

(2) Limits on information received under paragraph (1)(B)

A person may receive pursuant to paragraph (1)(B) only -

(A) the name and address of a consumer;

(B) an identifier that is not unique to the consumer and that is used by the person solely for the purpose of verifying the identity of the consumer; and

(C) other information pertaining to a consumer that does not identify the relationship or experience of the consumer with respect to a particular creditor or other entity.

(3) Information regarding inquiries

Except as provided in section 1681g(a)(5) of this title, a consumer reporting agency shall not furnish to any person a record of inquiries in connection with a credit or insurance transaction that is not initiated by a consumer.

(d) Reserved

(e) Election of consumer to be excluded from lists

(1) In general

A consumer may elect to have the consumer's name and address excluded from any list provided by a consumer reporting agency under subsection (c)(1)(B) of this section in connection with a credit or insurance transaction that is not initiated by the consumer, by notifying the agency in accordance with paragraph (2) that the consumer does not consent to any use of a consumer report relating to the consumer in connection with any credit or insurance transaction that is not initiated by the consumer.

(2) Manner of notification

A consumer shall notify a consumer reporting agency under paragraph (1) -

(A) through the notification system maintained by the agency under paragraph (5); or

(B) by submitting to the agency a signed notice of election form issued by the agency for purposes of this subparagraph.

(3) Response of agency after notification through system

Upon receipt of notification of the election of a consumer under paragraph (1) through the notification system maintained by the agency under paragraph (5), a consumer reporting agency shall-

(A) inform the consumer that the election is effective only for the 2-year period following the election if the consumer does not submit to the agency a signed notice of election form issued by the agency for purposes of paragraph (2)(B); and

(B) provide to the consumer a notice of election form, if requested by the consumer, not later than 5 business days after receipt of the notification of the election through the system established under paragraph (5), in the case of a request made at the time the consumer provides notification through the system.

(4) Effectiveness of election

An election of a consumer under paragraph (1) -

(A) shall be effective with respect to a consumer reporting agency beginning 5 business days after the date on which the consumer notifies the agency in accordance with paragraph (2);

(B) shall be effective with respect to a consumer reporting agency -

(i) subject to subparagraph (C), during the 2-year period beginning 5 business days after the date on which the consumer notifies the agency of the election, in the case of an election for which a consumer notifies the agency only in accordance with paragraph (2)(A); or

(ii) until the consumer notifies the agency under subparagraph (C), in the case of an election for which a consumer notifies the agency in accordance with paragraph (2)(B);

(C) shall not be effective after the date on which the consumer notifies the agency, through the notification system established by the agency under paragraph (5), that the election is no longer effective; and

(D) shall be effective with respect to each affiliate of the agency.

(5) Notification system

(A) In general

Each consumer reporting agency that, under subsection (c)(1)(B) of this section, furnishes a consumer report in connection with a credit or insurance transaction that is not initiated by a consumer, shall -

(i) establish and maintain a notification system, including a toll-free telephone number, which permits any consumer whose consumer report is maintained by the agency to notify the agency, with appropriate identification, of the consumer's election to have the consumer's name and address excluded from any such list of names and addresses provided by the agency for such a transaction; and

(ii) publish by not later than 365 days after September 30, 1996, and not less than annually thereafter, in a publication of general circulation in the area served by the agency -

(I) a notification that information in consumer files maintained by the agency may be used in connection with such transactions; and

(II) the address and toll-free telephone number for consumers to use to notify the agency of the consumer's election under clause (i).

(B) Establishment and maintenance as compliance

Establishment and maintenance of a notification system (including a toll-free telephone number) and publication by a consumer reporting agency on the agency's own behalf and on behalf of any of its affiliates in accordance with this paragraph is deemed to be compliance with this paragraph by each of those affiliates.

(6) Notification system by agencies that operate nationwide

Each consumer reporting agency that compiles and maintains files on consumers on a nationwide basis shall establish and maintain a notification system for purposes of paragraph (5) jointly with other such consumer reporting agencies.

(f) Certain use or obtaining of information prohibited

A person shall not use or obtain a consumer report for any purpose unless -

(1) the consumer report is obtained for a purpose for which the consumer report is authorized to be furnished under this section; and

(2) the purpose is certified in accordance with section 1681e of this title by a prospective user of the report through a general or specific certification.

(g) Furnishing reports containing medical information

A consumer reporting agency shall not furnish for employment purposes, or in connection with a credit or insurance transaction, a consumer report that contains medical information about a consumer, unless the consumer consents to the furnishing of the report.

Section 1681c. Requirements relating to information contained in consumer reports

(a) Information excluded from consumer reports

Except as authorized under subsection (b) of this section, no consumer reporting agency may make any consumer report containing any of the following items of information:

(1) Cases under title 11 or under the Bankruptcy Act that, from the date of entry of the order for relief or the date of adjudication, as the case may be, antedate the report by more than 10 years.

(2) Civil suits, civil judgments, and records of arrest that, from date of entry, antedate the report by more than seven years or until the governing statute of limitations has expired, whichever is the longer period.

(3) Paid tax liens which, from date of payment, antedate the report by more than seven years.

(4) Accounts placed for collection or charged to profit and loss which antedate the report by more than seven years.

(5) Any other adverse item of information, other than records of convictions of crimes which antedates the report by more than seven years.

(b) Exempted cases

The provisions of subsection (a) of this section are not applicable in the case of any consumer credit report to be used in connection with -

(1) a credit transaction involving, or which may reasonably be expected to involve, a principal amount of $150,000 or more;

(2) the underwriting of life insurance involving, or which may reasonably be expected to involve, a face amount of $150,000 or more; or

(3) the employment of any individual at an annual salary which equals, or which may reasonably be expected to equal $75,000, or more.

(c) Running of reporting period

(1) In general

The 7-year period referred to in paragraphs (4) and (6) of subsection (a) of this section shall begin, with respect to any delinquent account that is placed for collection (internally or by referral to a third party, whichever is earlier), charged to profit and loss, or subjected to any similar action, upon the expiration of the 180-day period beginning on the date of the commencement of the delinquency which immediately preceded the collection activity, charge to profit and loss, or similar action.

(2) Effective date

Paragraph (1) shall apply only to items of information added to the file of a consumer on or after the date that is 455 days after September 30, 1996.

(d) Information required to be disclosed

Any consumer reporting agency that furnishes a consumer report that contains information regarding any case involving the consumer that arises under title 11 shall include in the report an identification of the chapter of such title 11 under which such case arises if provided by the source of the information. If any case arising or filed under title 11 is withdrawn by the consumer before a final judgment, the consumer reporting agency shall include in the report that such case or filing was withdrawn upon receipt of documentation certifying such withdrawal.

(e) Indication of closure of account by consumer

If a consumer reporting agency is notified pursuant to section 1681s-2(a)(4) of this title that a credit account of a consumer was voluntarily closed by the consumer, the agency shall indicate that fact in any consumer report that includes information related to the account.

(f) Indication of dispute by consumer

If a consumer reporting agency is notified pursuant to section 1681s-2(a)(3) of this title that information regarding a consumer who was furnished to the agency is disputed by the consumer, the agency shall indicate that fact in each consumer report that includes the disputed information.

Section 1681d. Disclosure of investigative consumer reports

(a) Disclosure of fact of preparation

A person may not procure or cause to be prepared an investigative consumer report on any consumer unless -

(1) it is clearly and accurately disclosed to the consumer that an investigative consumer report including information as to his character, general reputation, personal characteristics, and mode of living, whichever are applicable, may be made, and such disclosure

(A) is made in a writing mailed, or otherwise delivered, to the consumer, not later than three days after the date on which the report was first requested, and

(B) includes a statement informing the consumer of his right to request the additional disclosures provided for under subsection (b) of this section and the written summary of the rights of the consumer prepared pursuant to section 1681g(c) of this title; and

(2) the person certifies or has certified to the consumer reporting agency that -

(A) the person has made the disclosures to the consumer required by paragraph (1); and

(B) the person will comply with subsection (b) of this section.

(b) Disclosure on request of nature and scope of investigation

Any person who procures or causes to be prepared an investigative consumer report on any consumer shall, upon written request made by the consumer within a reasonable period of time after the receipt by him of the disclosure required by subsection (a)(1) of this section, make a complete and accurate disclosure of the nature and scope of the investigation requested. This disclosure shall be made in a writing mailed, or otherwise delivered, to the consumer not later than five days after the date on which the request for such disclosure was received from the consumer or such report was first requested, whichever is the later.

(c) Limitation on liability upon showing of reasonable procedures for compliance with provisions

No person may be held liable for any violation of subsection (a) or (b) of this section if he shows by a preponderance of the evidence that at the time of the violation he maintained reasonable procedures to assure compliance with subsection (a) or (b) of this section.

(d) Prohibitions

(1) Certification

A consumer reporting agency shall not prepare or furnish an investigative consumer report unless the agency has received a certification under subsection (a)(2) of this section from the person who requested the report.

(2) Inquiries

A consumer reporting agency shall not make an inquiry for the purpose of preparing an investigative consumer report on a consumer for employment purposes if the making of the inquiry by an employer or prospective employer of the consumer would violate any applicable Federal or State equal employment opportunity law or regulation.

(3) Certain public record information

Except as otherwise provided in section 1681k of this title, a consumer reporting agency shall not furnish an investigative consumer report that includes information that is a matter of public record and that relates to an arrest, indictment, conviction, civil judicial action, tax lien, or outstanding judgment, unless the agency has verified the accuracy of the information during the 30-day period ending on the date on which the report is furnished.

(4) Certain adverse information

A consumer reporting agency shall not prepare or furnish an investigative consumer report on a consumer that contains information that is adverse to the interest of the consumer and that is obtained through a personal interview with a neighbor, friend, or associate of the consumer or with another person with whom the consumer is acquainted or who has knowledge of such item of information, unless -

(A) the agency has followed reasonable procedures to obtain confirmation of the information, from an additional source that has independent and direct knowledge of the information; or

(B) the person interviewed is the best possible source of the information.

Section 1681e. Compliance procedures

(a) Identity and purposes of credit users

Every consumer reporting agency shall maintain reasonable procedures designed to avoid violations of section 1681c of this title and to limit the furnishing of consumer reports to the purposes listed under section 1681b of this title. These procedures shall require that prospective users of the information identify themselves, certify the purposes for which the information is sought, and certify that the information will be used for no other purpose. Every consumer reporting agency shall make a reasonable effort to verify the identity of a new prospective user and the uses certified by such prospective user prior to furnishing such user a consumer report. No consumer reporting agency may furnish a consumer report to any person if it has reasonable grounds for believing that the consumer report will not be used for a purpose listed in section 1681b of this title.

(b) Accuracy of report

Whenever a consumer reporting agency prepares a consumer report it shall follow reasonable procedures to assure maximum possible accuracy of the information concerning the individual about whom the report relates.

(c) Disclosure of consumer reports by users allowed

A consumer reporting agency may not prohibit a user of a consumer report furnished by the agency on a consumer from disclosing the contents of the report to the consumer, if adverse action against the consumer has been taken by the user based in whole or in part on the report.

(d) Notice to users and furnishers of information

(1) Notice requirement

A consumer reporting agency shall provide to any person -

(A) who regularly and in the ordinary course of business furnishes information to the agency with respect to any consumer; or

(B) to whom a consumer report is provided by the agency; a notice of such person's responsibilities under this subchapter.

(2) Content of notice

The Federal Trade Commission shall prescribe the content of notices under paragraph (1), and a consumer reporting agency shall be in compliance with this subsection if it provides a notice under paragraph (1) that is substantially similar to the Federal Trade Commission prescription under this paragraph.

(e) Procurement of consumer report for resale

(1) Disclosure

A person may not procure a consumer report for purposes of reselling the report (or any information in the report) unless the person discloses to the consumer reporting agency that originally furnishes the report -

(A) the identity of the end-user of the report (or information); and

(B) each permissible purpose under section 1681b of this title for which the report is furnished to the end-user of the report (or information).

(2) Responsibilities of procurers for resale

A person who procures a consumer report for purposes of reselling the report (or any information in the report) shall -

(A) establish and comply with reasonable procedures designed to ensure that the report (or information) is resold by the person only for a purpose for which the report may be furnished under section 1681b of this title, including by requiring that each person to which the report (or information) is resold and that resells or provides the report (or information) to any other person -

(i) identifies each end user of the resold report (or information);

(ii) certifies each purpose for which the report (or information) will be used; and

(iii) certifies that the report (or information) will be used for no other purpose; and

(B) before reselling the report, make reasonable efforts to verify the identifications and certifications made under subparagraph (A).

(3) Resale of consumer report to a Federal agency or department

Notwithstanding paragraph (1) or (2), a person who procures a consumer report for purposes of reselling the report (or any information in the report) shall not disclose the identity of the end-user of the report under paragraph (1) or (2) if -

(A) the end user is an agency or department of the United States Government which procures the report from the person for purposes of determining the eligibility of the consumer concerned to receive access or continued access to classified information (as defined in section 1681b(b)(4)(E)(i) of this title); and

(B) the agency or department certifies in writing to the person reselling the report that nondisclosure is necessary to protect classified information or the safety of persons employed by or contracting with, or undergoing investigation for work or contracting with the agency or department.

Section 1681f. Disclosures to governmental agencies

Notwithstanding the provisions of section 1681b of this title, a consumer reporting agency may furnish identifying information respecting any consumer, limited to his name, address, former addresses, places of employment, or former places of employment, to a governmental agency.

Section 1681g. Disclosures to consumers

(a) Information on file; sources; report recipients

Every consumer reporting agency shall, upon request, and subject to section 1681h(a)(1) of this title, clearly and accurately disclose to the consumer:

(1) All information in the consumer's file at the time of the request, except that nothing in this paragraph shall be construed to require a consumer reporting agency to disclose to a consumer any information concerning credit scores or any other risk scores or predictors relating to the consumer.

(2) The sources of the information; except that the sources of information acquired solely for use in preparing an investigative consumer report and actually used for no other purpose need not be disclosed: Provided, That in the event an action is brought under this subchapter, such sources shall be available to the plaintiff under appropriate discovery procedures in the court in which the action is brought.

(3)   (A) Identification of each person (including each end-user identified under section 1681e(e)(1) of this title) that procured a consumer report -

(i) for employment purposes, during the 2-year period preceding the date on which the request is made; or

(ii) for any other purpose, during the 1-year period preceding the date on which the request is made.

(B) An identification of a person under subparagraph (A) shall include -

(i) the name of the person or, if applicable, the trade name (written in full) under which such person conducts business; and

(ii) upon request of the consumer, the address and telephone number of the person.

(C) Subparagraph (A) does not apply if -

(i) the end user is an agency or department of the United States Government that procures the report from

the person for purposes of determining the eligibility of the consumer to whom the report relates to receive access or continued access to classified information (as defined in section 1681b(b)(4)(E)(i) of this title); and

(ii) the head of the agency or department makes a written finding as prescribed under section 1681b(b)(4)(A) of this title.

(4) The dates, original payees, and amounts of any checks upon which is based any adverse characterization of the consumer, included in the file at the time of the disclosure.

(5) A record of all inquiries received by the agency during the 1-year period preceding the request that identified the consumer in connection with a credit or insurance transaction that was not initiated by the consumer.

(b) Exempt information

The requirements of subsection (a) of this section respecting the disclosure of sources of information and the recipients of consumer reports do not apply to information received or consumer reports furnished prior to the effective date of this subchapter except to the extent that the matter involved is contained in the files of the consumer reporting agency on that date.

(c) Summary of rights required to be included with disclosure

(1) Summary of rights

A consumer reporting agency shall provide to a consumer, with each written disclosure by the agency to the consumer under this section -

(A) a written summary of all of the rights that the consumer has under this subchapter; and

(B) in the case of a consumer reporting agency that compiles and maintains files on consumers on a nationwide basis, a toll-free telephone number established by the agency, at which personnel are accessible to consumers during normal business hours.

(2) Specific items required to be included

The summary of rights required under paragraph (1) shall include -

(A) a brief description of this subchapter and all rights of consumers under this subchapter;

(B) an explanation of how the consumer may exercise the rights of the consumer under this subchapter;

(C) a list of all Federal agencies responsible for enforcing any provision of this subchapter and the address and any appropriate phone number of each such agency, in a form that will assist the consumer in selecting the appropriate agency;

(D) a statement that the consumer may have additional rights under State law and that the consumer may wish to contact a State or local consumer protection agency or a State attorney general to learn of those rights; and

(E) a statement that a consumer reporting agency is not required to remove accurate derogatory information from a consumer's file, unless the information is outdated under section 1681c of this title or cannot be verified.

(3) Form of summary of rights

For purposes of this subsection and any disclosure by a consumer reporting agency required under this subchapter with respect to consumers' rights, the Federal Trade Commission (after consultation with each Federal agency referred to in section 1681s(b) of this title) shall prescribe the form and content of any such disclosure of the rights of consumers required under this subchapter. A consumer reporting agency shall be in compliance with this subsection if it provides disclosures under paragraph (1) that are substantially similar to the Federal Trade Commission prescription under this paragraph.

(4) Effectiveness

No disclosures shall be required under this subsection until the date on which the Federal Trade Commission prescribes the form and content of such disclosures under paragraph (3).

Section 1681h. Conditions and form of disclosure to consumers

(a) In general

(1) Proper identification

A consumer reporting agency shall require, as a condition of making the disclosures required under section 1681g of this title, that the consumer furnish proper identification.

(2) Disclosure in writing

Except as provided in subsection (b) of this section, the disclosures required to be made under section 1681g of this title shall be provided under that section in writing.

(b) Other forms of disclosure

(1) In general

If authorized by a consumer, a consumer reporting agency may make the disclosures required under section 1681g of this title –

(A) other than in writing; and

(B) in such form as may be -

(i) specified by the consumer in accordance with paragraph (2); and

(ii) available from the agency.

(2) Form

A consumer may specify pursuant to paragraph (1) that disclosures under section 1681g of this title shall be made -

(A) in person, upon the appearance of the consumer at the place of business of the consumer reporting agency where disclosures are regularly provided, during normal business hours, and on reasonable notice;

(B) by telephone, if the consumer has made a written request for disclosure by telephone;

(C) by electronic means, if available from the agency; or

(D) by any other reasonable means that is available from the agency.

(c) Trained personnel

Any consumer reporting agency shall provide trained personnel to explain to the consumer any information furnished to him pursuant to section 1681g of this title.

(d) Persons accompanying consumer

The consumer shall be permitted to be accompanied by one other person of his choosing, who shall furnish reasonable identification. A consumer reporting agency may require the consumer to furnish a written statement granting permission to the consumer reporting agency to discuss the consumer's file in such person's presence.

(e) Limitation of liability

Except as provided in sections 1681n and 1681o of this title, no consumer may bring any action or proceeding in the nature of defamation, invasion of privacy, or negligence with respect to the reporting of information against any consumer reporting agency, any user of information, or any person who furnishes information to a consumer reporting agency, based on information disclosed pursuant to section 1681g, 1681h, or 1681m of this title, or based on information disclosed by a user of a consumer report to or for a consumer against whom the user has taken adverse action, based in whole or in part on the report, except as to false information furnished with malice or willful intent to injure such consumer.

Section 1681i. Procedure in case of disputed accuracy

(a) Reinvestigations of disputed information

(1) Reinvestigation required

(A) In general

If the completeness or accuracy of any item of information contained in a consumer's file at a consumer reporting agency is disputed by the consumer and the consumer notifies the agency directly of such dispute, the agency shall reinvestigate free of charge and record the current status of the disputed information, or delete the item from the file in accordance with paragraph (5), before the end of the 30-day period beginning on the date on which the agency receives the notice of the dispute from the consumer.

(B) Extension of period to reinvestigate

Except as provided in subparagraph (C), the 30-day period described in subparagraph (A) may be extended for not more than 15 additional days if the consumer reporting agency receives information from the consumer during that 30-day period that is relevant to the reinvestigation.

(C) Limitations on extension of period to reinvestigate

Subparagraph (B) shall not apply to any reinvestigation in which, during the 30-day period described in subparagraph (A), the information that is the subject of the reinvestigation is found to be inaccurate or incomplete or the consumer reporting agency determines that the information cannot be verified.

(2) Prompt notice of dispute to furnisher of information

(A) In general

Before the expiration of the 5-business-day period beginning on the date on which a consumer reporting agency receives notice of a dispute from any consumer in accordance with paragraph (1), the agency shall provide notification of the dispute to any person who provided any item of information in dispute, at the address and in the manner established with the person. `The notice shall include all relevant information regarding the dispute that the agency has received from the consumer.

(B) Provision of other information from consumer

The consumer reporting agency shall promptly provide to the person who provided the information in dispute all relevant information regarding the dispute that is received by the agency from the consumer after the period referred to in subparagraph (A) and before the end of the period referred to in paragraph (1)(A).

(3) Determination that dispute is frivolous or irrelevant

(A) In general

Notwithstanding paragraph (1), a consumer reporting agency may terminate a reinvestigation of information disputed by a consumer under that paragraph if the agency reasonably determines that the dispute by the consumer is frivolous or irrelevant, including by reason of a failure by a consumer to provide sufficient information to investigate the disputed information.

(B) Notice of determination

Upon making any determination in accordance with subparagraph (A) that a dispute is frivolous or irrelevant, a consumer reporting agency shall notify the consumer of such determination not later than 5 business days after making such determination, by mail or, if authorized by the consumer for that purpose, by any other means available to the agency.

(C) Contents of notice

A notice under subparagraph (B) shall include -

(i) the reasons for the determination under subparagraph (A); and

(ii) identification of any information required to investigate the disputed information, which may consist of a standardized form describing the general nature of such information.

(4) Consideration of consumer information

In conducting any reinvestigation under paragraph (1) with respect to disputed information in the file of any consumer, the consumer reporting agency shall review and consider all relevant information submitted by the consumer in the period described in paragraph (1)(A) with respect to such disputed information.

(5) Treatment of inaccurate or unverifiable information

(A) In general

If, after any reinvestigation under paragraph (1) of any information disputed by a consumer, an item of the information is found to be inaccurate or incomplete or cannot be verified, the consumer reporting agency shall promptly delete that item of information from the consumer's file or modify that item of information, as appropriate, based on the results of the reinvestigation.

(B) Requirements relating to reinsertion of previously deleted material

(i) Certification of accuracy of information

If any information is deleted from a consumer's file pursuant to subparagraph (A), the information may not be reinserted in the file by the consumer reporting agency unless the person who furnishes the information certifies that the information is complete and accurate.

(ii) Notice to consumer

If any information that has been deleted from a consumer's file pursuant to subparagraph (A) is reinserted in the file, the consumer reporting agency shall notify the consumer of the reinsertion in writing not later than 5 business days after the reinsertion or, if authorized by the consumer for that purpose, by any other means available to the agency.

(iii) Additional information

As part of, or in addition to, the notice under clause (ii), a consumer reporting agency shall provide to a consumer in writing not later than 5 business days after the date of the reinsertion -

(I) a statement that the disputed information has been reinserted;

(II) the business name and address of any furnisher of information contacted and the telephone number of such furnisher, if reasonably available, or of any furnisher of information that contacted the consumer reporting agency, in connection with the reinsertion of such information; and

(III) a notice that the consumer has the right to add a statement to the consumer's file disputing the accuracy or completeness of the disputed information.

(C) Procedures to prevent reappearance

A consumer reporting agency shall maintain reasonable procedures designed to prevent the reappearance in a consumer's file, and in consumer reports on the consumer, of information that is deleted pursuant to this paragraph (other than information that is reinserted in accordance with subparagraph (B)(i).

(D) Automated reinvestigation system

Any consumer reporting agency that compiles and maintains files on consumers on a nationwide basis shall implement an automated system through which furnishers of information to that consumer reporting agency may report the results of a reinvestigation that finds incomplete or inaccurate information in a consumer's file to other such consumer reporting agencies.

(6) Notice of results of reinvestigation

(A) In general

A consumer reporting agency shall provide written notice to a consumer of the results of a reinvestigation under this subsection not later than 5 business days after the completion of the reinvestigation, by mail or, if authorized by the consumer for that purpose, by other means available to the agency.

(B) Contents

As part of, or in addition to, the notice under subparagraph (A), a consumer reporting agency shall provide to a consumer in writing before the expiration of the 5-day period referred to in subparagraph (A) –

(i) a statement that the reinvestigation is completed;

(ii) a consumer report that is based upon the consumer's file as that file is revised as a result of the reinvestigation;

(iii) a notice that, if requested by the consumer, a description of the procedure used to determine the accuracy and completeness of the information shall be provided to the consumer by the agency, including the business name and address of any furnisher of information contacted in connection with such information and the telephone number of such furnisher, if reasonably available;

(iv) a notice that the consumer has the right to add a statement to the consumer's file disputing the accuracy or completeness of the information; and

(v) a notice that the consumer has the right to request under subsection (d) of this section that the consumer reporting agency furnish notifications under that subsection.

(7) Description of reinvestigation procedure

A consumer reporting agency shall provide to a consumer a `description referred to in paragraph (6)(B)(iii) by not later than 15 days after receiving a request from the consumer for that description.

(8) Expedited dispute resolution

If a dispute regarding an item of information in a consumer's file at a consumer reporting agency is resolved in accordance with paragraph (5)(A) by the deletion of the disputed information by not later than 3 business days after the date on which the agency receives notice of the dispute from the consumer in accordance with paragraph (1)(A), then the agency shall not be required to comply with paragraphs (2), (6), and (7) with respect to that dispute if the agency -

(A) provides prompt notice of the deletion to the consumer by telephone;

(B) includes in that notice, or in a written notice that accompanies a confirmation and consumer report provided in accordance with subparagraph (C), a statement of the consumer's right to request under subsection (d) of this section that the agency furnish notifications under that subsection; and

(C) provides written confirmation of the deletion and a copy of a consumer report on the consumer that is based on the consumer's file after the deletion, not later than 5 business days after making the deletion.

(b) Statement of dispute

If the reinvestigation does not resolve the dispute, the consumer may file a brief statement setting forth the nature of the dispute. The consumer reporting agency may limit such statements to not more than one hundred words if it provides the consumer with assistance in writing a clear summary of the dispute.

(c) Notification of consumer dispute in subsequent consumer reports

Whenever a statement of a dispute is filed, unless there is reasonable grounds to believe that it is frivolous or irrelevant, the consumer reporting agency shall, in any subsequent consumer report containing the information in question, clearly note that it is disputed by the consumer and provide either the consumer's statement or a clear and accurate codification or summary thereof.

(d) Notification of deletion of disputed information

Following any deletion of information which is found to be inaccurate or whose accuracy can no longer be verified or any notation as to disputed information, the consumer reporting agency shall, at the request of the consumer, furnish notification that the item has been deleted or the statement, codification or summary pursuant to subsection (b) or (c) of this section to any person specifically designated by the consumer who has within two years prior thereto received a consumer report for employment purposes, or within six months prior thereto received a consumer report for any other purpose, which contained the deleted or disputed information.

Section 1681j. Charges for certain disclosures

(a) Reasonable charges allowed for certain disclosures

(1) In general

Except as provided in subsections (b), (c), and (d) of this section, a consumer reporting agency may impose a reasonable charge on a consumer -

(A) for making a disclosure to the consumer pursuant to section 1681g of this title, which charge -

(i) shall not exceed $8; and

(ii) shall be indicated to the consumer before making the disclosure; and

(B) for furnishing, pursuant to section 1681i(d) of this title, following a reinvestigation under section 1681i(a) of this title, a statement, codification, or summary to a person designated by the con-

sumer under that section after the 30-day period beginning on the date of notification of the consumer under paragraph (6) or (8) of section 1681i(a) of this title with respect to the reinvestigation, which charge -

(i) shall not exceed the charge that the agency would impose on each designated recipient for a consumer report; and

(ii) shall be indicated to the consumer before furnishing such information.

(2) Modification of amount

The Federal Trade Commission shall increase the amount referred to in paragraph (1)(A)(i) on January 1 of each year, based proportionally on changes in the Consumer Price Index, with fractional changes rounded to the nearest fifty cents.

(b) Free disclosure after adverse notice to consumer

Each consumer reporting agency that maintains a file on a consumer shall make all disclosures pursuant to section 1681g of this title without charge to the consumer if, not later than 60 days after receipt by such consumer of a notification pursuant to section 1681m of this title, or of a notification from a debt collection agency affiliated with that consumer reporting agency stating that the consumer's credit rating may be or has been adversely affected, the consumer makes a request under section 1681g of this title.

(c) Free disclosure under certain other circumstances

Upon request of the consumer, a consumer reporting agency shall make all disclosures pursuant to section 1681g of this title once during any 12-month period without charge to that consumer if the consumer certifies in writing that the consumer -

(1) is unemployed and intends to apply for employment in the 60-day period beginning on the date on which the certification is made;

(2) is a recipient of public welfare assistance; or

(3) has reason to believe that the file on the consumer at the agency contains inaccurate information due to fraud.

(d) Other charges prohibited

A consumer reporting agency shall not impose any charge on a consumer for providing any notification required by this subchapter or making any disclosure required by this subchapter, except as authorized by subsection (a) of this section.

Section 1681k. Public record information for employment purposes

(a) In general

A consumer reporting agency which furnishes a consumer report for employment purposes and which for that purpose compiles and reports items of information on consumers which are matters of public record and are likely to have an adverse effect upon a consumer's ability to obtain employment shall -

(1) at the time such public record information is reported to the user of such consumer report, notify the consumer of the fact that public record information is being reported by the consumer reporting agency, together with the name and address of the person to whom such information is being reported; or

(2) maintain strict procedures designed to insure that whenever public record information which is likely to have an adverse effect on a consumer's ability to obtain employment is reported it is complete and up to date. For purposes of this paragraph, items of public record relat-

ing to arrests, indictments, convictions, suits, tax liens, and outstanding judgments shall be considered up to date if the current public record status of the item at the time of the report is reported.

(b) Exemption for national security investigations

Subsection (a) of this section does not apply in the case of an agency or department of the United States Government that seeks to obtain and use a consumer report for employment purposes, if the head of the agency or department makes a written finding as prescribed under section 1681b(b)(4)(A) of this title.

Section 1681l. Restrictions on investigative consumer reports

Whenever a consumer reporting agency prepares an investigative consumer report, no adverse information in the consumer report (other than information which is a matter of public record) may be included in a subsequent consumer report unless such adverse information has been verified in the process of making such subsequent consumer report, or the adverse information was received within the three-month period preceding the date the subsequent report is furnished.

Section 1681m. Requirements on users of consumer reports

(a) Duties of users taking adverse actions on basis of information contained in consumer reports

If any person takes any adverse action with respect to any consumer that is based in whole or in part on any information contained in a consumer report, the person shall -

(1) provide oral, written, or electronic notice of the adverse action to the consumer;

(2) provide to the consumer orally, in writing, or electronically -

(A) the name, address, and telephone number of the consumer reporting agency (including a toll-free telephone number established by the agency if the agency compiles and maintains files on consumers on a nationwide basis) that furnished the report to the person; and

(B) a statement that the consumer reporting agency did not make the decision to take the adverse action and is unable to provide the consumer the specific reasons why the adverse action was taken; and

(3) provide to the consumer an oral, written, or electronic notice of the consumer's right -

(A) to obtain, under section 1681j of this title, a free copy of a consumer report on the consumer from the consumer reporting agency referred to in paragraph (2), which notice shall include an indication of the 60-day period under that section for obtaining such a copy; and

(B) to dispute, under section 1681i of this title, with a consumer reporting agency the accuracy or completeness of any information in a consumer report furnished by the agency.

(b) Adverse action based on information obtained from third parties other than consumer reporting agencies

(1) In general

Whenever credit for personal, family, or household purposes involving a consumer is denied or the charge for such credit is increased either wholly or partly because of information obtained from a person other than a consumer reporting agency bearing upon the consumer's creditworthiness, credit standing, credit capacity, character, general reputation, personal characteristics, or mode of living, the user of such information shall, within a reasonable period of time, upon the consumer's written request for the reasons for such adverse action received within sixty days after learning of such adverse action, disclose the nature of the information to the consumer. The user of such information shall clearly and accurately disclose to the consumer his right to make such written request at the time such adverse action is communicated to the consumer.

(2) Duties of person taking certain actions based on information provided by affiliate

(A) Duties, generally

If a person takes an action described in subparagraph (B) with respect to a consumer, based in whole or in part on information described in subparagraph (C), the person shall -

(i) notify the consumer of the action, including a statement that the consumer may obtain the information in accordance with clause (ii); and

(ii) upon a written request from the consumer received within 60 days after transmittal of the notice required by clause (i), disclose to the consumer the nature of the information upon which the action is based by not later than 30 days after receipt of the request.

(B) Action described

An action referred to in subparagraph (A) is an adverse action described in section 1681a(k)(1)(A) of this title, taken in connection with a transaction initiated by the consumer, or any adverse action described in clause (i) or (ii) of section 1681a(k)(1)(B) of this title.

(C) Information described

Information referred to in subparagraph (A) -

(i) except as provided in clause (ii), is information that-

(I) is furnished to the person taking the action by a person related by common ownership or affiliated by common corporate control to the person taking the action; and

(II) bears on the creditworthiness, credit standing, credit capacity, character, general reputation, personal characteristics, or mode of living of the consumer; and

(ii) does not include –

(I) information solely as to transactions or experiences between the consumer and the person furnishing the information; or

(II) information in a consumer report.

(c) Reasonable procedures to assure compliance

No person shall be held liable for any violation of this section if he shows by a preponderance of the evidence that at the time of the alleged violation he maintained reasonable procedures to assure compliance with the provisions of this section.

(d) Duties of users making written credit or insurance solicitations on basis of information contained in consumer files

(1) In general

Any person who uses a consumer report on any consumer in connection with any credit or insurance transaction that is not initiated by the consumer, that is provided to that person under section 1681b(c)(1)(B) of this title, shall provide with each written solicitation made to the consumer regarding the transaction a clear and conspicuous statement that -

(A) information contained in the consumer's consumer report was used in connection with the transaction;

(B) the consumer received the offer of credit or insurance because the consumer satisfied the criteria for creditworthiness or insurability under which the consumer was selected for the offer;

(C) if applicable, the credit or insurance may not be extended if, after the consumer responds to the offer, the consumer does not meet the criteria used to select the consumer for the offer or any applicable criteria bearing on creditworthiness or insurability or does not furnish any `required collateral;

(D) the consumer has a right to prohibit information contained in the consumer's file with any consumer reporting agency from being used in connection with any credit or insurance transaction that is not initiated by the consumer; and

(E) the consumer may exercise the right referred to in subparagraph (D) by notifying a notification system established under section 1681b(e) of this title.

(2) Disclosure of address and telephone number

A statement under paragraph (1) shall include the address and toll-free telephone number of the appropriate notification system established under section 1681b(e) of this title.

(3) Maintaining criteria on file

A person who makes an offer of credit or insurance to a consumer under a credit or insurance transaction described in paragraph (1) shall maintain on file the criteria used to select the consumer to receive the offer, all criteria bearing on creditworthiness or insurability, as applicable, that are the basis for determining whether or not to extend credit or insurance pursuant to the offer, and any requirement for the furnishing of collateral as a condition of the extension of credit or insurance, until the expiration of the 3-year period beginning on the date on which the offer is made to the consumer.

(4) Authority of Federal agencies regarding unfair or deceptive acts or practices not affected

This section is not intended to affect the authority of any Federal or State agency to enforce a prohibition against unfair or deceptive acts or practices, including the making of false or misleading statements in connection with a credit or insurance transaction that is not initiated by the consumer.

Section 1681n. Civil liability for willful noncompliance

(a) In general

Any person who willfully fails to comply with any requirement imposed under this subchapter with respect to any consumer is liable to that consumer in an amount equal to the sum of -

(1)   (A) any actual damages sustained by the consumer as a result of the failure or damages of not less than $100 and not more than $1,000; or

(B) in the case of liability of a natural person for obtaining a consumer report under false pretenses or knowingly without

a permissible purpose, actual damages sustained by the consumer as a result of the failure or $1,000, whichever is greater;

(2) such amount of punitive damages as the court may allow; and

(3) in the case of any successful action to enforce any liability under this section, the costs of the action together with reasonable attorney's fees as determined by the court.

(b) Civil liability for knowing noncompliance

Any person who obtains a consumer report from a consumer reporting agency under false pretenses or knowingly without a permissible purpose shall be liable to the consumer reporting agency for actual damages sustained by the consumer reporting agency or $1,000, whichever is greater.

(c) Attorney's fees

Upon a finding by the court that an unsuccessful pleading, motion, or other paper filed in connection with an action under this section was filed in bad faith or for purposes of harassment, the court shall award to the prevailing party attorney's fees reasonable in relation to the work expended in responding to the pleading, motion, or other paper.

Section 1681o. Civil liability for negligent noncompliance

(a) In general

Any person who is negligent in failing to comply with any requirement imposed under this subchapter with respect to any consumer is liable to that consumer in an amount equal to the sum of -

(1) any actual damages sustained by the consumer as a result of the failure;

(2) in the case of any successful action to enforce any liability under this section, the costs of the action together with reasonable attorney's fees as determined by the court.

(b) Attorney's fees

On a finding by the court that an unsuccessful pleading, motion, or other paper filed in connection with an action under this section was filed in bad faith or for purposes of harassment, the court shall award to the prevailing party attorney's fees reasonable in relation to the work expended in responding to the pleading, motion, or other paper.

Section 1681p. Jurisdiction of courts; limitation of actions

An action to enforce any liability created under this subchapter may be brought in any appropriate United States district court without regard to the amount in controversy, or in any other court of competent jurisdiction, within two years from the date on which the liability arises, except that where a defendant has materially and willfully misrepresented any information required under this subchapter to be disclosed to an individual and the information so misrepresented is material to the establishment of the defendant's liability to that individual under this subchapter, the action may be brought at any time within two years after discovery by the individual of the misrepresentation.

Section 1681q. Obtaining information under false pretenses

Any person who knowingly and willfully obtains information on a consumer from a consumer reporting agency under false pretenses shall be fined under title 18, imprisoned for not more than 2 years, or both.

Section 1681r. Unauthorized disclosures by officers or employees

Any officer or employee of a consumer reporting agency who knowingly and willfully provides information concerning an individual from the agency's files to a person not authorized to receive that information shall be fined under title 18, imprisoned for not more than 2 years, or both.

Section 1681s. Administrative enforcement

(a) Enforcement by Federal Trade Commission

(1) Compliance with the requirements imposed under this subchapter shall be enforced under the Federal Trade Commission Act (15 U.S.C. 41 et seq.) by the Federal Trade Commission with respect to consumer reporting agencies and all other persons subject thereto, except to the extent that enforcement of the requirements imposed under this subchapter is specifically committed to some other government agency under subsection (b) hereof. `For the purpose of the exercise by the Federal Trade Commission of its functions and powers under the Federal Trade Commission Act, a violation of any requirement or prohibition imposed under this subchapter shall constitute an unfair or deceptive act or practice in commerce in violation of section 5(a) of the Federal Trade Commission Act (15 U.S.C. 45(a)) and shall be subject to enforcement by the Federal Trade Commission under section 5(b) thereof (15 U.S.C. 45(b)) with respect to any consumer reporting agency or person subject to enforcement by the Federal Trade Commission pursuant to this subsection, irrespective of whether that person is engaged in commerce or meets any other jurisdictional tests in the Federal Trade Commission Act. The Federal Trade Commission shall have such procedural, investigative, and enforcement powers, including the power to issue procedural rules in enforcing compliance with the requirements imposed under this subchapter and to require the filing of reports, the production of documents, and the appearance of witnesses as though the applicable terms and conditions of the Federal Trade Commission Act were part of this subchapter. `Any person violating any of the provisions of this subchapter shall be subject to the penalties and entitled to the privileges and immunities provided in the Federal Trade Commission Act as though the applicable terms and provisions thereof were part of this subchapter.

(2)   (A) In the event of a knowing violation, which constitutes a pattern or practice of violations of this subchapter, the Commission may commence a civil action to recover a civil penalty in a district court of the United States against any person that violates this subchapter. `In such action, such person shall be liable for a civil penalty of not more than $2,500 per violation.

(B) In determining the amount of a civil penalty under subparagraph (A), the court shall take into account the degree of culpability, any history of prior such conduct, ability to pay, effect on ability to continue to do business, and such other matters as justice may require.

(3) Notwithstanding paragraph (2), a court may not impose any civil penalty on a person for a violation of section 1681s-2(a)(1) of this title unless the person has been enjoined from committing the violation, or ordered not to commit the violation, in an action or proceeding brought by or on behalf of the Federal Trade Commission, and has violated the injunction or order, and the court may not impose any civil penalty for any violation occurring before the date of the violation of the injunction or order.

(4) Neither the Commission nor any other agency referred to in subsection (b) of this section may prescribe trade regulation rules or other regulations with respect to this subchapter.

(b) Enforcement by other agencies

Compliance with the requirements imposed under this subchapter with respect to consumer reporting agencies, persons who use consumer reports from such agencies, persons who furnish information to such agencies, and users of information that are subject to subsection (d) of section 1681m of this title shall be enforced under -

(1) section 8 of the Federal Deposit Insurance Act (12 U.S.C. 1818), in the case of -

(A) national banks, and Federal branches and Federal agencies of foreign banks, by the Office of the Comptroller of the Currency;

(B) member banks of the Federal Reserve System (other than national banks), branches and agencies of foreign banks (other than Federal branches, Federal agencies, and insured State branches of foreign banks), commercial lending companies owned or controlled by foreign banks, and organizations operating under section 25 or 25(a) of the Federal Reserve Act (12 U.S.C. 601 et seq., 611 et seq.), by the Board of Governors of the Federal Reserve System; and

(C) banks insured by the Federal Deposit Insurance Corporation (other than members of the Federal Reserve System) and insured State branches of foreign banks, by the Board of Directors of the Federal Deposit Insurance Corporation;

(2) section 8 of the Federal Deposit Insurance Act (12 U.S.C. 1818), by the Director of the Office of Thrift Supervision, in the case of a savings association the deposits of which are insured by the Federal Deposit Insurance Corporation;

(3) the Federal Credit Union Act (12 U.S.C. 1751 et seq.), by the Administrator of the National Credit Union Administration with respect to any Federal credit union;

(4) subtitle IV of title 49, by the Secretary of Transportation, with respect to all carriers subject to the jurisdiction of the Surface Transportation Board;

(5) part A of subtitle VII of title 49, by the Secretary of Transportation with respect to any air carrier or foreign air carrier subject to that part; and

(6) the Packers and Stockyards Act, 1921 (7 U.S.C. 181 et seq.) (except as provided in section 406 of that Act (7 U.S.C. 226, 227)), by the Secretary of Agriculture with respect to any activities subject to that Act. The terms used in paragraph (1) that are not defined in this subchapter or otherwise defined in section 3(s) of the Federal Deposit Insurance Act (12 U.S.C. 1813(s)) shall have the meaning given to them in section 1(b) of the International Banking Act of 1978 (12 U.S.C. 3101).

(c) State action for violations

(1) Authority of States

In addition to such other remedies as are provided under State law, if the chief law enforcement officer of a State, or an official or agency designated by a State, has reason to believe that any person has violated or is violating this subchapter, the State -

(A) may bring an action to enjoin such violation in any appropriate United States district court or in any other court of competent jurisdiction;

(B) subject to paragraph (5), may bring an action on behalf of the residents of the State to recover -

(i) damages for which the person is liable to such residents under sections 1681n and 1681o of this title as a result of the violation;

(ii) in the case of a violation of section 1681s-2(a) of this title, damages for which the person would, but for section 1681s-2(c) of this title, be liable to such residents `as a result of the violation; or

(iii) damages of not more than $1,000 for each willful or negligent violation; and

(C) in the case of any successful action under subparagraph (A) or (B), shall be awarded the costs of the action and reasonable attorney fees as determined by the court.

(2) Rights of Federal regulators

The State shall serve prior written notice of any action under paragraph (1) upon the Federal Trade Commission or the appropriate Federal regulator determined under subsection (b) of this section and provide the Commission or appropriate Federal regulator with a copy of its complaint, except in any case in which such prior notice is not feasible, in which case the State shall serve such notice immediately upon instituting such action. The Federal Trade Commission or appropriate Federal regulator shall have the right -

(A) to intervene in the action;

(B) upon so intervening, to be heard on all matters arising therein;

(C) to remove the action to the appropriate United States district court; and

(D) to file petitions for appeal.

(3) Investigatory powers

For purposes of bringing any action under this subsection, nothing in this subsection shall prevent the chief law enforcement officer, or an official or agency designated by a State, from exercising the powers conferred on the chief law enforcement officer or such official by the laws of such State to conduct investigations or to administer oaths or affirmations or to compel the attendance of witnesses or the production of documentary and other evidence.

(4) Limitation on State action while Federal action pending If the Federal Trade Commission or the appropriate Federal regulator has instituted a civil action or an administrative action under section 8 of the Federal Deposit Insurance Act (12 U.S.C. 1818) for a violation of this subchapter, no State may, during the pendency of such action, bring an action under this section against any defendant named in the complaint of the Commission or the appropriate Federal regulator for any violation of this subchapter that is alleged in that complaint.

(5) Limitations on State actions for violation of section 1681s-2(a)(1)

(A) Violation of injunction required

A State may not bring an action against a person under paragraph (1)(B) for a violation of section 1681s-2(a)(1) of this title, unless -

(i) the person has been enjoined from committing the violation, in an action brought by the State under paragraph (1)(A); and

(ii) the person has violated the injunction.

(B) Limitation on damages recoverable

In an action against a person under paragraph (1)(B) for a violation of section 1681s-2(a)(1) of this title, a State may not recover any damages incurred before the date of the violation of an injunction on which the action is based.

(d) Enforcement under other authority

For the purpose of the exercise by any agency referred to in subsection (b) of this section of its powers under any Act referred to in that subsection, a violation of any requirement imposed under this subchapter shall be deemed to be a violation of a requirement imposed under that Act. In addition to its powers under any provision of law specifically referred to in subsection (b) of this section, each of the agencies referred to in that subsection may exercise, for the purpose of enforcing compliance with any requirement imposed under this subchapter any other authority conferred on it by law. Notwithstanding the preceding, no agency referred to in subsection (b) of this section may conduct an examination of a bank, savings association, or credit union regarding compliance with the provisions of this subchapter, except in response to a complaint (or if the agency otherwise has knowledge) that the bank, savings association, or credit union has violated a provision of this subchapter, in which case, the agency may conduct an examination as necessary to investigate the complaint. `If an agency determines during an investigation in response to a complaint that a violation of this subchapter has occurred, the agency may, during its next 2 regularly scheduled examinations of the bank, savings association, or credit union, examine for compliance with this subchapter.

(e) Interpretive authority

The Board of Governors of the Federal Reserve System may issue interpretations of any provision of this subchapter as such provision may apply to any persons identified under paragraphs (1), (2), and (3) of subsection (b) of this section, or to the holding companies and affiliates of such persons, in consultation with Federal agencies identified in paragraphs (1), (2), and (3) of subsection (b) of this section.

Section 1681s-1. Information on overdue child support obligations

Notwithstanding any other provision of this subchapter, a consumer reporting agency shall include in any consumer report furnished by the agency in accordance with section 1681b of this title, any information on the failure of the consumer to pay overdue support which -

(1) is provided -

(A) to the consumer reporting agency by a State or local child support enforcement agency; or

(B) to the consumer reporting agency and verified by any local, State, or Federal Government agency; and

(2) antedates the report by 7 years or less.

Section 1681s-2. Responsibilities of furnishers of information to consumer reporting agencies

(a) Duty of furnishers of information to provide accurate information

(1) Prohibition

(A) Reporting information with actual knowledge of errors

A person shall not furnish any information relating to a consumer to any consumer reporting agency if the person knows or consciously avoids knowing that the information is inaccurate.

(B) Reporting information after notice and confirmation of errors

A person shall not furnish information relating to a consumer to any consumer reporting agency if -

(i) the person has been notified by the consumer, at the address specified by the person for such notices, that specific information is inaccurate; and

(ii) the information is, in fact, inaccurate.

(C) No address requirement

A person who clearly and conspicuously specifies to the consumer an address for notices referred to in subparagraph (B) shall not be subject to subparagraph (A); however, nothing in subparagraph (B) shall require a person to specify such an address.

(2) Duty to correct and update information

A person who -

(A) regularly and in the ordinary course of business furnishes information to one or more consumer reporting agencies about the person's transactions or experiences with any consumer; and

(B) has furnished to a consumer reporting agency information that the person determines is not complete or accurate, shall promptly notify the consumer reporting agency of that determination and provide to the agency any corrections to that information, or any additional information, that is necessary to make the information provided by the person to the agency complete and accurate, and shall not thereafter furnish to the agency any of the information that remains not complete or accurate.

(3) Duty to provide notice of dispute

If the completeness or accuracy of any information furnished by any person to any consumer reporting agency is disputed to such person by a consumer, the person may not furnish the information to any consumer reporting agency without notice that such information is disputed by the consumer.

(4) Duty to provide notice of closed accounts

A person who regularly and in the ordinary course of business furnishes information to a consumer reporting agency regarding a consumer who has a credit account with that person shall notify the agency of the voluntary closure of the account by the consumer, in information regularly furnished for the period in which the account is closed.

(5) Duty to provide notice of delinquency of accounts

A person who furnishes information to a consumer reporting agency regarding a delinquent account being placed for collection, charged to profit or loss, or subjected to any similar action shall, not later than 90 days after furnishing the information, notify the agency of the month and year of the commencement of the delinquency that immediately preceded the action.

(b) Duties of furnishers of information upon notice of dispute

(1) In general

After receiving notice pursuant to section 1681i(a)(2) of this title of a dispute with regard to the completeness or accuracy of any information provided by a person to a consumer reporting agency, the person shall -

(A) conduct an investigation with respect to the disputed information;

(B) review all relevant information provided by the consumer reporting agency pursuant to section 1681i(a)(2) of this title;

(C) report the results of the investigation to the consumer reporting agency; and

(D) if the investigation finds that the information is incomplete or inaccurate, report those results to all other consumer reporting agencies to which the person furnished the information and that compile and maintain files on consumers on a nationwide basis.

(2) Deadline

A person shall complete all investigations, reviews, and reports required under paragraph (1) regarding information provided by the person to a consumer reporting agency, before the expiration of the period under section 1681i(a)(1) of this title within which the consumer reporting agency is required to complete actions required by that section regarding that information.

(c) Limitation on liability

Sections 1681n and 1681o of this title do not apply to any failure to comply with subsection (a) of this section, except as provided in section 1681s(c)(1)(B) of this title.

(d) Limitation on enforcement

Subsection (a) of this section shall be enforced exclusively under section 1681s of this title by the Federal agencies and officials and the State officials identified in that section.

Section 1681t. Relation to State laws

(a) In general

Except as provided in subsections (b) and (c) of this section, this subchapter does not annul, alter, affect, or exempt any person subject to the provisions of this subchapter from complying with the laws of any State with respect to the collection, distribution, or use of any information on consumers, except to the extent that those laws are inconsistent with any provision of this subchapter, and then only to the extent of the inconsistency.

(b) General exceptions

No requirement or prohibition may be imposed under the laws of any State -

(1) with respect to any subject matter regulated under -

(A) subsection (c) or (e) of section 1681b of this title, relating to the prescreening of consumer reports;

(B) section 1681i of this title, relating to the time by which a consumer reporting agency must take any action, including the provision of notification to a consumer or other person, in any procedure related to the disputed accuracy of information in a consumer's file, except that this subparagraph shall not apply to any State law in effect on September 30, 1996;

(C) subsections (a) and (b) of section 1681m of this title, relating to the duties of a person who takes any adverse action with respect to a consumer;

(D) section 1681m(d) of this title, relating to the duties of persons who use a consumer report of a consumer in connection with any credit or insurance transaction that is not initiated by the consumer and that consists of a firm offer of credit or insurance;

(E) section 1681c of this title, relating to information contained in consumer reports, except that this subparagraph shall not apply to any State law in effect on September 30, 1996; or

(F) section 1681s-2 of this title, relating to the responsibilities of persons who furnish information to consumer reporting agencies, except that this paragraph shall not apply -

(i) with respect to section 54A(a) of chapter 93 of the Massachusetts Annotated Laws (as in effect on September 30, 1996); or

(ii) with respect to section 1785.25(a) of the California Civil Code (as in effect on September 30, 1996);

(2) with respect to the exchange of information among persons affiliated by common ownership or common corporate control, except that this paragraph shall not apply with respect to subsection (a) or (c)(1) of section 2480e of title 9, Vermont Statutes Annotated (as in effect on September 30, 1996); or

(3) with respect to the form and content of any disclosure required to be made under section 1681g(c) of this title.

(c) "Firm offer of credit or insurance" defined

Notwithstanding any definition of the term "firm offer of credit or insurance" (or any equivalent term) under the laws of any State, the definition of that term contained in section 1681a(l) of this title shall be construed to apply in the enforcement and interpretation of the laws of any State governing consumer reports.

(d) Limitations

Subsections (b) and (c) of this section -

(1) do not affect any settlement, agreement, or consent judgment between any State Attorney General and any consumer reporting agency in effect on September 30, 1996; and

(2) do not apply to any provision of State law (including any provision of a State constitution) that -

(A) is enacted after January 1, 2004;

(B) states explicitly that the provision is intended to supplement this subchapter; and

(C) gives greater protection to consumers than is provided under this subchapter.

EQUAL CREDIT OPPORTUNITY ACT
UNITED STATES CODE
TITLE 15
CHAPTER 41
SUBCHAPTER IV

Section 1691. Scope of prohibition

(a) Activities constituting discrimination

It shall be unlawful for any creditor to discriminate against any applicant, with respect to any aspect of a credit transaction -

(1) on the basis of race, color, religion, national origin, sex or marital status, or age (provided the applicant has the capacity to contract);

(2) because all or part of the applicant's income derives from any public assistance program; or

(3) because the applicant has in good faith exercised any right under this chapter.

(b) Activities not constituting discrimination

It shall not constitute discrimination for purposes of this subchapter for a creditor -

(1) to make an inquiry of marital status if such inquiry is for the purpose of ascertaining the creditor's rights and remedies applicable to the particular extension of credit and not to discriminate in a determination of creditworthiness;

(2) to make an inquiry of the applicant's age or of whether the applicant's income derives from any public assistance program if such inquiry is for the purpose of determining the amount and probable continuance of income levels, credit history, or other pertinent element of creditworthiness as provided in regulations of the Board;

(3) to use any empirically derived credit system which considers age if such system is demonstrably and statistically sound in accordance with regulations of the Board, except that in the operation of such system the age of an elderly applicant may not be assigned a negative factor or value; or

(4) to make an inquiry or to consider the age of an elderly applicant when the age of such applicant is to be used by the creditor in the extension of credit in favor of such applicant.

(c) Additional activities not constituting discrimination

It is not a violation of this section for a creditor to refuse to extend credit offered pursuant to -

(1) any credit assistance program expressly authorized by law for an economically disadvantaged class of persons;

(2) any credit assistance program administered by a nonprofit organization for its members or an economically disadvantaged class of persons; or

(3) any special purpose credit program offered by a profit-making organization to meet special social needs which meets standards prescribed in regulations by the Board; if such refusal is required by or made pursuant to such program.

(d) Reason for adverse action; procedure applicable; "adverse action" defined

(1) Within thirty days (or such longer reasonable time as specified in regulations of the Board for any class of credit transaction) after receipt of a completed application for credit, a creditor shall notify the applicant of its action on the application.

(2) Each applicant against whom adverse action is taken shall be entitled to a statement of reasons for such action from the creditor. `A creditor satisfies this obligation by -

(A) providing statements of reasons in writing as a matter of course to applicants against whom adverse action is taken; or

(B) giving written notification of adverse action which discloses (i) the applicant's right to a statement of reasons within thirty days after receipt by the creditor of a request made within sixty days after such notification, and (ii) the identity of the person or office from which such statement may be obtained. Such statement may be given orally if the written notification advises the applicant of his right to have the statement of reasons confirmed in writing on written request.

(3) A statement of reasons meets the requirements of this section only if it contains the specific reasons for the adverse action taken.

(4) Where a creditor has been requested by a third party to make a specific extension of credit directly or indirectly to an applicant, the notification and statement of reasons required by this subsection may be made directly by such creditor, or indirectly through the third party, provided in either case that the identity of the creditor is disclosed.

(5) The requirements of paragraph (2), (3), or (4) may be satisfied by verbal statements or notifications in the case of any creditor who did not act on more than one hundred and fifty applications during the calendar year preceding the calendar year in which the adverse action is taken, as determined under regulations of the Board.

(6) For purposes of this subsection, the term "adverse action" means a denial or revocation of credit, a change in the terms of an existing credit arrangement, or a refusal to grant credit in substantially the amount or on substantially the terms requested. Such term does not include a refusal to extend additional credit under an existing credit arrangement where the applicant is delinquent or otherwise in default, or where such additional credit would exceed a previously established credit limit.

(e) Appraisals; copies of reports to applicants; costs

Each creditor shall promptly furnish an applicant, upon written request by the applicant made within a reasonable period of time of the application, a copy of the appraisal report used in connection with the applicant's application for a loan that is or would have been secured by a lien on residential real property. `The creditor may require the applicant to reimburse the creditor for the cost of the appraisal.

Section 1691a. Definitions; rules of construction

(a) The definitions and rules of construction set forth in this section are applicable for the purposes of this subchapter.

(b) The term "applicant" means any person who applies to a creditor directly for an extension, renewal, or continuation of credit, or applies to a creditor indirectly by use of an existing credit plan for an amount exceeding a previously established credit limit.

(c) The term "Board" refers to the Board of Governors of the Federal Reserve System.

(d) The term "credit" means the right granted by a creditor to a debtor to defer payment of debt or to incur debts and defer its payment or to purchase property or services and defer payment therefor.

(e) The term "creditor" means any person who regularly extends, renews, or continues credit; any person who regularly arranges for the extension, renewal, or continuation of credit; or any assignee of an original creditor who participates in the decision to extend, renew, or continue credit.

(f) The term "person" means a natural person, a corporation, government or governmental subdivision or agency, trust, estate, partnership, cooperative, or association.

(g) Any reference to any requirement imposed under this subchapter or any provision thereof includes reference to the regulations of the Board under this subchapter or the provision thereof in question.

Section 1691b. Promulgation of regulations by Board; establishment of Consumer Advisory Council by Board; duties, membership, etc., of Council

(a) Regulations

(1) The Board shall prescribe regulations to carry out the purposes of this subchapter. These regulations may contain but are not limited to such classifications, differentiation, or other provision, and may provide for such adjustments and exceptions for any class of transactions, as in the judgment of the Board are necessary or proper to effectuate the purposes of this subchapter, to prevent circumvention or evasion thereof, or to facilitate or substantiate compliance therewith.

(2) Such regulations may exempt from the provisions of this subchapter any class of transactions that are not primarily for personal, family, or household purposes, or business or commercial loans made available by a financial institution, except that a particular type within a class of such transactions may be exempted if the Board determines, after making an express finding that the application of this subchapter or of any provision of this subchapter of such transaction would not contribute substantially to effecting the purposes of this subchapter.

(3) An exemption granted pursuant to paragraph (2) shall be for no longer than five years and shall be extended only if the Board makes a subsequent determination, in the manner described by such paragraph, that such exemption remains appropriate.

(4) Pursuant to Board regulations, entities making business or commercial loans shall maintain such records or other data relating to such loans as may be necessary to evidence compliance with this subsection or enforce any action pursuant to the authority of this chapter. In no event shall such records or data be maintained for a period of less than one year. `The Board shall promulgate regulations to implement this paragraph in the manner prescribed by chapter 5 of title 5.

(5) The Board shall provide in regulations that an applicant for a business or commercial loan shall be provided a written notice of such applicant's right to receive a written statement of the reasons for the denial of such loan.

(b) Consumer Advisory Council

The Board shall establish a Consumer Advisory Council to advise and consult with it in the exercise of its functions under this chapter and to advise and consult with it concerning other consumer related matters it may place before the Council. In appointing the members of the Council, the Board shall seek to achieve a fair representation of the interests of creditors and consumers. `The Council shall meet from time to time at the call of the Board. Members of the Council who are not regular full-time employees of the United States shall, while attending meetings of such Council, be entitled to receive compensation at a rate fixed by the Board, but not exceeding $100 per day, including travel time. `Such members may be allowed travel expenses, including transportation and subsistence, while away from their homes or regular place of business.

Section 1691c. Administrative enforcement

(a) Enforcing agencies

Compliance with the requirements imposed under this subchapter shall be enforced under:

(1) section 8 of the Federal Deposit Insurance Act (12 U.S.C. 1818), in the case of -

(A) national banks, and Federal branches and Federal agencies of foreign banks, by the Office of the Comptroller of the Currency;

(B) member banks of the Federal Reserve System (other than national banks), branches and agencies of foreign banks (other than Federal branches, Federal agencies, and insured State branches of foreign banks), commercial lending companies owned or controlled by foreign banks, and organizations operating under section 25 or 25(a) of the Federal Reserve Act (12 U.S.C. 601 et seq., 611 et seq.), by the Board; and

(C) banks insured by the Federal Deposit Insurance Corporation (other than members of the Federal Reserve System) and insured State branches of foreign banks, by the Board of Directors of the Federal Deposit Insurance Corporation;

(2) Section 8 of the Federal Deposit Insurance Act (12 U.S.C. 1818), by the Director of the Office of Thrift Supervision, in the case of a savings association the deposits of which are insured by the Federal Deposit Insurance Corporation.

(3) The Federal Credit Union Act (12 U.S.C. 1751 et seq.), by the Administrator of the National Credit Union Administration with respect to any Federal Credit Union.

(4) Subtitle IV of title 49, by the Secretary of Transportation, with respect to all carriers subject to the jurisdiction of the Surface Transportation Board.

(5) Part A of subtitle VII of title 49, by the Secretary of Transportation with respect to any air carrier or foreign air carrier subject to that part.

(6) The Packers and Stockyards Act, 1921 (7 U.S.C. 181 et seq.) (except as provided in section 406 of that Act (7 U.S.C. 226, 227)), by the Secretary of Agriculture with respect to any activities subject to that Act.

(7) The Farm Credit Act of 1971 (12 U.S.C. 2001 et seq.), by the Farm Credit Administration with respect to any Federal land bank, Federal land bank association, Federal intermediate credit bank, and production credit association;

(8) The Securities Exchange Act of 1934 (15 U.S.C. 78a et seq.), by the Securities and Exchange Commission with respect to brokers and dealers; and

(9) The Small Business Investment Act of 1958 (15 U.S.C. 661 et seq.), by the Small Business Administration, with respect to small business investment companies. The terms used in paragraph (1) that are not defined in this subchapter or otherwise defined in section 3(s) of the Federal Deposit Insurance Act (12 U.S.C. 1813(s)) shall have the meaning given to them in section 1(b) of the International Banking Act of 1978 (12 U.S.C. 3101).

(b) Violations of subchapter deemed violations of preexisting statutory requirements; additional agency powers

For the purpose of the exercise by any agency referred to in subsection (a) of this section of its powers under any Act referred to in that subsection, a violation of any requirement imposed under this subchapter shall be deemed to be a violation of a requirement imposed under that Act. In addition to its powers under any provision of law specifically referred to in subsection (a) of this section, each of the agencies referred to in that subsection may exercise for the purpose of enforcing compliance with any requirement imposed under this subchapter, any other authority conferred on it by law. The exercise of the authorities of any of the agencies referred to in subsection (a) of this section for the purpose of enforcing compliance with any requirement imposed under this subchapter shall in no way preclude the exercise of such authorities for the purpose of enforcing compliance with any other provision of law not relating to the prohibition of discrimination on the basis of sex or marital status with respect to any aspect of a credit transaction.

(c) Overall enforcement authority of Federal Trade Commission

Except to the extent that enforcement of the requirements imposed under this subchapter is specifically committed to some other Government agency under subsection (a) of this section, the Federal Trade Commission shall enforce such requirements. `For the purpose of the exercise by the Federal Trade Commission of its functions and powers under the Federal Trade Commission Act (15 U.S.C. 41 et seq.), a violation of any requirement imposed under this subchapter shall be deemed

a violation of a requirement imposed under that Act. All of the functions and powers of the Federal Trade Commission under the Federal Trade Commission Act are available to the Commission to enforce compliance by any person with the requirements imposed under this subchapter, irrespective of whether that person is engaged in commerce or meets any other jurisdictional tests in the Federal Trade Commission Act, including the power to enforce any Federal Reserve Board regulation promulgated under this subchapter in the same manner as if the violation had been a violation of a Federal Trade Commission trade regulation rule.

(d) Rules and regulations by enforcing agencies

The authority of the Board to issue regulations under this subchapter does not impair the authority of any other agency designated in this section to make rules respecting its own procedures in enforcing compliance with requirements imposed under this subchapter.

Section 1691c-1. Incentives for self-testing and self-correction

(a) Privileged information

(1) Conditions for privilege

A report or result of a self-test (as that term is defined by regulations of the Board) shall be considered to be privileged under paragraph (2) if a creditor -

(A) conducts, or authorizes an independent third party to conduct, a self-test of any aspect of a credit transaction by a creditor, in order to determine the level or effectiveness of compliance with this subchapter by the creditor; and

(B) has identified any possible violation of this subchapter by the creditor and has taken, or is taking, appropriate corrective action to address any such possible violation.

(2) Privileged self-test

If a creditor meets the conditions specified in subparagraphs (A) and (B) of paragraph (1) with respect to a self-test described in that paragraph, any report or results of that self-test -

(A) shall be privileged; and

(B) may not be obtained or used by any applicant, department, or agency in any -

(i) proceeding or civil action in which one or more violations of this subchapter are alleged; or

(ii) examination or investigation relating to compliance with this subchapter.

(b) Results of self-testing

(1) In general

No provision of this section may be construed to prevent an applicant, department, or agency from obtaining or using a report or results of any self-test in any proceeding or civil action in which a violation of this subchapter is alleged, or in any examination or investigation of compliance with this subchapter if -

(A) the creditor or any person with lawful access to the report or results -

(i) voluntarily releases or discloses all, or any part of, the report or results to the applicant, department, or agency, or to the general public; or

(ii) refers to or describes the report or results as a defense to charges of violations of this subchapter against the creditor to whom the self-test relates; or

(B) the report or results are sought in conjunction with an adjudication or admission of a violation of this subchapter for the sole purpose of determining an appropriate penalty or remedy.

(2) Disclosure for determination of penalty or remedy

Any report or results of a self-test that are disclosed for the purpose specified in paragraph (1)(B) -

(A) shall be used only for the particular proceeding in which the adjudication or admission referred to in paragraph (1)(B) is made; and

(B) may not be used in any other action or proceeding.

(c) Adjudication

An applicant, department, or agency that challenges a privilege asserted under this section may seek a determination of the existence and application of that privilege in -

(1) a court of competent jurisdiction; or

(2) an administrative law proceeding with appropriate jurisdiction.

Section 1691d. Applicability of other laws

(a) Requests for signature of husband and wife for creation of valid lien, etc.

A request for the signature of both parties to a marriage for the purpose of creating a valid lien, passing clear title, waiving inchoate rights to property, or assigning earnings, shall not constitute discrimination under this subchapter: Provided, however, That this provision shall not be construed to permit a creditor to take sex or marital status into account in connection with the evaluation of creditworthiness of any applicant.

(b) State property laws affecting creditworthiness

Consideration or application of State property laws directly or indirectly affecting creditworthiness shall not constitute discrimination for purposes of this subchapter.

(c) State laws prohibiting separate extension of consumer credit to husband and wife

Any provision of State law which prohibits the separate extension of consumer credit to each party to a marriage shall not apply in any case where each party to a marriage voluntarily applies for separate credit from the same creditor: Provided, That in any case where such a State law is so preempted, each party to the marriage shall be solely responsible for the debt so contracted.

(d) Combining credit accounts of husband and wife with same creditor to determine permissible finance charges or loan ceilings under Federal or State laws

When each party to a marriage separately and voluntarily applies for and obtains separate credit accounts with the same creditor, those accounts shall not be aggregated or otherwise combined for purposes of determining permissible finance charges or permissible loan ceilings under the laws of any State or of the United States.

(e) Election of remedies under subchapter or State law; nature of relief determining applicability

Where the same act or omission constitutes a violation of this subchapter and of applicable State law, a person aggrieved by such conduct may bring a legal action to recover monetary damages either under this subchapter or under such State law, but not both. This election of remedies shall not apply to court actions in which the relief sought does not include monetary damages or to administrative actions.

(f) Compliance with inconsistent State laws; determination of inconsistency

This subchapter does not annul, alter, or affect, or exempt any person subject to the provisions of this subchapter from complying with, the laws of any State with respect to credit discrimination, except to the extent that those laws are inconsistent with any provision of this subchapter, and then only to the extent of the inconsistency. `The Board is authorized to determine whether such inconsistencies exist. `The Board may not determine that any State law is inconsistent with any provision of this subchapter if the Board determines that such law gives greater protection to the applicant.

(g) Exemption by regulation of credit transactions covered by State law; failure to comply with State law

The Board shall by regulation exempt from the requirements of sections 1691 and 1691a of this title any class of credit transactions within any State if it determines that under the law of that State that class of transactions is subject to requirements substantially similar to those imposed under this subchapter or that such law gives greater protection to the applicant, and that there is adequate provision for enforcement. Failure to comply with any requirement of such State law in any transaction so exempted shall constitute a violation of this subchapter for the purposes of section 1691e of this title.

Section 1691e. Civil liability

(a) Individual or class action for actual damages

Any creditor who fails to comply with any requirement imposed under this subchapter shall be liable to the aggrieved applicant for any actual damages sustained by such applicant acting either in an individual capacity or as a member of a class.

(b) Recovery of punitive damages in individual and class action for actual damages; exemptions; maximum amount of punitive damages in individual actions; limitation on total recovery in class actions; factors determining amount of award

Any creditor, other than a government or governmental subdivision or agency, who fails to comply with any requirement imposed under this subchapter shall be liable to the aggrieved applicant for punitive damages in an amount not greater than $10,000, in addition to any actual damages provided in subsection (a) of this section, except that in the case of a class action the total recovery under this subsection shall not exceed the lesser of $500,000 or 1 per centum of the net worth of the creditor. `In determining the amount of such damages in any action, the court shall consider, among other relevant factors, the amount of any actual damages awarded, the frequency and persistence of failures of compliance by the creditor, the resources of the creditor, the number of persons adversely affected, and the extent to which the creditor's failure of compliance was intentional.

(c) Action for equitable and declaratory relief

Upon application by an aggrieved applicant, the appropriate United States district court or any other court of competent jurisdiction may grant such equitable and declaratory relief as is necessary to enforce the requirements imposed under this subchapter.

(d) Recovery of costs and attorney fees

In the case of any successful action under subsection (a), (b), or (c) of this section, the costs of the action, together with a reasonable attorney's fee as determined by the court, shall be added to any damages awarded by the court under such subsection.

(e) Good faith compliance with rule, regulation, or interpretation of Board or interpretation or approval by an official or employee of Federal Reserve System duly authorized by Board

No provision of this subchapter imposing liability shall apply to any act done or omitted in good faith in conformity with any official rule, regulation, or interpretation thereof by the Board or in conformity with any interpretation or approval by an official or employee of the Federal Reserve System duly authorized by the Board to issue such interpretations or approvals under such procedures as the Board may prescribe therefor, notwithstanding that after such act or omission has occurred, such rule, regulation, interpretation, or approval is amended, rescinded, or determined by judicial or other authority to be invalid for any reason.

(f) Jurisdiction of courts; time for maintenance of action; exceptions

Any action under this section may be brought in the appropriate United States district court without regard to the amount in controversy, or in any other court of competent jurisdiction. No such action shall be brought later than two years from the date of the occurrence of the violation, except that -

(1) whenever any agency having responsibility for administrative enforcement under section 1691c of this title commences an enforcement proceeding within two years from the date of the occurrence of the violation,

(2) whenever the Attorney General commences a civil action under this section within two years from the date of the occurrence of the violation, then any applicant who has been a victim of the discrimination which is the subject of such proceeding or civil action may bring an action under this section not later than one year after the commencement of that proceeding or action.

(g) Request by responsible enforcement agency to Attorney General for civil action

The agencies having responsibility for administrative enforcement under section 1691c of this title, if unable to obtain compliance with section 1691 of this title, are authorized to refer the matter to the Attorney General with a recommendation that an appropriate civil action be instituted. Each agency referred to in paragraphs `(1), (2), and (3) of section 1691c(a) of this title shall refer the matter to the Attorney General whenever the agency has reason to believe that 1 or more creditors has engaged in a pattern or practice of discouraging or denying applications for credit in violation of section 1691(a) of this title. Each such agency may refer the matter to the Attorney General whenever the agency has reason to believe that 1 or more creditors has violated section 1691(a) of this title.

(h) Authority for Attorney General to bring civil action; jurisdiction

When a matter is referred to the Attorney General pursuant to subsection (g) of this section, or whenever he has reason to believe that one or more creditors are engaged in a pattern or practice in violation of this subchapter, the Attorney General may bring a civil action in any appropriate United States district court for such relief as may be appropriate, including actual and punitive damages and injunctive relief.

(i) Recovery under both subchapter and fair housing enforcement provisions prohibited for violation based on same transaction

No person aggrieved by a violation of this subchapter and by a violation of section 3605 of title 42 shall recover under this subchapter and section 3612 of title 42, if such violation is based on the same transaction.

(j) Discovery of creditor's granting standards

Nothing in this subchapter shall be construed to prohibit the discovery of a creditor's credit granting standards under appropriate discovery procedures in the court or agency in which an action or proceeding is brought.

(k) Notice to HUD of violations

Whenever an agency referred to in paragraph (1), (2), or (3) of section 1691c(a) of this title -

(1) has reason to believe, as a result of receiving a consumer complaint, conducting a consumer compliance examination, or otherwise, that a violation of this subchapter has occurred;

(2) has reason to believe that the alleged violation would be a violation of the Fair Housing Act (42 U.S.C. 3601 et seq.); and

(3) does not refer the matter to the Attorney General pursuant to subsection (g) of this section, the agency shall notify the Secretary of Housing and Urban Development of the violation, and shall notify the applicant that the Secretary of Housing and Urban Development has been notified of the alleged violation and that remedies for the violation may be available under the Fair Housing Act.

FAIR DEBT COLLECTION PRACTICES ACT
UNITED STATES CODE
TITLE 15
CHAPTER 41
SUBCHAPTER V

Section 1692. Congressional findings and declaration of purpose

(a) Abusive practices

There is abundant evidence of the use of abusive, deceptive, and unfair debt collection practices by many debt collectors. `Abusive debt collection practices contribute to the number of personal bankruptcies, to marital instability, to the loss of jobs, and to invasions of individual privacy.

(b) Inadequacy of laws

Existing laws and procedures for redressing these injuries are inadequate to protect consumers.

(c) Available non-abusive collection methods

Means other than misrepresentation or other abusive debt collection practices are available for the effective collection of debts.

(d) Interstate commerce

Abusive debt collection practices are carried on to a substantial extent in interstate commerce and through means and instrumentalities of such commerce. Even where abusive debt collection practices are purely intrastate in character, they nevertheless directly affect interstate commerce.

(e) Purposes

It is the purpose of this subchapter to eliminate abusive debt collection practices by debt collectors, to insure that those debt collectors who refrain from using abusive debt collection practices are not competitively disadvantaged, and to promote consistent State action to protect consumers against debt collection abuses.

Section 1692a. Definitions

As used in this subchapter -

(1) The term "Commission" means the Federal Trade Commission.

(2) The term "communication" means the conveying of information regarding a debt directly or indirectly to any person through any medium.

(3) The term "consumer" means any natural person obligated or allegedly obligated to pay any debt.

(4) The term "creditor" means any person who offers or extends credit creating a debt or to whom a debt is owed, but such term does not include any person to the extent that he receives an assignment or transfer of a debt in default solely for the purpose of facilitating collection of such debt for another.

(5) The term "debt" means any obligation or alleged obligation of a consumer to pay money arising out of a transaction in which the money, property, insurance, or services which are the subject of the transaction are primarily for personal, family, or household purposes, whether or not such obligation has been reduced to judgment.

(6) The term "debt collector" means any person who uses any instrumentality of interstate commerce or the mails in any business the principal purpose of which is the collection of any debts, or who regularly collects or attempts to collect, directly or indirectly, debts owed or due or asserted to be owed or due another. Notwithstanding the exclusion provided by clause (F) of the last sentence of this paragraph, the term includes any creditor who, in the process of collecting his own debts, uses any name other than his own which would indicate that a third person is collecting or attempting to collect such debts. For the purpose of section 1692f(6) of this title, such term also includes any person who uses any instrumentality of interstate commerce or the mails in any business the principal purpose of which is the enforcement of security interests. The term does not include -

(A) any officer or employee of a creditor while, in the name of the creditor, collecting debts for such creditor;

(B) any person while acting as a debt collector for another person, both of whom are related by common ownership or affiliated by corporate control, if the person acting as a debt collector does so only for persons to whom it is so related or affiliated and if the principal business of such person is not the collection of debts;

(C) any officer or employee of the United States or any State to the extent that collecting or attempting to collect any debt is in the performance of his official duties;

(D) any person while serving or attempting to serve legal process on any other person in connection with the judicial enforcement of any debt;

(E) any nonprofit organization which, at the request of consumers, performs bona fide consumer credit counseling and assists consumers in the liquidation of their debts by receiving payments from such consumers and distributing such amounts to creditors; and

(F) any person collecting or attempting to collect any debt owed or due or asserted to be owed or due another to the extent such activity

(i) is incidental to a bona fide fiduciary obligation or a bona fide escrow arrangement;

(ii) concerns a debt which was originated by such person;

(iii) concerns a debt which was not in default at the time it was obtained by such person; or

(iv) concerns a debt obtained by such person as a secured party in a commercial credit transaction involving the creditor.

(7) The term "location information" means a consumer's place of abode and his telephone number at such place, or his place of employment.

(8) The term "State" means any State, territory, or possession of the United States, the District of Columbia, the Commonwealth of Puerto Rico, or any political subdivision of any of the foregoing.

Section 1692b. Acquisition of location information

Any debt collector communicating with any person other than the consumer for the purpose of acquiring location information about the consumer shall -

(1) identify himself, state that he is confirming or correcting location information concerning the consumer, and, only if expressly requested, identify his employer;

(2) not state that such consumer owes any debt;

(3) not communicate with any such person more than once unless requested to do so by such person or unless the debt collector reasonably believes that the earlier response of such person is erroneous or incomplete and that such person now has correct or complete location information;

(4) not communicate by post card;

(5) not use any language or symbol on any envelope or in the contents of any communication effected by the mails or telegram that indicates that the debt collector is in the debt collection business or that the communication relates to the collection of a debt; and

(6) after the debt collector knows the consumer is represented by an attorney with regard to the subject debt and has knowledge of, or can readily ascertain, such attorney's name and address, not communicate with any person other than that attorney, unless the attorney fails to respond within a reasonable period of time to communication from the debt collector.

Section 1692c. Communication in connection with debt collection

(a) Communication with the consumer generally

Without the prior consent of the consumer given directly to the debt collector or the express permission of a court of competent jurisdiction, a debt collector may not communicate with a consumer in connection with the collection of any debt -

(1) at any unusual time or place or a time or place known or which should be known to be inconvenient to the consumer. `In the absence of knowledge of circumstances to the contrary, a debt collector shall assume that the convenient time for communicating with a consumer is after 8 o'clock antemeridian and before 9 o'clock postmeridian, local time at the consumer's location;

(2) if the debt collector knows the consumer is represented by an attorney with respect to such debt and has knowledge of, or can readily ascertain, such attorney's name and address, unless the attorney fails to respond within a reasonable period of time to a communication from

the debt collector or unless the attorney consents to direct communication with the consumer; or

(3) at the consumer's place of employment if the debt collector knows or has reason to know that the consumer's employer prohibits the consumer from receiving such communication.

(b) Communication with third parties

Except as provided in section 1692b of this title, without the prior consent of the consumer given directly to the debt collector, or the express permission of a court of competent jurisdiction, or as reasonably necessary to effectuate a postjudgment judicial remedy, a debt collector may not communicate, in connection with the collection of any debt, with any person other than the consumer, his attorney, a consumer reporting agency if otherwise permitted by law, the creditor, the attorney of the creditor, or the attorney of the debt collector.

(c) Ceasing communication

If a consumer notifies a debt collector in writing that the consumer refuses to pay a debt or that the consumer wishes the debt collector to cease further communication with the consumer, the debt collector shall not communicate further with the consumer with respect to such debt, except –

(1) to advise the consumer that the debt collector's further efforts are being terminated;

(2) to notify the consumer that the debt collector or creditor may invoke specified remedies which are ordinarily invoked by such debt collector or creditor; or

(3) where applicable, to notify the consumer that the debt collector or creditor intends to invoke a specified remedy. If such notice from the consumer is made by mail, notification shall be complete upon receipt.

(d) "Consumer" defined

For the purpose of this section, the term "consumer" includes the consumer's spouse, parent (if the consumer is a minor), guardian, executor, or administrator.

Section 1692d. Harassment or abuse

A debt collector may not engage in any conduct the natural consequence of which is to harass, oppress, or abuse any person in connection with the collection of a debt. Without limiting the general application of the foregoing, the following conduct is a violation of this section:

(1) The use or threat of use of violence or other criminal means to harm the physical person, reputation, or property of any person.

(2) The use of obscene or profane language or language the natural consequence of which is to abuse the hearer or reader.

(3) The publication of a list of consumers who allegedly refuse to pay debts, except to a consumer reporting agency or to persons meeting the requirements of section 1681a(f) or 1681b(3) of this title.

(4) The advertisement for sale of any debt to coerce payment of the debt.

(5) Causing a telephone to ring or engaging any person in telephone conversation repeatedly or continuously with intent to annoy, abuse, or harass any person at the called number.

(6) Except as provided in section 1692b of this title, the placement of telephone calls without meaningful disclosure of the caller's identity.

Section 1692e. False or misleading representations

A debt collector may not use any false, deceptive, or misleading representation or means in connection with the collection of any debt. Without limiting the general application of the foregoing, the following conduct is a violation of this section:

(1) The false representation or implication that the debt collector is vouched for, bonded by, or affiliated with the United States or any State, including the use of any badge, uniform, or facsimile thereof.

(2) The false representation of –

(A) the character, amount, or legal status of any debt; or

(B) any services rendered or compensation which may be lawfully received by any debt collector for the collection of a debt.

(3) The false representation or implication that any individual is an attorney or that any communication is from an attorney.

(4) The representation or implication that nonpayment of any debt will result in the arrest or imprisonment of any person or the seizure, garnishment, attachment, or sale of any property or wages of any person unless such action is lawful and the debt collector or creditor intends to take such action.

(5) The threat to take any action that cannot legally be taken or that is not intended to be taken.

(6) The false representation or implication that a sale, referral, or other transfer of any interest in a debt shall cause the consumer to –

(A) lose any claim or defense to payment of the debt; or

(B) become subject to any practice prohibited by this subchapter.

(7) The false representation or implication that the consumer committed any crime or other conduct in order to disgrace the consumer.

(8) Communicating or threatening to communicate to any person credit information which is known or which should be known to be false, including the failure to communicate that a disputed debt is disputed.

(9) The use or distribution of any written communication which simulates or is falsely represented to be a document authorized, issued, or approved by any court, official, or agency of the United States or any State, or which creates a false impression as to its source, authorization, or approval.

(10) The use of any false representation or deceptive means to collect or attempt to collect any debt or to obtain information concerning a consumer.

(11) The failure to disclose in the initial written communication with the consumer and, in addition, if the initial communication with the consumer is oral, in that initial oral communication, that the debt collector is attempting to collect a debt and that any information obtained will be used for that purpose, and the failure to disclose in subsequent communications that the communication is from a debt collector, except that this paragraph shall not apply to a formal pleading made in connection with a legal action.

(12) The false representation or implication that accounts have been turned over to innocent purchasers for value.

(13) The false representation or implication that documents are legal process.

(14) The use of any business, company, or organization name other than the true name of the debt collector's business, company, or organization.

(15) The false representation or implication that documents are not legal process forms or do not require action by the consumer.

(16) The false representation or implication that a debt collector operates or is employed by a consumer reporting agency as defined by section 1681a(f) of this title.

Section 1692f. Unfair practices

A debt collector may not use unfair or unconscionable means to collect or attempt to collect any debt. Without limiting the general application of the foregoing, the following conduct is a violation of this section:

(1) The collection of any amount (including any interest, fee, charge, or expense incidental to the principal obligation) unless such amount is expressly authorized by the agreement creating the debt or permitted by law.

(2) The acceptance by a debt collector from any person of a check or other payment instrument postdated by more than five days unless such person is notified in writing of the debt collector's intent to deposit such check or instrument not more than ten nor less than three business days prior to such deposit.

(3) The solicitation by a debt collector of any postdated check or other postdated payment instrument for the purpose of threatening or instituting criminal prosecution.

(4) Depositing or threatening to deposit any postdated check or other postdated payment instrument prior to the date on such check or instrument.

(5) Causing charges to be made to any person for communications by concealment of the true purpose of the communication. `Such charges include, but are not limited to, collect telephone calls and telegram fees.

(6) Taking or threatening to take any nonjudicial action to effect dispossession or disablement of property if -

(A) there is no present right to possession of the property claimed as collateral through an enforceable security interest;

(B) there is no present intention to take possession of the property; or

(C) the property is exempt by law from such dispossession or disablement.

(7) Communicating with a consumer regarding a debt by post card.

(8) Using any language or symbol, other than the debt collector's address, on any envelope when communicating with a consumer by use of the mails or by telegram, except that a debt collector may use his business name if such name does not indicate that he is in the debt collection business.

Section 1692g. Validation of debts

(a) Notice of debt; contents

Within five days after the initial communication with a consumer in connection with the collection of any debt, a debt collector shall, unless the following information is contained in the initial communication or the consumer has paid the debt, send the consumer a written notice containing -

(1) the amount of the debt;

(2) the name of the creditor to whom the debt is owed;

(3) a statement that unless the consumer, within thirty days after receipt of the notice, disputes the validity of the debt, or any portion thereof, the debt will be assumed to be valid by the debt collector;

(4) a statement that if the consumer notifies the debt collector in writing within the thirty-day period that the debt, or any portion thereof, is disputed, the debt collector will obtain verification of the debt or a copy of a judgment against the consumer and a copy of such verification or judgment will be mailed to the consumer by the debt collector; and

(5) a statement that, upon the consumer's written request within the thirty-day period, the debt collector will provide the consumer with the name and address of the original creditor, if different from the current creditor.

(b) Disputed debts

If the consumer notifies the debt collector in writing within the thirty-day period described in subsection (a) of this section that the debt, or any portion thereof, is disputed, or that the consumer requests the name and address of the original creditor, the debt collector shall cease collection of the debt, or any disputed portion thereof, until the debt collector obtains verification of the debt or a copy of a judgment, or the name and address of the original creditor, and a copy of such verification or judgment, or name and address of the original creditor, is mailed to the consumer by the debt collector.

(c) Admission of liability

The failure of a consumer to dispute the validity of a debt under this section may not be construed by any court as an admission of liability by the consumer.

Section 1692h. Multiple debts

If any consumer owes multiple debts and makes any single payment to any debt collector with respect to such debts, such debt collector may not apply such payment to any debt which is disputed by the consumer and, where applicable, shall apply such payment in accordance with the consumer's directions.

Section 1692i. Legal actions by debt collectors

(a) Venue

Any debt collector who brings any legal action on a debt against any consumer shall -

(1) in the case of an action to enforce an interest in real property securing the consumer's obligation, bring such action only in a judicial district or similar legal entity in which such real property is located; or

(2) in the case of an action not described in paragraph (1), bring such action only in the judicial district or similar legal entity -

(A) in which such consumer signed the contract sued upon; or

(B) in which such consumer resides at the commencement of the action.

(b) Authorization of actions

Nothing in this subchapter shall be construed to authorize the bringing of legal actions by debt collectors.

Section 1692j. Furnishing certain deceptive forms

(a) It is unlawful to design, compile, and furnish any form knowing that such form would be used to create the false belief in a consumer that a person other than the creditor of such consumer is participating in the collection of or in an attempt to collect a debt such consumer allegedly owes such creditor, when in fact such person is not so participating.

(b) Any person who violates this section shall be liable to the same extent and in the same manner as a debt collector is liable under section 1692k of this title for failure to comply with a provision of this subchapter.

Section 1692k. Civil liability

(a) Amount of damages

Except as otherwise provided by this section, any debt collector who fails to comply with any provision of this subchapter with respect to any person is liable to such person in an amount equal to the sum of -

(1) any actual damage sustained by such person as a result of such failure;

(2) (A) in the case of any action by an individual, such additional damages as the court may allow, but not exceeding $1,000; or

(B) in the case of a class action,

(i) such amount for each named plaintiff as could be recovered under subparagraph (A), and

(ii) such amount as the court may allow for all other class members, without regard to a minimum individual recovery, not to exceed the lesser of $500,000 or 1 per centum of the net worth of the debt collector; and

(3) in the case of any successful action to enforce the foregoing liability, the costs of the action, together with a reasonable attorney's fee as determined by the court. `On a finding by the court that an action under this section was brought in bad faith and for the purpose of harassment, the court may award to the defendant attorney's fees reasonable in relation to the work expended and costs.

(b) Factors considered by court

In determining the amount of liability in any action under subsection (a) of this section, the court shall consider, among other relevant factors -

(1) in any individual action under subsection (a)(2)(A) of this section, the frequency and persistence of noncompliance by the debt collector, the nature of such noncompliance, and the extent to which such noncompliance was intentional; or

(2) in any class action under subsection (a)(2)(B) of this section, the frequency and persistence of noncompliance by the debt collector, the nature of such noncompliance, the resources of the debt collector, the number of persons adversely affected, and the extent to which the debt collector's noncompliance was intentional.

(c) Intent

A debt collector may not be held liable in any action brought under this subchapter if the debt collector shows by a preponderance of evidence that the violation was not intentional and resulted from a bona fide error notwithstanding the maintenance of procedures reasonably adapted to avoid any such error.

(d) Jurisdiction

An action to enforce any liability created by this subchapter may be brought in any appropriate United States district court without regard to the amount in controversy, or in any other court of competent jurisdiction, within one year from the date on which the violation occurs.

(e) Advisory opinions of Commission

No provision of this section imposing any liability shall apply to any act done or omitted in good faith in conformity with any advisory opinion of the Commission, notwithstanding that after such act or omission has occurred, such opinion is amended, rescinded, or determined by judicial or other authority to be invalid for any reason.

Section 1692l. Administrative enforcement

(a) Federal Trade Commission

Compliance with this subchapter shall be enforced by the Commission, except to the extent that enforcement of the requirements imposed under this subchapter is specifically committed to another agency under subsection (b) of this section. `For purpose of the exercise by the Commission of its functions and powers under the Federal Trade Commission Act (15 U.S.C. 41 et seq.), a violation of this subchapter shall be deemed an unfair or deceptive act or practice in violation of that Act. All of the functions and powers of the Commission under the Federal Trade Commission Act are available to the Commission to enforce compliance by any person with this subchapter, irrespective of whether that person is engaged in commerce or meets any other jurisdictional tests in the Federal Trade Commission Act, including the power to enforce the provisions of this subchapter in the same manner as if the violation had been a violation of a Federal Trade Commission trade regulation rule.

(b) Applicable provisions of law

Compliance with any requirements imposed under this subchapter shall be enforced under -

(1) section 8 of the Federal Deposit Insurance Act (12 U.S.C. 1818), in the case of -

(A) national banks, and Federal branches and Federal agencies of foreign banks, by the Office of the Comptroller of the Currency;

(B) member banks of the Federal Reserve System (other than national banks), branches and agencies of foreign banks (other than Federal branches, Federal agencies, and insured State branches of foreign banks), commercial lending companies owned or controlled by foreign banks, and organizations operating under section 25 or 25(a) of the Federal Reserve Act (12 U.S.C. 601 et seq., 611 et seq.), by the Board of Governors of the Federal Reserve System; and

(C) banks insured by the Federal Deposit Insurance Corporation (other than members of the Federal Reserve System) and insured State branches of foreign banks, by the Board of Directors of the Federal Deposit Insurance Corporation;

(2) section 8 of the Federal Deposit Insurance Act (12 U.S.C. 1818), by the Director of the Office of Thrift Supervision, in the case of a savings association the deposits of which are insured by the Federal Deposit Insurance Corporation;

(3) the Federal Credit Union Act (12 U.S.C. 1751 et seq.), by the National Credit Union Administration Board with respect to any Federal credit union;

(4) subtitle IV of title 49, by the Secretary of Transportation, with respect to all carriers subject to the jurisdiction of the Surface Transportation Board;

(5) part A of subtitle VII of title 49, by the Secretary of Transportation with respect to any air carrier or any foreign air carrier subject to that part; and

(6) the Packers and Stockyards Act, 1921 (7 U.S.C. 181 et seq.) `(except as provided in section 406 of that Act (7 U.S.C. 226, 227)),

by the Secretary of Agriculture with respect to any activities subject to that Act. The terms used in paragraph (1) that are not defined in this subchapter or otherwise defined in section 3(s) of the Federal Deposit Insurance Act (12 U.S.C. 1813(s)) shall have the meaning given to them in section 1(b) of the International Banking Act of 1978 (12 U.S.C. 3101).

(c) Agency powers

For the purpose of the exercise by any agency referred to in subsection (b) of this section of its powers under any Act referred to in that subsection, a violation of any requirement imposed under this subchapter shall be deemed to be a violation of a requirement imposed under that Act. In addition to its powers under any provision of law specifically referred to in subsection (b) of this section, each of the agencies referred to in that subsection may exercise, for the purpose of enforcing compliance with any requirement imposed under this subchapter any other authority conferred on it by law, except as provided in subsection (d) of this section.

(d) Rules and regulations

Neither the Commission nor any other agency referred to in subsection (b) of this section may promulgate trade regulation rules or other regulations with respect to the collection of debts by debt collectors as defined in this subchapter.

CREDIT REPAIR ORGANIZATIONS ACT UNITED STATES CODE TITLE 15 CHAPTER 41 SUBCHAPTER II-A

Section 1679. Findings and purposes

(a) Findings

The Congress makes the following findings:

(1) Consumers have a vital interest in establishing and maintaining their creditworthiness and credit standing in order to obtain and use credit. As a result, consumers who have experienced credit problems may seek assistance from credit repair organizations which offer to improve the credit standing of such consumers.

(2) Certain advertising and business practices of some companies engaged in the business of credit repair services have worked a financial hardship upon consumers, particularly those of limited economic means and who are inexperienced in credit matters.

(b) Purposes

The purposes of this subchapter are -

(1) to ensure that prospective buyers of the services of credit repair organizations are provided with the information necessary to make an informed decision regarding the purchase of such services; and

(2) to protect the public from unfair or deceptive advertising and business practices by credit repair organizations.

Section 1679a. Definitions

For purposes of this subchapter, the following definitions apply:

(1) Consumer

The term "consumer" means an individual.

(2) Consumer credit transaction

The term "consumer credit transaction" means any transaction in which credit is offered or extended to an individual for personal, family, or household purposes.

(3) Credit repair organization

The term "credit repair organization" -

(A) means any person who uses any instrumentality of interstate commerce or the mails to sell, provide, or perform (or represent that such person can or will sell, provide, or perform) any service, in return for the payment of money or other valuable consideration, for the express or implied purpose of -

(i) improving any consumer's credit record, credit history, or credit rating; or

(ii) providing advice or assistance to any consumer with regard to any activity or service described in clause (i); and

(B) does not include -

(i) any nonprofit organization which is exempt from taxation under section 501(c)(3) of title 26;

(ii) any creditor (as defined in section 1602 of this title), with respect to any consumer, to the extent the creditor is assisting the consumer to restructure any debt owed by the consumer to the creditor; or

(iii) any depository institution (as that term is defined in section 1813 of title 12) or any Federal or State credit union (as those terms are defined in section 1752 of title 12), or any affiliate or subsidiary of such a depository institution or credit union.

(4) Credit

The term "credit" has the meaning given to such term in section 1602(e) of this title.

Section 1679b. Prohibited practices

(a) In general

No person may -

(1) make any statement, or counsel or advise any consumer to make any statement, which is untrue or misleading (or which, upon the exercise of reasonable care, should be known by the credit repair organization, officer, employee, agent, or other person to be untrue or misleading) with respect to any consumer's creditworthiness, credit standing, or credit capacity to -

(A) any consumer reporting agency (as defined in section 1681a(f) of this title); or

(B) any person -

(i) who has extended credit to the consumer; or

(ii) to whom the consumer has applied or is applying for an extension of credit;

(2) make any statement, or counsel or advise any consumer to make any statement, the intended effect of which is to alter the consumer's identification to prevent the display of the consumer's credit record, history, or rating for the purpose of concealing adverse information that is accurate and not obsolete to -

(A) any consumer reporting agency;

(B) any person -

(i) who has extended credit to the consumer; or

(ii) to whom the consumer has applied or is applying for an extension of credit;

(3) make or use any untrue or misleading representation of the services of the credit repair organization; or

(4) engage, directly or indirectly, in any act, practice, or course of business that constitutes or results in the commission of, or an attempt to commit, a fraud or deception on any person in connection with the offer or sale of the services of the credit repair organization.

(b) Payment in advance

No credit repair organization may charge or receive any money or other valuable consideration for the performance of any service which the credit repair organization has agreed to perform for any consumer before such service is fully performed.

Section 1679c. Disclosures

(a) Disclosure required

Any credit repair organization shall provide any consumer with the following written statement before any contract or agreement between the consumer and the credit repair organization is executed:

"CONSUMER CREDIT FILE RIGHTS UNDER STATE AND FEDERAL LAW

"You have a right to dispute inaccurate information in your credit report by contacting the credit bureau directly. However, neither you nor any 'credit repair' company or credit repair organization has the right to have accurate, current, and verifiable information removed from your credit report. The credit bureau must remove accurate, negative information from your report only if it is over 7 years old. Bankruptcy information can be reported for 10 years.

"You have a right to obtain a copy of your credit report from a credit bureau. You may be charged a reasonable fee. There is no fee, however, if you have been turned down for credit, employment, insurance, or a rental dwelling because of information in your credit report within the preceding 60 days. The credit bureau must provide someone to help you interpret the information in your credit file. You are entitled to receive a free copy of your credit report if you are unemployed and intend to apply for employment in the next 60 days, if you are a recipient of public welfare assistance, or if you have reason to believe that there is inaccurate information in your credit report due to fraud.

"You have a right to sue a credit repair organization that violates the Credit Repair Organization Act. This law prohibits deceptive practices by credit repair organizations.

"You have the right to cancel your contract with any credit repair organization for any reason within 3 business days from the date you signed it.

"Credit bureaus are required to follow reasonable procedures to ensure that the information they report is accurate. However, mistakes may occur.

"You may, on your own, notify a credit bureau in writing that you dispute the accuracy of information in your credit file. The credit bureau must then reinvestigate and modify or remove inaccurate or incomplete information. The credit bureau may not charge any fee for this service. Any pertinent information and copies of all documents you have concerning an error should be given to the credit bureau.

"If the credit bureau's reinvestigation does not resolve the dispute to your satisfaction, you may send a brief statement to the credit bureau, to be kept in your file, explaining why you think the record is inaccurate. The credit bureau must include a summary of your statement about disputed information with any report it issues about you.

"The Federal Trade Commission regulates credit bureaus and credit repair organizations. For more information contact:

"THE PUBLIC REFERENCE BRANCH
"FEDERAL TRADE COMMISSION
"WASHINGTON, D.C. 20580".

(b) Separate statement requirement

The written statement required under this section shall be provided as a document which is separate from any written contract or other agreement between the credit repair organization and the consumer or any other written material provided to the consumer.

(c) Retention of compliance records

(1) In general

The credit repair organization shall maintain a copy of the statement signed by the consumer acknowledging receipt of the statement.

(2) Maintenance for 2 years

The copy of any consumer's statement shall be maintained in the organization's files for 2 years after the date on which the statement is signed by the consumer.

Section 1679d. Credit repair organizations contracts

(a) Written contracts required

No services may be provided by any credit repair organization for any consumer -

(1) unless a written and dated contract (for the purchase of such services) which meets the requirements of subsection (b) of this section has been signed by the consumer; or

(2) before the end of the 3-business-day period beginning on the date the contract is signed.

(b) Terms and conditions of contract

No contract referred to in subsection (a) of this section meets the requirements of this subsection unless such contract includes (in writing) -

(1) the terms and conditions of payment, including the total amount of all payments to be made by the consumer to the credit repair organization or to any other person;

(2) a full and detailed description of the services to be performed by the credit repair organization for the consumer, including -

(A) all guarantees of performance; and

(B) an estimate of -

(i) the date by which the performance of the services (to be performed by the credit repair organization or any other person) will be complete; or

(ii) the length of the period necessary to perform such services;

(3) the credit repair organization's name and principal business address; and

(4) a conspicuous statement in bold face type, in immediate proximity to the space reserved for the consumer's signature on the contract, which reads as follows: "You may cancel this contract without penalty or obligation at any time before midnight of the 3rd business day after the date on which you signed the contract. See the attached notice of cancellation form for an explanation of this right.".

Section 1679e. Right to cancel contract

(a) In general

Any consumer may cancel any contract with any credit repair organization without penalty or obligation by notifying the credit repair organization of the consumer's intention to do so at any time before midnight of the 3rd business day which begins after the date on which the contract or agreement between the consumer and the credit repair organization is executed or would, but for this subsection, become enforceable against the parties.

(b) Cancellation form and other information

Each contract shall be accompanied by a form, in duplicate, which has the heading "Notice of Cancellation" and contains in bold face type the following statement:

"You may cancel this contract, without any penalty or obligation, at any time before midnight of the 3rd day which begins after the date the contract is signed by you.

"To cancel this contract, mail or deliver a signed, dated copy of this cancellation notice, or any other written notice to (name of credit repair organization) at (address of credit repair organization) before midnight on (date)

"I hereby cancel this transaction, (date) (purchaser's signature)."

(c) Consumer copy of contract required

Any consumer who enters into any contract with any credit repair organization shall be given, by the organization -

(1) a copy of the completed contract and the disclosure statement required under section 1679c of this title; and

(2) a copy of any other document the credit repair organization requires the consumer to sign, at the time the contract or the other document is signed.

Section 1679f. Noncompliance with this subchapter

(a) Consumer waivers invalid

Any waiver by any consumer of any protection provided by or any right of the consumer under this subchapter -

(1) shall be treated as void; and

(2) may not be enforced by any Federal or State court or any other person.

(b) Attempt to obtain waiver

Any attempt by any person to obtain a waiver from any consumer of any protection provided by or any right of the consumer under this subchapter shall be treated as a violation of this subchapter.

(c) Contracts not in compliance

Any contract for services which does not comply with the applicable provisions of this subchapter -

(1) shall be treated as void; and

(2) may not be enforced by any Federal or State court or any other person.

Section 1679g. Civil liability

(a) Liability established

Any person who fails to comply with any provision of this subchapter with respect to any other person shall be liable to such person in an amount equal to the sum of the amounts determined under each of the following paragraphs:

(1) Actual damages

The greater of -

(A) the amount of any actual damage sustained by such person as a result of such failure; or

(B) any amount paid by the person to the credit repair organization.

(2) Punitive damages

(A) Individual actions

In the case of any action by an individual, such additional amount as the court may allow.

(B) Class actions

In the case of a class action, the sum of -

(i) the aggregate of the amount which the court may allow for each named plaintiff; and

(ii) the aggregate of the amount which the court may allow for each other class member, without regard to any minimum individual recovery.

(3) Attorneys' fees

In the case of any successful action to enforce any liability under paragraph (1) or (2), the costs of the action, together with reasonable attorneys' fees.

(b) Factors to be considered in awarding punitive damages

In determining the amount of any liability of any credit repair organization under subsection (a)(2) of this section, the court shall consider, among other relevant factors -

(1) the frequency and persistence of noncompliance by the credit repair organization;

(2) the nature of the noncompliance;

(3) the extent to which such noncompliance was intentional; and

(4) in the case of any class action, the number of consumers adversely affected.

Section 1679h. Administrative enforcement

(a) In general

Compliance with the requirements imposed under this subchapter with respect to credit repair organizations shall be enforced under the Federal Trade Commission Act (15 U.S.C. 41 et seq.) by the Federal Trade Commission.

(b) Violations of this subchapter treated as violations of Federal Trade Commission Act

(1) In general

For the purpose of the exercise by the Federal Trade Commission of the Commission's functions and powers under the Federal Trade Commission Act (15 U.S.C. 41 et seq.), any violation of any requirement or prohibition imposed under this subchapter with respect to credit repair organizations shall constitute an unfair or deceptive act or practice in commerce in violation of section 5(a) of the Federal Trade Commission Act (15 U.S.C. 45(a)).

(2) Enforcement authority under other law

All functions and powers of the Federal Trade Commission under the Federal Trade Commission Act shall be available to the Commission to enforce compliance with this subchapter by any person subject to enforcement by the Federal Trade Commission pursuant to this subsection, including the power to enforce the provisions of this subchapter in the same manner as if the violation had been a violation of any Federal Trade Commission trade regulation rule, without regard to whether the credit repair organization -

(A) is engaged in commerce; or

(B) meets any other jurisdictional tests in the Federal Trade Commission Act.

(c) State action for violations

(1) Authority of States

In addition to such other remedies as are provided under State law, whenever the chief law enforcement officer of a State, or an official or agency designated by a State, has reason to believe that any person has violated or is violating this subchapter, the State -

(A) may bring an action to enjoin such violation;

(B) may bring an action on behalf of its residents to recover damages for which the person is liable to such residents under section 1679g of this title as a result of the violation; and

(C) in the case of any successful action under subparagraph (A) or (B), shall be awarded the costs of the action and reasonable attorney fees as determined by the court.

(2) Rights of Commission

(A) Notice to Commission

The State shall serve prior written notice of any civil action under paragraph (1) upon the Federal Trade Commission and provide the Commission with a copy of its complaint, except in any case where such prior notice is not feasible, in which case the State shall serve such notice immediately upon instituting such action.

(B) Intervention

The Commission shall have the right -

(i) to intervene in any action referred to in subparagraph (A);

(ii) upon so intervening, to be heard on all matters arising in the action; and

(iii) to file petitions for appeal.

(3) Investigatory powers

For purposes of bringing any action under this subsection, nothing in this subsection shall prevent the chief law enforcement officer, or an official or agency designated by a State, from exercising the powers conferred on the chief law enforcement officer or such official by the laws of such State to conduct investigations or to administer oaths or affirmations or to compel the attendance of witnesses or the production of documentary and other evidence.

(4) Limitation

Whenever the Federal Trade Commission has instituted a civil action for violation of this subchapter, no State may, during the pendency of such action, bring an action under this section against any defendant named in the complaint of the Commission for any violation of this subchapter that is alleged in that complaint.

Section 1679i. Statute of limitations

Any action to enforce any liability under this subchapter may be brought before the later of -

(1) the end of the 5-year period beginning on the date of the occurrence of the violation involved; or

(2) in any case in which any credit repair organization has materially and willfully misrepresented any information which -

(A) the credit repair organization is required, by any provision of this subchapter, to disclose to any consumer; and

(B) is material to the establishment of the credit repair organization's liability to the consumer under this subchapter, the end of the 5-year period beginning on the date of the discovery by the consumer of the misrepresentation.

CONSUMER LEASING ACT
UNITED STATES CODE
TITLE 15
CHAPTER 41
SUBCHAPTER I
PART E

Section 1667. Definitions

For purposes of this part -

(1) The term "consumer lease" means a contract in the form of a lease or bailment for the use of personal property by a natural person for a period of time exceeding four months, and for a total contractual obligation not exceeding $25,000, primarily for personal, family, or household purposes, whether or not the lessee has the option to purchase or otherwise become the owner of the property at the expiration of the lease, except that such term shall not include any credit sale as defined in section 1602(g) of this title. Such term does not include a lease for agricultural, business, or commercial purposes, or to a government or governmental agency or instrumentality, or to an organization.

(2) The term "lessee" means a natural person who leases or is offered a consumer lease.

(3) The term "lessor" means a person who is regularly engaged in leasing, offering to lease, or arranging to lease under a consumer lease.

(4) The term "personal property" means any property which is not real property under the laws of the State where situated at the time offered or otherwise made available for lease.

(5) The terms "security" and "security interest" mean any interest in property which secures payment or performance of an obligation.

Section 1667a. Consumer lease disclosures

Each lessor shall give a lessee prior to the consummation of the lease a dated written statement on which the lessor and lessee are identified setting out accurately and in a clear and conspicuous manner the following information with respect to that lease, as applicable:

(1) A brief description or identification of the leased property;

(2) The amount of any payment by the lessee required at the inception of the lease;

(3) The amount paid or payable by the lessee for official fees, registration, certificate of title, or license fees or taxes;

(4) The amount of other charges payable by the lessee not included in the periodic payments, a description of the charges and that the lessee shall be liable for the differential, if any, between the anticipated fair market value of the leased property and its appraised actual value at the termination of the lease, if the lessee has such liability;

(5) A statement of the amount or method of determining the amount of any liabilities the lease imposes upon the lessee at the end of

the term and whether or not the lessee has the option to purchase the leased property and at what price and time;

(6) A statement identifying all express warranties and guarantees made by the manufacturer or lessor with respect to the leased property, and identifying the party responsible for maintaining or servicing the leased property together with a description of the responsibility;

(7) A brief description of insurance provided or paid for by the lessor or required of the lessee, including the types and amounts of the coverages and costs;

(8) A description of any security interest held or to be retained by the lessor in connection with the lease and a clear identification of the property to which the security interest relates;

(9) The number, amount, and due dates or periods of payments under the lease and the total amount of such periodic payments;

(10) Where the lease provides that the lessee shall be liable for the anticipated fair market value of the property on expiration of the lease, the fair market value of the property at the inception of the lease, the aggregate cost of the lease on expiration, and the differential between them; and

(11) A statement of the conditions under which the lessee or lessor may terminate the lease prior to the end of the term and the amount or method of determining any penalty or other charge for delinquency, default, late payments, or early termination. The disclosures required under this section may be made in the lease contract to be signed by the lessee. The Board may provide by regulation that any portion of the information required to be disclosed under this section may be given in the form of estimates where the lessor is not in a position to know exact information.

Section 1667b. Lessee's liability on expiration or termination of lease

(a) Estimated residual value of property as basis; presumptions; action by lessor for excess liability; mutually agreeable final adjustment

Where the lessee's liability on expiration of a consumer lease is based on the estimated residual value of the property such estimated residual value shall be a reasonable approximation of the anticipated actual fair market value of the property on lease expiration. There shall be a rebuttable presumption that the estimated residual value is unreasonable to the extent that the estimated residual value exceeds the actual residual value by more than three times the average payment allocable to a monthly period under the lease. In addition, where the lessee has such liability on expiration of a consumer lease there shall be a rebuttable presumption that the lessor's estimated residual value is not in good faith to the extent that the estimated residual value exceeds the actual residual value by more than three times the average payment allocable to a monthly period under the lease and such lessor shall not collect from the lessee the amount of such excess liability on expiration of a consumer lease unless the lessor brings a successful action with respect to such excess liability. In all actions, the lessor shall pay the lessee's reasonable attorney's fees. The presumptions stated in this section shall not apply to the extent the excess of estimated over actual residual value is due to physical damage to the property beyond reasonable wear and use, or to excessive use, and the lease may set standards for such wear and use if such standards are not unreasonable. Nothing in this subsection shall preclude the right of a willing lessee to make any mutually agreeable final adjustment with respect to such excess residual liability, provided such an agreement is reached after termination of the lease.

(b) Penalties and charges for delinquency, default, or early termination

Penalties or other charges for delinquency, default, or early termination may be specified in the lease but only at an amount which is reasonable in the light of the anticipated or actual harm caused by the delinquency, default, or early termination, the difficulties of proof of loss, and the inconvenience or nonfeasibility of otherwise obtaining an adequate remedy.

(c) Independent professional appraisal of residual value of property at termination of lease; finality

If a lease has a residual value provision at the termination of the lease, the lessee may obtain at his expense, a professional appraisal of the leased property by an independent third party agreed to by both parties. Such appraisal shall be final and binding on the parties.

Section 1667c. Consumer lease advertising; liability of advertising media

(a) In general

If an advertisement for a consumer lease includes a statement of the amount of any payment or a statement that any or no initial payment is required, the advertisement shall clearly and conspicuously state, as applicable -

(1) the transaction advertised is a lease;

(2) the total amount of any initial payments required on or before consummation of the lease or delivery of the property, whichever is later;

(3) that a security deposit is required;

(4) the number, amount, and timing of scheduled payments; and

(5) with respect to a lease in which the liability of the consumer at the end of the lease term is based on the anticipated residual value of the property, that an extra charge may be imposed at the end of the lease term.

(b) Advertising medium not liable

No owner or employee of any entity that serves as a medium in which an advertisement appears or through which an advertisement is disseminated, shall be liable under this section.

(c) Radio advertisements

(1) In general

An advertisement by radio broadcast to aid, promote, or assist, directly or indirectly, any consumer lease shall be deemed to be in compliance with the requirements of subsection (a) of this section if such advertisement clearly and conspicuously -

(A) states the information required by paragraphs (1) and (2) of subsection (a) of this section;

(B) states the number, amounts, due dates or periods of scheduled payments, and the total of such payments under the lease;

(C) includes -

(i) a referral to -

(I) a toll-free telephone number established in accordance with paragraph (2) that may be used by consumers to obtain the information required under subsection (a) of this section; or

(II) a written advertisement that -

(aa) appears in a publication in general circulation in the community served by the radio station on which such advertisement is broadcast during the period beginning 3 days before any such broadcast and ending 10 days after such broadcast; and

(bb) includes the information required to be disclosed under subsection (a) of this section; and

(ii) the name and dates of any publication referred to in clause (i)(II); and

(D) includes any other information which the Board determines necessary to carry out this part.

(2) Establishment of toll-free number

(A) In general

In the case of a radio broadcast advertisement described in paragraph (1) that includes a referral to a toll-free telephone number, the lessor who offers the consumer lease shall -

(i) establish such a toll-free telephone number not later than the date on which the advertisement including the referral is broadcast;

(ii) maintain such telephone number for a period of not less than 10 days, beginning on the date of any such broadcast; and

(iii) provide the information required under subsection (a) of this section with respect to the lease to any person who calls such number.

(B) Form of information

The information required to be provided under subparagraph (A)(iii) shall be provided verbally or, if requested by the consumer, in written form.

(3) No effect on other law

Nothing in this subsection shall affect the requirements of Federal law as such requirements apply to advertisement by any medium other than radio broadcast.

Section 1667d. Civil liability of lessors

(a) Grounds for maintenance of action

Any lessor who fails to comply with any requirement imposed under section 1667a or 1667b of this title with respect to any person is liable to such person as provided in section 1640 of this title.

(b) Additional grounds for maintenance of action; "creditor" defined

Any lessor who fails to comply with any requirement imposed under section 1667c of this title with respect to any person who suffers actual damage from the violation is liable to such person as provided in section 1640 of this title. For the purposes of this section, the term "creditor" as used in sections 1640 and 1641 of this title shall include a lessor as defined in this part.

(c) Jurisdiction of courts; time limitation

Notwithstanding section 1640(e) of this title, any action under this section may be brought in any United States district court or in any other court of competent jurisdiction. Such actions alleging a failure to disclose or otherwise comply with the requirements of this part shall be brought within one year of the termination of the lease agreement.

Section 1667e. Applicability of State laws; exemptions by Board from leasing requirements

(a) This part does not annul, alter, or affect, or exempt any person subject to the provisions of this part from complying with, the laws of any State with respect to consumer leases, except to the extent that those laws are inconsistent with any provision of this part, and then only to the extent of the inconsistency. The Board is authorized to determine whether such inconsistencies exist. The Board may not determine that any State law is inconsistent with any provision of this part if the Board determines that such law gives greater protection and benefit to the consumer.

(b) The Board shall by regulation exempt from the requirements of this part any class of lease transactions within any State if it determines that under the law of that State that class of transactions is subject to requirements substantially similar to those imposed under this part or that such law gives greater protection and benefit to the consumer, and that there is adequate provision for enforcement.

Section 1667f. Regulations

(a) Regulations authorized

(1) In general

The Board shall prescribe regulations to update and clarify the requirements and definitions applicable to lease disclosures and contracts, and any other issues specifically related to consumer leasing, to the extent that the Board determines such action to be necessary -

(A) to carry out this part;

(B) to prevent any circumvention of this part; or

(C) to facilitate compliance with the requirements of this part.

(2) Classifications, adjustments

Any regulations prescribed under paragraph (1) may contain classifications and differentiations, and may provide for adjustments and exceptions for any class of transactions, as the Board considers appropriate.

(b) Model disclosure

(1) Publication

The Board shall establish and publish model disclosure forms to facilitate compliance with the disclosure requirements of this part and to aid the consumer in understanding the transaction to which the subject disclosure form relates.

(2) Use of automated equipment

In establishing model forms under this subsection, the Board shall consider the use by lessors of data processing or similar automated equipment.

(3) Use optional

A lessor may utilize a model disclosure form established by the Board under this subsection for purposes of compliance with this part, at the discretion of the lessor.

(4) Effect of use

Any lessor who properly uses the material aspects of any model disclosure form established by the Board under this subsection shall be deemed to be in compliance with the disclosure requirements to which the form relates.

Appendix C:
Forms and Letters

The forms in this appendix can be torn out for use. However, it would be best to copy them in case you make a mistake, need more than one copy, or to use as a rough draft. All of the letters would serve you best if you put them on your own stationary or letterhead.

Table of Forms

DEBT ASSESSMENT

Fill in the blanks to list all of your monthly debts. Total the items at the bottom to get the number for your total monthly debts.

NAME OF CREDITOR	ACCOUNT NUMBER	TOTAL DUE	MONTHLY PAYMENT
_____	_____	_____	_____
_____	_____	_____	_____
_____	_____	_____	_____
_____	_____	_____	_____
_____	_____	_____	_____
_____	_____	_____	_____
_____	_____	_____	_____
_____	_____	_____	_____
_____	_____	_____	_____
_____	_____	_____	_____
_____	_____	_____	_____
_____	_____	_____	_____
_____	_____	_____	_____
_____	_____	_____	_____
_____	_____	_____	_____
_____	_____	_____	_____
_____	_____	_____	_____
_____	_____	_____	_____

Total amount due:_____

Total monthly payments due:_____

ASSET ASSESSMENT

Salary:

    Monthly amount earned:_____

    Yearly amount earned:_____

Other income (such as child support, alimony, etc):

    Monthly amount: _____

    Yearly amount:_____

Other income (include interest, unrepoted income, etc.):

    Monthly amount: _____

    Yearly amount:_____

Total Income:

    Monthly: _____

    Yearly: _____

Other Assets: list name of item, account number if applicable and value.

NAME/DESCRIPTION	ACCOUNT NUMBER	VALUE
_____	_____	_____
_____	_____	_____
_____	_____	_____
_____	_____	_____
_____	_____	_____
_____	_____	_____
_____	_____	_____
_____	_____	_____
_____	_____	_____

Total value of other assets:_____

TOTAL ASSESSMENT

Monthly

Total monthly income: _____

Total monthly debts: _____

Subtract debts from assets and you get this:_____.

If this is a negative number, you know you need to make some changes. If this is a positive number but is not enough to pay your expenses, such as food and gas, you need to make some changes.

Total assets: _____

Total debts:_____

Compare these two numbers. If your assets are larger than your debts, you are in good shape. If your debts are larger than your assets, you know this is something you need to work on.

LETTER COMPLAINING OF UNFAIR DEBT COLLECTION PRACTICES

_____(your name and address)

_____

_____

_____ (name and address of creditor/ collection agency)

_____

_____

_____ (date)

Dear Sir or Madam:

I am writing to inform you that your agency/company violated the Fair Debt Collection Practices Act, a federal law, in your dealings with me. The incident(s) occurred on _____ and was/were as follows:

_____

_____

_____

_____

_____.

I am requesting that you take steps to change your practices. I am also forwarding a copy of this letter to the Federal Trade Commission and the state Attorney General.

Sincerely,

cc: Federal Trade Commission
    State Attorney General

LETTER REQUESTING CREDIT REPORT

_____ (your name and address)

_____

_____

_____ (credit reporting agency name and address)

_____

_____

_____ (date)

Dear Sir or Madam:

I am writing to request a copy of my credit report.

___ I have been denied credit or employment in the last 60 days based on my credit report and request my free copy.

___ I am enclosing $___ as required in my state and request that you send me my credit report.

Please use the following information for verification purposes:

Social Security #_____

Employer:_____

My last previous address:_____

One credit card name and account number I hold:_____

Please forward my report to me at the above address.

Sincerely,

CORRESPONDENCE LOG

Date	Business Name	Name of contact	Account number or item	Type of correspondence	Action	Steps to Take
1.						
2.						
3.						
4.						
5.						
6.						
7.						
8.						
9.						
10.						

LETTER REQUESTING MERGER OF SPOUSE'S REPORT

_____ (your name and address)

_____

_____

_____ (name and address of credit reporting agency)

_____

_____

_____ (date)

Dear Sir or Madam:

Please merge my spouse's credit report with mine.

My Social Security number:_____

Number of my file or report number from your agency:_____

My spouse's name: _____

My spouse's social security number: _____

Sincerely,

LETTER REQUESTING INDIVIDUALIZATION OF CREDIT REPORT

_____ (your name and address)

_____

_____

_____ (name and address of credit reporting agency)

_____

_____

_____ (date)

Dear Sir or Madam:

I recently received a copy of my credit report and noticed that it contains information about my spouse, as well as about me. I would like my spouse's information removed from my report.

My social security number: _____

Number of my file or report from your agency:_____

My spouse's name: _____

My spouse's social security number:_____

Sincerely,

LETTER TO CREDITOR REGARDING BILLING ERROR

_____ (your name and address)

_____

_____

_____ (creditor's name and address)

_____

_____

_____ (date)

Dear Sir or Madam:

I recently received a bill from you that contains an error.

My account number is _____.

The item that is incorrect is _____ for $_____ dated _____.

This is incorrect because _____

_____ and should be for _____.

I would appreciate it if you could correct this item and send me a corrected statement.

Sincerely,

LETTER DISPUTING CREDIT REPORT

_____ (your name and address)

_____

_____

_____ (name and address of credit reporting agency)

_____

_____

_____ (date)

Dear Sir or Madam:

Recently I received my credit report from your agency. My file or report number is _____. In reviewing my report, I noticed the following error(s):

1._____

   This item is incorrect because _____

   and should instead indicate _____.

2. _____

   This item is incorrect because _____

   and should instead indicate _____.

3. _____

   This item is incorrect because _____

   and should instead indicate _____.

I would appreciate it if these errors could be corrected. I look forward to hearing from you within thirty days.

Sincerely,

SECOND REQUEST FOR REINVESTIGATION

_____ (your name and address)

_____

_____

_____ (name and address of credit reporting agency)

_____

_____

_____ (date)

Dear Sir or Madam:

On _____ I sent you a written request for reinvestigation (your file or report number _____) of the following errors on my credit report:

1._____

2. _____

3._____

I am enclosing a copy of the letter I sent you. Thirty days have passed and I have not received any response from you regarding this matter. I would appreciate it if you would please notify me of the status of this request as soon as possible.

Sincerely,

LETTER REQUESTING CORRECTION OF REAPPEARING INCORRECT ITEM

_____(your name and address)

_____

_____

_____ (name and address of credit reporting agency)

_____

_____

_____ (date)

Dear Sir or Madam:

I am writing in regard to my credit report, your file or report number _____.   On _____ you removed the following incorrect information from my report:

_____

_____

_____

_____ at my request because _____

_____

_____.

On the latest copy of my credit report, dated _____, this incorrect information has reappeared. I am requesting that you immediately remove this incorrect information and replace it with the following correct information:_____

_____

_____.

Please advise me when the correction has been made and send me a corrected credit report.

Sincerely,

LETTER TO CREDITOR REGARDING INCORRECT CREDIT REPORT

_____ (your name and address)

_____

_____

_____ (name and address of creditor)

_____

_____

_____ (date)

Dear Sir or Madam:

I am writing to you in regard to my account, number _____. I recently received a copy of my credit report from the following credit reporting agency: _____. My account with you is incorrectly listed as _____, when in fact it is _____. I have asked that the credit reporting agency verify this with you and was told you did not verify the correct information.

I am requesting that you immediately contact this credit reporting agency with the correct information regarding this account. Please provide me with a copy of your correspondence correcting this. I am prepared to enforce my rights under the Fair Credit Reporting Act if you do not report the correct information to this agency.

Sincerely,

LETTER SHOWING CREDITOR ERROR

_____ (your name and address)

_____

_____

_____ (name and address of credit reporting agency)

_____

_____

____ (date)

Dear Sir or Madam:

I am writing in regard to my file or report number _____. There is an error on this report. _____ is listed incorrectly. I have contacted the creditor directly and the creditor has admitted that it made an error in reporting this account to you. I am enclosing written proof of this and am requesting that you change this listing on my report as soon as possible and send me a corrected copy of my report.

Sincerely,

LETTER REQUESTING DISCHARGE

_____ (your name and address)

_____

_____

_____ (name and address of creditor)

_____

_____

____ (date)

Dear Sir or Madam:

I am writing in regard to account number _____, which resulted in a judgment in your company's favor dated _____ for $_____. This judgment has been paid in full and I requesting that your company complete and file a formal discharge with the court immediately. Please send me a copy of the discharge and report it to credit reporting agencies as well.

Sincerely,

LETTER REQUESTING INCLUSION OF ACCOUNTS

_____ (your name and address)

_____

_____

_____ (name and address of credit reporting agency)

_____

_____

_____ (date)

Dear Sir or Madam:

I recently received my credit report (your file or report number _____) from you. I noticed that some accounts of mine do not appear on the report. Since these reports demonstrate excellent payment histories, I would appreciate it if you could include them on my credit report. The name of the creditors, addresses and account numbers are listed below. I am attaching copies of my most recent statements from these accounts for verification purposes.

Name of Creditor   Address   Account Number

Please notify me when the information has been included.

Sincerely,

LETTER REQUESTING ADDITION OF INFORMATION

_____ (your name and address)

_____

_____

_____ (name and address of credit reporting agency)

_____

_____

_____ (date)

Dear Sir or Madam:

I recently received a copy of my credit report from your agency (your file or report number _____). I would like you to include the information listed below on my report. This information is not included on the current report and demonstrates stability and would thus make my report more favorable. I would appreciate your assistance with this.

_____

_____

_____

_____

_____

_____

_____

Sincerely,

LETTER WITH 100 WORD STATEMENT

_____ (your name and address)

_____

_____

_____ (name and address of credit reporting agency)

_____

_____

_____ (date)

Dear Sir or Madam:

I would like the following 100 word statement to be included on my credit report (your file or report number _____).

_____

_____

_____

_____

_____

_____

_____

Sincerely,

DEBT PRIORITIZATION

Look at the debts on your **DEBT ASSESSMENT**. List them in order or importance below, so that you can pay or settle the most urgent items first.

PRIORITY	ITEM	AMOUNT
1.	_____	_____
2.	_____	_____
3.	_____	_____
4.	_____	_____
5.	_____	_____
6.	_____	_____
7.	_____	_____
8.	_____	_____
9.	_____	_____
10.	_____	_____
11.	_____	_____
12.	_____	_____
13.	_____	_____
14.	_____	_____
15.	_____	_____
16.	_____	_____
17.	_____	_____
18.	_____	_____
19.	_____	_____
20.	_____	_____

STATEMENT OF CIRCUMSTANCES

_____ (your name and address)

_____

_____

_____ (name and address of potential creditor)

_____

_____

_____ (date)

Dear Sir or Madam:

I am writing in reference to my application to you for credit. I have seen my credit report and realize that there may be items on it that concern you. Please allow me to explain. I have experienced the following circumstances: _____

_____

_____

_____

which caused the problems you see on the credit report. My current circumstances are: ____

_____

_____

and I would ask you to understand that my situation has improved. I will be able to make all payments to without any problem and hope that you will give my application consideration.

Sincerely,

REQUEST TO OPT OUT

_____ (your name and address)

_____

_____

_____ (name and address of credit reporting agency opt out program)

_____

_____

_____ (date)

Dear Sir or Madam:

I do not wish to have any information released about me to companies seeking to send me promotional materials. Please do not release any such information about me. I do not wish to receive mailings or phone calls from companies soliciting their services.

Sincerely,

BUDGET

for the month of _____

Enter in your estimated monthly expenses on this form. You should include everything you spend money on. Be sure you include expenses and incomes for your entire household.

HOUSEHOLD EXPENSES

Rent/mortgage _____

Home equity loan payment _____

Real estate taxes (if not included in mortgage) _____

Renter's/homeowner's insurance _____

Electric _____

Gas _____

Water _____

Telephone (local and long distance) _____

Cable _____

Internet access _____

Home repairs _____

Food _____

Alcohol _____

Bank fees _____

Household supplies _____

Household items _____

Furniture purchases and maintenance _____

Lawn/yard expenses _____

Other _____

PERSONAL EXPENSES

Clothing _____

Laundry/dry cleaning _____

Haircuts and styling _____

Other personal care (nails, salon) _____

Gym membership _____

Other clubs or memberships _____

Life insurance _____

Health insurance _____

Prescription plan _____

Co-pays _____

Optical _____

Dental _____

Other medical _____

Grooming/personal care items _____

Charity _____

Baby sitter _____

Household help _____

Hobbies _____

Cigarettes _____

Income taxes _____

Children's allowances _____

Pet expenses _____

Other _____

AUTOMOTIVE EXPENSES

Car loan or lease payment _____

Bus/train/plane/ taxi fares _____

Gas _____

Car wash _____

Parking/tolls _____

Other _____

ENTERTAINMENT EXPENSES

Restaurants/take out _____

Movies, theater, etc. _____

Books, newspapers and magazines _____

Video rentals _____

Other _____

FRIENDS AND FAMILY

Party supplies _____

Birthday, anniversary, wedding gifts _____

Cards and wrapping paper   _____

Payment on personal loan   _____

Other   _____

CREDIT CARDS AND LOANS

(list each separately with the monthly payment)

_____   _____

_____   _____

_____   _____

_____   _____

_____   _____

_____   _____

SAVINGS

Investment   _____

Savings account   _____

College savings plan   _____

Retirement plan   _____

EDUCATION (FOR ALL HOUSEHOLD MEMBERS)

Tuition   _____

Student loan payment   _____

School supplies and materials   _____

Other   _____

YEARLY EXPENSES (DIVIDED BY 12)

Car repairs/maintenance   _____

Driver's license   _____

Car registration   _____

Car insurance   _____

Car inspection   _____

Vacation   _____

Holiday gifts   _____

Club memberships   _____

OTHER

_____   _____

_____   _____

_____   _____

_____   _____

                                    TOTAL EXPENSES _____

MONTHLY INCOME

    Salary   _____

    Child support/alimony   _____

    Other income (non-reported, interest, etc.)   _____

                                    TOTAL INCOME _____

SPENDING LOG

For _____ (month and year)

Date	Item	Cost	Daily Total
_____	_____	_____	_____
_____	_____	_____	_____
_____	_____	_____	_____
_____	_____	_____	_____
_____	_____	_____	_____
_____	_____	_____	_____
_____	_____	_____	_____
_____	_____	_____	_____
_____	_____	_____	_____
_____	_____	_____	_____
_____	_____	_____	_____
_____	_____	_____	_____
_____	_____	_____	_____
_____	_____	_____	_____
_____	_____	_____	_____
_____	_____	_____	_____
_____	_____	_____	_____
_____	_____	_____	_____
_____	_____	_____	_____
_____	_____	_____	_____
_____	_____	_____	_____
_____	_____	_____	_____
_____	_____	_____	_____
_____	_____	_____	_____
_____	_____	_____	_____
_____	_____	_____	_____

Date	Item	Cost	Daily Total
_____	_____	_____	_____
_____	_____	_____	_____
_____	_____	_____	_____
_____	_____	_____	_____
_____	_____	_____	_____
_____	_____	_____	_____
_____	_____	_____	_____
_____	_____	_____	_____
_____	_____	_____	_____
_____	_____	_____	_____
_____	_____	_____	_____
_____	_____	_____	_____
_____	_____	_____	_____
_____	_____	_____	_____
_____	_____	_____	_____
_____	_____	_____	_____
_____	_____	_____	_____
_____	_____	_____	_____
_____	_____	_____	_____
_____	_____	_____	_____
_____	_____	_____	_____
_____	_____	_____	_____
_____	_____	_____	_____
_____	_____	_____	_____
_____	_____	_____	_____
_____	_____	_____	_____
_____	_____	_____	_____
_____	_____	_____	_____
_____	_____	_____	_____
_____	_____	_____	_____
_____	_____	_____	_____

Monthly Total: _____

LETTER OFFERING TO RETURN SECURED PROPERTY

_____ (your name and address)

_____

_____

_____ (name and address of creditor)

_____

_____

_____ (date)

Dear Sir or Madam:

I am writing in regard to my account with you, number _____, which I used to purchase the following items on a secured basis:

_____

_____

_____.

As you may be aware, I have been experiencing financial difficulties lately. I wish to propose the following settlement offer for this account. I will return the secured property to you in exchange for cancellation of the debt and a neutral/positive rating for this account being reported to credit reporting agencies. Please respond to this offer in writing within fourteen days.

Sincerely,

LETTER REQUESTING PAYMENT PLAN

_____ (your name and address)

_____

_____

_____ (name and address of creditor)

_____

_____

_____ (date)

Dear Sir or Madam:

I am the holder of account number _____. I have been experiencing some financial diffi-culties and have been having trouble paying on this account. I fully intend to pay you for the full amount due, but I find that right now my finances are not able to pay for this account. I would like to arrange a payment plan as follows: _____

_____

_____.

I would also propose that as part of this plan, you will report my account to credit reporting agencies as follows:_____

_____

_____.

Please respond to this proposal in writing within fourteen days.

Sincerely,

LETTER EXPLAINING JUDGMENT PROOF STATUS

_____ (your name and address)

_____

_____

_____ (name and address of creditor)

_____

_____

_____ (date)

Dear Sir or Madam:

I am aware that I am behind on payments to my account number _____. I am unable to make payments because I am experiencing financial difficulties. I would like to notify you that I am without income or assets and have nothing for you to pursue. Since I am judgment proof, please do not waste your time and energy pursuing this matter. I will resume making payments as soon as possible.

Sincerely,

LETTER EXPLAINING PLAN TO GO BANKRUPT

_____ (your name and address)

_____

_____

_____ (name and address of creditor)

_____

_____

_____ (date)

Dear Sir or Madam:

I am writing in regard to my account number _____. Please be advised that I am about to file for bankruptcy and that I will be including this debt in the proceeding. Please contact my attorney _____ at _____ about this matter in the future.

Sincerely,

LETTER REQUESTING NO PAYMENT

_____ (your name and address)

_____

_____

_____ (name and address of creditor)

_____

_____

_____ (date)

Dear Sir or Madam:

I am writing in regard to my account number _____. I am behind on my payments and am experiencing some temporary financial difficulties. I fully intend to repay this account in full, however I am unable to make any payments at this time for a period of _____. I am requesting that you allow me to miss _____ payment(s) while I get back on my feet financially. I would be very appreciative if you could help me in this way. Please let me know in writing if this is possible.

Sincerely,

LETTER CLOSING ACCOUNT

_____ (your name and address)

_____

_____

_____ (name and address of creditor)

_____

_____

_____ (date)

Dear Sir or Madam:

Please close my account number _____ with you. I will no longer be using this account.

Sincerely,

IRS

Department of the Treasury
Internal Revenue Service

www.irs.gov

Form 656 (Rev. 5-2001)
Catalog Number 16728N

Form 656
Offer in Compromise

IRS RECEIVED DATE

Item 1 — Taxpayer's Name and Home or Business Address

Name _____

Name _____

Street Address _____

City _____ State _____ ZIP Code _____

Mailing Address *(if different from above)*

DATE RETURNED

Street Address _____

City _____ State _____ ZIP Code _____

Item 2 — Social Security Numbers

(a) Primary _____

(b) Secondary _____

Item 3 — Employer Identification Number *(included in offer)*

_____

Item 4 — Other Employer Identification Numbers *(not included in offer)* _____
_____
_____

Item 5 — To: Commissioner of Internal Revenue Service

I/We (includes all types of taxpayers) submit this offer to compromise the tax liabilities plus any interest, penalties, additions to tax, and additional amounts required by law (tax liability) for the tax type and period marked below: (Please mark an "X" in the box for the correct description and fill-in the correct tax period(s), adding additional periods if needed).

❑ **1040/1120 Income Tax** — Year(s) _____
_____

❑ **941 Employer's Quarterly Federal Tax Return** — Quarterly period(s) _____
_____

❑ **940 Employer's Annual Federal Unemployment (FUTA) Tax Return** — Year(s) _____
_____

❑ **Trust Fund Recovery Penalty** as a responsible person of (enter corporation name) _____
_____ ,
for failure to pay withholding and Federal Insurance Contributions Act Taxes (Social Security taxes), for period(s) ending _____ .

❑ **Other Federal Tax(es)** [specify type(s) and period(s)] _____
_____

Note: If you need more space, use another sheet titled "Attachment to Form 656 Dated _____ ."
Sign and date the attachment following the listing of the tax periods.

Item 6 — I/We submit this offer for the reason(s) checked below:

❑ **Doubt as to Liability** — "I do not believe I owe this amount." You must include a detailed explanation of the reason(s) why you believe you do not owe the tax in Item 9.

❑ **Doubt as to Collectibility** — "I have insufficient assets and income to pay the full amount." You must include a complete Collection Information Statement, Form 433-A and/or Form 433-B.

❑ **Effective Tax Administration** — "I owe this amount and have sufficient assets to pay the full amount, but due to my exceptional circumstances, requiring full payment would cause an economic hardship or would be unfair and inequitable." You must include a complete Collection Information Statement, Form 433-A and/or Form 433B **and** complete Item 9.

Item 7

I/We offer to pay $ _____ (must be more than zero). Complete item 10 to explain where you will obtain the funds to make this offer.

Check one of the following:

❑ **Cash Offer (Offered amount will be paid in 90 days or less.)**

Balance to be paid in: ❑ 10; ❑ 30; ❑ 60; or ❑ 90 days from written notice of acceptance of the offer.

❑ **Short-Term Deferred Payment Offer (Offered amount will be paid in MORE than 90 days but within 24 months from written notice of acceptance of the offer.)**

$_____ within_____ days (not more than 90 — See Instructions Section, **Determine Your Payment Terms**) from written notice of acceptance of the offer; and

beginning in the _____ month after written notice of acceptance of the offer, $_____ on the _____ day of each month for a total of _____ months. (Cannot extend more than 24 months from written notice of acceptance of the offer.)

❑ **Deferred Payment Offer (Offered amount will be paid over the life of the collection statute.)**

$_____ within_____ days (not more than 90 — See Instructions Section, **Determine Your Payment Terms**) from written notice of acceptance of the offer; and

beginning in the first month after written notice of acceptance of the offer, $_____ on the _____ day of each month for a total of _____ months.

NOTE: Signature(s) of taxpayer required on last page of Form 656

Item 8 — By submitting this offer, I/we understand and agree to the following conditions:

(a) I/We voluntarily submit all payments made on this offer.

(b) The IRS will apply payments made under the terms of this offer in the best interest of the government.

(c) If the IRS rejects or returns the offer or I/we withdraw the offer, the IRS will return any amount paid with the offer. If I/we agree in writing, IRS will apply the amount paid with the offer to the amount owed. If I/we agree to apply the payment, the date the IRS received the offer remittance will be considered the date of payment. I/We understand that the IRS will not pay interest on any amount I/we submit with the offer.

(d) I/We will comply with all provisions of the Internal Revenue Code relating to filing my/our returns and paying my/our required taxes for 5 years or until the offered amount is paid in full, whichever is longer. In the case of a jointly submitted offer to compromise joint tax liabilities, I/we understand that default with respect to the compliance provisions described in this paragraph by one party to this agreement will not result in the default of the entire agreement. The default provisions described in Item 8(n) of this agreement will be applied only to the party failing to comply with the requirements of this paragraph. This provision does not apply to offers based on Doubt as to Liability.

(e) I/We waive and agree to the suspension of any statutory periods of limitation (time limits provided for by law) for the IRS assessment of the tax liability for the periods identified in Item 5. I/We understand that I/we have the right not to waive these statutory periods or to limit the waiver to a certain length or to certain issues. I/We understand, however, that the IRS may not consider this offer if I/we refuse to waive the statutory periods for assessment or if we provide only a limited waiver. The amount of any Federal tax due for the periods described in Item 5 may be assessed at any time prior to the acceptance of this offer or within one year of the rejection of this offer.

(f) The IRS will keep all payments and credits made, received or applied to the total original tax liability before submission of this offer. The IRS may keep any proceeds from a levy served prior to submission of the offer, but not received at the time the offer is submitted. If I/we have an installment agreement prior to submitting the offer, I/we must continue to make the payments as agreed while this offer is pending. Installment agreement payments will not be applied against the amount offered.

(g) As additional consideration beyond the amount of my/our offer, the IRS will keep any refund, including interest, due to me/us because of overpayment of any tax or other liability, for tax periods extending through the calendar year that the IRS accepts the offer. I/We may not designate an overpayment ordinarily subject to refund, to which the IRS is entitled, to be applied to estimated tax payments for the following year. This condition does not apply if the offer is based on Doubt as to Liability.

(h) I/We will return to the IRS any refund identified in (g) received after submission of this offer. This condition does not apply to offers based on Doubt as to Liability.

(i) The IRS cannot collect more than the full amount of the tax liability under this offer.

(j) I/We understand that I/we remain responsible for the full amount of the tax liability, unless and until the IRS accepts the offer in writing and I/we have met all the terms and conditions of the offer. The IRS will not remove the original amount of the tax liability from its records until I/we have met all the terms of the offer.

NOTE: Signature(s) of taxpayer required on last page of Form 656

(k) I/We understand that the tax I/we offer to compromise is and will remain a tax liability until I/we meet all the terms and conditions of this offer. If I/we file bankruptcy before the terms and conditions of this offer are completed, any claim the IRS files in the bankruptcy proceedings will be a tax claim.

(l) Once the IRS accepts the offer in writing, I/we have no right to contest, in court or otherwise, the amount of the tax liability.

(m) The offer is pending starting with the date an authorized IRS official signs this form. The offer remains pending until an authorized IRS official accepts, rejects, returns or acknowledges withdrawal of the offer in writing. If I/we appeal an IRS rejection decision on the offer, the IRS will continue to treat the offer as pending until the Appeals Office accepts or rejects the offer in writing. If I/we don't file a protest within 30 days of the date the IRS notifies me/us of the right to protest the decision, I/we waive the right to a hearing before the Appeals Office about the offer in compromise.

(n) If I/We fail to meet any of the terms and conditions of the offer and the offer defaults, then the IRS may:

- immediately file suit to collect the entire unpaid balance of the offer

- immediately file suit to collect an amount equal to the original amount of the tax liability as liquidating damages, minus any payment already received under the terms of this offer

- disregard the amount of the offer and apply all amounts already paid under the offer against the original amount of the tax liability

- file suit or levy to collect the original amount of the tax liability, without further notice of any kind.

The IRS will continue to add interest, as Section 6601 of the Internal Revenue Code requires, on the amount the IRS determines is due after default. The IRS will add interest from the date the offer is defaulted until I/we completely satisfy the amount owed.

(o) The IRS generally files a Notice of Federal Tax Lien to protect the Government's interest on deferred payment offers. This tax lien will be released when the payment terms of the offer agreement have been satisfied.

(p) I/We understand that the IRS employees may contact third parties in order to respond to this request and I authorize the IRS to make such contacts. Further, by authorizing the Internal Revenue Service to contact third parties, I understand that I will not receive notice, pursuant to section 7602(c) of the Internal Revenue Code, of third parties contacted in connection with this request.

NOTE: Signature(s) of taxpayer required on last page of Form 656

Item 9 — Explanation of Circumstances

I am requesting an offer in compromise for the reason(s) listed below:

*Note: If you are requesting compromise based on doubt as to liability, explain why you don't believe you owe the tax.
If you believe you have special circumstances affecting your ability to fully pay the amount due, explain your situation.
You may attach additional sheets if necessary.*

_____

_____

_____

_____

_____

_____

_____

_____

_____

_____

_____

_____

_____

_____

Item 10 — Source of Funds

I/we shall obtain the funds to make this offer from the following source(s):

_____

_____

_____

Item 11

If I/we submit this offer on a substitute form, I/we affirm that this form is a verbatim duplicate of the official Form 656, and I/we agree to be bound by all the terms and conditions set forth in the official Form 656.

Under penalties of perjury, I declare that I have examined this offer, including accompanying schedules and statements, and to the best of my knowledge and belief, it is true, correct and complete.

_____

11(a) Signature of Taxpayer

_____

Date

For Official Use Only

I accept the waiver of the statutory period of limitations for the Internal Revenue Service.

_____

Signature of Authorized Internal Revenue Service Official

_____

Title

_____

Date

What You Need to Know Before Submitting an Offer in Compromise

What is an Offer in Compromise?

An *Offer in Compromise* (OIC) is an agreement between a taxpayer and the Internal Revenue Service (IRS) that resolves the taxpayer's tax liability. The IRS has the authority to settle, or *compromise*, federal tax liabilities by accepting less than full payment under certain circumstances. The IRS may legally compromise for one of the following reasons:

■ **Doubt as to Liability** — Doubt exists that the assessed tax is correct.

■ **Doubt as to Collectibility** — Doubt exists that you could ever pay the full amount of tax owed.

■ **Effective Tax Administration** — There is no doubt the tax is correct and no doubt the amount owed could be collected, but an exceptional circumstance exists that allows us to consider your offer. To be eligible for compromise on this basis, you must demonstrate that collection of the tax would create an economic hardship or would be unfair and inequitable.

Form 656, Offer in Compromise, and Substitute Forms

Form 656, *Offer in Compromise*, is the official compromise agreement. Substitute forms, whether computer-generated or photocopies, must affirm that:

1. The substitute form is a verbatim duplicate of the official Form 656, and

2. You agree to be bound by all terms and conditions set forth in the official Form 656.

You must initial and date all pages of the substitute form, in addition to signing and dating the signature page.

You can get Form 656 by calling 1–800–829–1040 or 1–800–829–FORM, by visiting your local Internal Revenue Service (IRS) office, or by accessing our website at www.irs.gov

Am I Eligible for Consideration of an Offer in Compromise?

You may be eligible for consideration of an *Offer in Compromise* if:

1. In your judgment, you don't owe the tax liability (**Doubt as to Liability**). You must submit a detailed written statement explaining why you believe you don't owe the tax liability you want to compromise. You won't be required to submit a collection information statement if you're submitting an offer on this basis alone.

2. In your judgment, you can't pay the entire tax liability in full (**Doubt as to Collectibility**). You must submit a collection information statement showing your current financial situation.

3. You agree the tax liability is correct and you're able to pay the balance due in full, but you have exceptional circumstances you'd like us to consider (**Effective Tax Administration**). To receive consideration on this basis, you must submit:

a. a collection information statement, and

b. a detailed written narrative. The narrative must explain your exceptional circumstances and why paying the tax liability in full would either create an economic hardship or would be unfair and inequitable.

We'll also consider your overall history of filing and paying taxes.

Note: If you request consideration on the basis of effective tax administration, we're first required to establish that there is no doubt as to liability and no doubt as to collectibility. We can only consider an offer on the basis of effective tax administration after we've determined the liability is correct and collectible.

◄

When Am I Not Eligible for Consideration of an Offer in Compromise?

You are not eligible for consideration of an *Offer in Compromise* on the basis of **doubt as to collectibility** or **effective tax administration** if:

1. You haven't filed all required federal tax returns, or

2. You're involved in an open bankruptcy proceeding.

Note: If you are an in-business taxpayer, you must have filed and deposited all employment taxes on time for the two (2) quarters preceding your offer, as well as, deposit all employment taxes on time during the quarter you submit your offer.

What We Need to Process Your Offer in Compromise

For us to process your offer, you must provide a complete and correct Form 656 and:

■ Form 433-A, *Collection Information Statement for Wage Earners and Self-Employed Individuals*, if you are submitting an offer as an **individual** or **self-employed taxpayer**.

■ Form 433-B, *Collection Information Statement for Businesses*, if you are submitting an offer as a **corporation** or **other business** taxpayer. We may also require Forms 433-A from corporate officers or individual partners.

For a more detailed explanation of the information required to complete these forms, see the section entitled, "Financial Information" on page 3.

Note: We don't need a collection information statement for an offer based solely on doubt as to liability.

Please complete all applicable items on Form 656 and provide all required documentation. We may contact you for any missing required information. If we don't receive a response to our request or receive the required information, we won't recommend your offer for acceptance and will return your Form 656 to you by mail. We will explain our reason(s) for returning your offer in our letter. The reasons for return are:

■ The pre-printed terms and conditions listed on Form 656 have changed

■ A taxpayer name is missing

■ A Social Security Number or Employer Identification Number is missing, incomplete, or incorrect

■ An offer amount or payment term is unstated

■ A signature is missing

■ A collection information statement (Form 433-A or Form 433-B) is missing or incomplete, if your offer is based on doubt as to collectibility or effective tax administration

■ We did not receive collection information statement verification

■ Our records show you don't have a tax liability

■ Your offer is submitted to delay collection or cause a delay which will jeopardize our ability to collect the tax

Note: You should personally sign your offer and any required collection information statements unless unusual circumstances prevent you from doing so. If someone with an authorized power of attorney signs your offer because of unusual circumstances, you must include a completed Form 2848, Power of Attorney and Declaration of Representative, with your offer.

What You Should Do If You Want to Submit an Offer in Compromise

Determine Your Offer Amount

All offer amounts (**doubt as to liability, doubt as to collectibility,** or **effective tax administration**) must exceed $0.00.

■ **Doubt as to Liability**

Complete Item 9, *Explanation of Circumstances,* on Form 656, explaining why, in your judgment, you don't owe the tax liability you want to compromise. Offer the correct tax, penalty, and interest owed based on your judgment.

■ **Doubt as to Collectibility**

Complete Form 433-A, *Collection Information Statement for Wage Earners and Self-Employed Individuals,* or Form 433-B, *Collection Information Statement for Businesses,* as appropriate, and attach to your Form 656. For assistance in determining your offer amount, visit our website at www.irs.ustreas.gov/ind_info/oic/index.html. If you are a wage earner or self-employed individual, figure your offer amount by completing the worksheet on pages 10–11.

You must offer an amount greater than or equal to the "reasonable collection potential" (RCP). The RCP equals the net equity of your assets plus the amount we could collect from your future income. Please see page 8, **Terms and Definitions,** for more detailed definitions of these and other terms.

If special circumstances cause you to offer an amount less than the RCP, you must also complete Item 9, *Explanation of Circumstances,* on Form 656, explaining your situation. Special circumstances may include factors such as advanced age, serious illness from which recovery is unlikely, or unusual circumstances that impact upon your ability to pay the total RCP and continue to provide for the necessary expenses for you and your family.

■ **Effective Tax Administration**

Complete Form 433-A or Form 433-B, as appropriate, and attach to Form 656.

Complete Item 9, *Explanation of Circumstances,* on Form 656, explaining your exceptional circumstances and why requiring payment of the tax liability in full would either create an economic hardship or would be unfair and inequitable.

Enter your offer amount on Item 7 of Form 656.

Financial Information

Note: We do not require this information if your offer is based solely on doubt as to liability.

You must provide financial information when you submit offers based on **doubt as to collectibility** and **effective tax administration**.

If you are submitting an offer as a wage earner or self-employed individual, you must file Form 433-A, *Collection Information Statement for Wage Earners and Self-Employed Individuals,* with your Form 656. If you are a corporation or other business taxpayer, you must file Form 433-B, *Collection Information Statement for Businesses.* We may also request Forms 433-A from corporate officers or individual partners.

You must send us current information that reflects your financial situation for at least the past six months. Collection information statements must show all your assets and income, even those unavailable to us through direct collection action, because you can use them to fund your offer. The offer examiner needs this information to evaluate your offer and may ask you to update it or verify certain financial information. We may also return offer packages without complete collection information statements.

When only one spouse has a tax liability but both have incomes, only the spouse responsible for the debt is required to prepare the necessary collection information statements. In states with community property laws, however, we require collection information statements from both spouses. We may also request financial information on the non-liable spouse for offer verification purposes, even when community property laws do not apply.

Determine Your Payment Terms

There are three payment plans you and the IRS may agree to:

- **Cash** (paid in 90 days or less)

- **Short-Term Deferred Payment** (more than 90 days, up to 24 months)

- **Deferred Payment** (offers with payment terms over the remaining statutory period for collecting the tax).

Cash Offer

You must pay cash offers within 90 days of acceptance.

You should offer the realizable value of your assets plus the total amount we could collect over 48 months of payments (or the remainder of the ten-year statutory period for collection, whichever is less).

*Note: **We require full payment of accepted doubt as to liability offers at the time of mutual agreement of the corrected liability. If you're unable to pay the corrected amount, you must also request compromise on the basis of doubt as to collectibility.***

Short-Term Deferred Payment Offer

This payment plan requires you to pay the offer within two years of acceptance.

The offer must include the realizable value of your assets plus the amount we could collect over 60 months of payments (or the remainder of the ten-year statutory period for collection, whichever is less).

You can pay the short-term deferred payment plan in three ways:

Plan One

- Full payment of the realizable value of your assets within 90 days from the date we accept your offer, and

- Payment within two years of acceptance of the amount we could collect over 60 months (future income) or the remaining life of the collection statute, whichever is less.

Plan Two

- Cash payment for a portion of the realizable value of your assets within 90 days from the date we accept your offer, and

- The balance of the realizable value plus the amount we could collect over 60 months (future income) or the remaining life of the collection statute, whichever is less, within two years of acceptance.

Plan Three

- The entire offer amount in monthly payments extending over a period not to exceed two years from date of acceptance (e.g., four payments within 120 days of acceptance).

For example, on a short-term deferred payment total offer of $16,000, you might propose to pay your realizable value of assets (e.g., $13,000) within 90 days of acceptance and the amount of your future income (e.g., $50 per month for 60 months, or $3,000) over 6 monthly payments of $500 each, beginning the first month after acceptance.

We may file a Notice of Federal Tax Lien on tax liabilities compromised under short-term deferred payment offers.

Deferred Payment Offer

This payment plan requires you to pay the offer amount over the remaining statutory period for collecting the tax.

The offer must include the realizable value of your assets plus the amount we could collect through monthly payments during the remaining life of the collection statute.

For wage earners and self-employed individuals who want to submit a deferred payment offer, we will help you determine your future income amount. To compute this amount, we must calculate the remaining time left on the collection statute for each period of the tax liability.

- Call 1–800–829–1040 to assist you in this calculation.

- Using Form 433-A Worksheet, multiply the amount from Item 12, Box O, by the number of months remaining on the collection statute. Add that amount to Item 11, Box N, and use the total as the basis for your offer amount in Item 7 of Form 656.

You can pay the deferred payment plan in three ways:

Plan One

- Full payment of the realizable value of your assets within 90 days from the date we accept your offer, and

- Your "future income" in monthly payments during the remaining life of the collection statute

Plan Two

- Cash payment for a portion of the realizable value of your assets within 90 days from the date we accept your offer, and

- Monthly payments during the remaining life of the collection statute for both the balance of the realizable value and your future income

Plan Three

- The entire offer amount in monthly payments over the life of the collection statute

For example, on a deferred payment offer with 7 years (84 months) remaining on the statutory period for collection and a total offer of $25,000, you might propose to pay your realizable value of assets (e.g., $10,000) within 90 days and your future income (e.g., $179 per month for 7 years, or $15,000) in 84 monthly installments of $179. Alternately, you could also pay the same total $25,000 offer in 84 monthly installments of $298.

Just as with short-term deferred payment offers, we may file a Notice of Federal Tax Lien.

Note: *The worksheet on page 10 instructs wage earners and self-employed individuals how to figure the appropriate amount for a Cash, Short-Term Deferred Payment, or Deferred Payment Offer.*

How We Consider Your Offer

An offer examiner will evaluate your offer and may request additional documentation from you to verify financial or other information you provide. The examiner will then make a recommendation to accept it or reject the offer. The examiner may also return your offer if you don't provide the requested information.

The examiner may decide that a larger offer amount is necessary to justify acceptance. You will have the opportunity to amend your offer.

Additional Agreements

When you submit certain offers, we may also request that you sign an additional agreement requiring you to:

■ Pay a percentage of your future earnings

■ Waive certain present or future tax benefits

Withholding Collection Activities

We will withhold collection activities while we consider your offer. We will not act to collect the tax liability:

■ While we investigate and evaluate your offer

■ For 30 days after we reject an offer

■ While you appeal an offer rejection

The above do not apply if we find any indication that you submitted your offer to delay collection or cause a delay which will jeopardize our ability to collect the tax.

If you currently have an installment agreement when you submit an offer, you must continue making the agreed upon monthly payments while we consider your offer.

If We Accept Your Offer

If we accept your offer, we will notify you by mail. When you receive your acceptance letter, you must:

■ Promptly pay any unpaid amounts that become due under the terms of the offer agreement

■ Comply with all the terms and conditions of the offer, along with those of any additional agreement

■ Promptly notify us of any change of address until you meet the conditions of your offer. Your acceptance letter will indicate which IRS office to contact if your address changes. Your notification allows us to contact you immediately regarding the status of your offer

We will release all Notices of Federal Tax Lien when you satisfy the payment terms of the offered amount. For an immediate release of a lien, you can submit certified funds with a request letter.

In the future, not filing returns or paying taxes when due could result in the default of an accepted offer (see Form 656, Item 8(d), the *future compliance provision*). If you default your agreement, we will reinstate the unpaid amount of the original tax liability, file a Notice of Federal Tax Lien on any tax liability without a filed notice, and resume collection activities. The future compliance provision applies to offers based on **doubt as to collectibility**. In certain cases, the future compliance provision may apply to offers based on **effective tax administration**.

We won't default your offer agreement when you have filed a joint offer with your spouse or ex-spouse as long as you've kept or are keeping all the terms of the agreement, even if your spouse or ex-spouse violates the future compliance provision.

Except for offers based on **doubt as to liability**, the offer agreement requires you to forego certain refunds, and to return those refunds to us if they are issued to you by mistake. These conditions are also listed on Form 656, Items 8(g) and 8(h).

Note: *The law requires us to make certain information from accepted Offers in Compromise available for public inspection and review in your local IRS Territory Office. Therefore, information regarding your Offer in Compromise may become publicly known.*

If We Reject Your Offer

We'll notify you by mail if we reject your offer. In our letter, we will explain our reason for the rejection. If your offer is rejected, you have the right to:

■ Appeal our decision to the Office of Appeals within thirty days from the date of our letter. The letter will include detailed instructions on how to appeal the rejection.

■ Submit another offer. You must increase an offer we've rejected as being too low, when your financial situation remains unchanged. However, you must provide updated financial information when your financial situation has changed or when the original offer is more than six months old.

Terms and Definitions

An understanding of the following terms and conditions will help you to prepare your offer.

Fair Market Value (FMV) – The amount you could reasonably expect from the sale of an asset. Provide an accurate valuation of each asset. Determine value from realtors, used car dealers, publications, furniture dealers, or other experts on specific types of assets. Please include a copy of any written estimate with your Collection Information Statement.

Quick Sale Value (QSV) – The amount you could reasonably expect from the sale of an asset if you sold it quickly, typically in ninety days or less. This amount generally is less than fair market value, but may be equal to or higher, based on local circumstances.

Realizable Value – The quick sale value amount minus what you owe to a secured creditor. The creditor must have priority over a filed Notice of Federal Tax Lien before we allow a subtraction from the asset's value.

Future Income – We generally determine the amount we could collect from your future income by subtracting necessary living expenses from your monthly income over a set number of months. For a cash offer, you must offer what you could pay in monthly payments over forty-eight months (or the remainder of the ten-year statutory period for collection, whichever is less). For a short-term deferred offer, you must offer what you could pay in monthly payments over sixty months (or the remainder of the statutory period for collection, whichever is less). For a deferred payment offer, you must offer what you could pay in monthly payments during the remaining time we could legally receive payments.

Reasonable Collection Potential (RCP) – The total realizable value of your assets plus your future income. The total is generally your minimum offer amount.

Necessary Expenses – The allowable payments you make to support you and your family's health and welfare and/or the production of income. This expense allowance does not apply to business entities. Our Publication 1854 explains the National Standard Expenses and gives the allowable amounts. We derive these amounts from the Bureau of Labor Statistics (BLS) Consumer Expenditure Survey. We also use information from the Bureau of the Census to determine local expenses for housing, utilities, and transportation.

Note: If the IRS determines that the facts and circumstances of your situation indicate that using the scheduled allowance of necessary expenses is inadequate, we will allow you an adequate means for providing basic living expenses. However, you must provide documentation that supports a determination that using national and local expense standards leaves you an inadequate means of providing for basic living expenses.

Expenses Not Generally Allowed – We typically do not allow you to claim tuition for private schools, public or private college expenses, charitable contributions, voluntary retirement contributions, payments on unsecured debts such as credit card bills, cable television charges and other similar expenses as necessary living expenses. However, we can allow these expenses when you can prove that they are necessary for the health and welfare of you or your family or for the production of income.

Completing Form 656, Offer in Compromise

We have included two Offer in Compromise forms. Use one form to submit your offer in compromise. You may use the other form as a worksheet and retain it for your personal records.

Note: If you have any questions about completing this form, you may call 1–800–829–1040 or visit your local IRS office or our website at www.irs.ustreas.gov/ind_info/oic/index.html. We may return your offer if you don't follow these instructions.

Item 1: Enter your name and home or business address. You should also include a mailing address, if it is different from your street address.

Show both names on joint offers for joint liabilities. If you owe one liability by yourself (such as employment taxes), and other liabilities jointly (such as income taxes), but only you are submitting an offer, list all tax liabilities on one Form 656. If you owe one liability yourself and another jointly, and both parties submit an offer, **complete two Forms 656**, one for the individual liability and one for the joint liability.

Item 2: Enter the social security number(s) for the person(s) submitting the offer. For example, enter the social security number of both spouses when submitting a joint offer for a joint tax liability. However, when only one spouse submits an offer, enter only that spouse's social security number.

Item 3: Enter the employer identification number for offers from businesses.

Item 4: Show the employer identification numbers for all other businesses (excluding corporate entities) that you own or in which you have an ownership interest.

Item 5: Identify your tax liability and enter the tax year or period. Letters and notices from us and Notices of Federal Tax Lien show the tax periods for trust fund recovery penalties.

Item 6: Check the appropriate box (es) describing the basis for your offer.

Doubt as to Liability offers require a statement describing in detail why you think you do not owe the liability. Complete Item 9, "Explanation of Circumstances," explaining your situation.

Doubt as to Collectibility offers require you to complete a Form 433-A, *Collection Information Statement for Wage Earners and Self-Employed Individuals*, if you are an individual taxpayer, or a Form 433-B, *Collection Information Statement for Businesses*, if you are a corporation or other business taxpayer.

Effective Tax Administration offers require you to complete a Form 433-A, *Collection Information Statement for Wage Earners and Self-Employed Individuals*, if you are an individual taxpayer, or a Form 433-B, *Collection Information Statement for Businesses*, if you are a corporation or other business taxpayer. Complete Item 9, "Explanation of Circumstances."

Note: Staple in the upper left corner the six (6) pages of the collection information statement before you send it to us.

Item 7:	Enter the total amount of your offer (see page 3, "Determine Your Offer Amount"). Your offer amount cannot include a refund we owe you or amounts you have already paid.	Check the appropriate payment box (cash, short-term deferred payment or deferred payment — see page 4, "Determine Your Payment Terms") and describe your payment plan in the spaces provided.
Item 8:	It is important that you understand the requirements listed in this section. Pay particular attention to Items 8(d)	and 8(g), as they address the future compliance provision and refunds.
Item 9:	Explain your reason(s) for submitting your offer in the "Explanation of	Circumstances." You may attach additional sheets if necessary.
Item 10:	Explain where you will get the funds to pay the amount you are offering.	
Item 11:	All persons submitting the offer must sign and date Form 656. Include titles of authorized corporate officers, executors, trustees, Powers of Attorney, etc. where applicable.	*Note: Staple in the upper left corner the four (4) pages of Form 656 before you send it to us.*

Where to File

IF YOU RESIDE IN

the states of Alaska, Alabama, Arizona, California, Colorado, Hawaii, Idaho, Kentucky, Louisiana, Mississippi, Montana, Nevada, New Mexico, Oregon, Tennessee, Texas, Utah, Washington, Wisconsin or Wyoming,

AND	AND
You are a wage earner or a self-employed individual without employees,	You are **OTHER** than wage earner or a self-employed individual without employees,
THEN MAIL	THEN MAIL
Form 656 and attachments to:	Form 656 and attachments to:
Memphis Internal Revenue Service Center COIC Unit **PO Box 30803, AMC** Memphis, TN 38130-0803	Memphis Internal Revenue Service Center COIC Unit **PO Box 30804, AMC** Memphis, TN 38130-0804

IF YOU RESIDE IN

Arkansas, Connecticut, Delaware, District of Columbia, Florida, Georgia, Illinois, Indiana, Iowa, Kansas, Maine, Maryland, Massachusetts, Michigan, Minnesota, Missouri, Nebraska, New Hampshire, New Jersey, New York, North Carolina, North Dakota, Ohio, Oklahoma, Pennsylvania, Puerto Rico, Rhode Island, South Carolina, South Dakota, Vermont, Virginia, West Virginia or have a foreign address,

AND	AND
You are a wage earner or a self-employed individual without employees,	You are **OTHER** than wage earner or a self-employed individual without employees,
THEN MAIL	THEN MAIL
Form 656 and attachments to:	Form 656 and attachments to:
Brookhaven Internal Revenue Service Center COIC Unit **PO Box 9007** Holtsville, NY 11742-9007	Brookhaven Internal Revenue Service Center COIC Unit **PO Box 9008** Holtsville, NY 11742-9008

Collection Information Statement for Wage Earners and Self-Employed Individuals

**Department of the Treasury
Internal Revenue Service**

www.irs.gov

Form 433-A (Rev. 5-2001)
Catalog Number 20312N

Complete all entry spaces with the most current data available.

Important! Write "N/A" (not applicable) in spaces that do not apply. We may require additional information to support "N/A" entries.

Failure to complete all entry spaces may result in rejection or significant delay in the resolution of your account.

Section 1
Personal Information

1. Full Name(s) _____

1a. Home Telephone (____) _____   Best Time To Call: _____ am _____ pm (Enter Hour)

Street Address _____

City _____ State _____ Zip _____

County of Residence _____

How long at this address? _____

2. Marital Status:
☐ Married   ☐ Separated
☐ Unmarried (single, divorced, widowed)

3. Your Social Security No.(SSN) _____
3a. Your Date of Birth (mm/dd/yyyy) _____

4. Spouse's Social Security No. _____
4a. Spouse's Date of Birth (mm/dd/yyyy) _____

5. ☐ Own Home   ☐ Rent   ☐ Other (specify, i.e. share rent, live with relative) _____

6. List the dependents you can claim on your tax return: (Attach sheet if more space is needed.)

First Name	Relationship	Age	Does this person live with you?	First Name	Relationship	Age	Does this person live with you?
_____			☐ No ☐ Yes	_____			☐ No ☐ Yes
_____			☐ No ☐ Yes	_____			☐ No ☐ Yes

☐ Check this box when all spaces in Sect. 1 are filled in.

Section 2
Your Business Information

7. Are you or your spouse self-employed or operate a business? (Check "Yes" if either applies)

☐ No   ☐ Yes   If yes, provide the following information:

7a. Name of Business _____
7b. Street Address _____
City _____ State _____ Zip _____

7c. Employer Identification No., if available : _____
7d. Do you have employees? ☐ No ☐ Yes
7e. Do you have accounts/notes receivable? ☐ No ☐ Yes
If yes, please complete Section 8 on page 5.

ATTACHMENTS REQUIRED: Please include proof of self-employment income for the **prior 3 months** (e.g., invoices, commissions, sales records, income statement).

☐ Check this box when all spaces in Sect. 2 are filled in and attachments provided.

Section 3
Employment Information

8. Your Employer _____
Street Address _____
City _____ State _____ Zip _____
Work telephone no. (____) _____
May we contact you at work? ☐ No ☐ Yes
8a. How long with this employer? _____
8b. Occupation _____

9. Spouse's Employer _____
Street Address _____
City _____ State _____ Zip _____
Work telephone no. (____) _____
May we contact you at work? ☐ No ☐ Yes
9a. How long with this employer? _____
9b. Occupation _____

ATTACHMENTS REQUIRED: Please provide proof of gross earnings and deductions for the past 3 months from each employer (e.g., pay stubs, earnings statements). If year-to-date information is available, send only 1 such statement as long as a **minimum of 3 months** is represented.

☐ Check this box when all spaces in Sect. 3 are filled in and attachments provided.

Section 4
Other Income Information

10. Do you receive income from sources other than your own business or your employer? (Check all that apply.)

☐ Pension   ☐ Social Security   ☐ Other (specify, i.e. child support, alimony, rental) _____

ATTACHMENTS REQUIRED: Please provide proof of pension/social security/other income for the past 3 months from each payor, including any statements showing deductions. If year-to-date information is available, send only 1 such statement as long as a **minimum of 3 months** is represented.

☐ Check this box when all spaces in Sect. 4 are filled in and attachments provided.

Section 5 begins on page 2 →
(Rev. 5-2001)

Collection Information Statement for Wage Earners and Self-Employed Individuals　　　**Form 433-A**

Name_____　SSN_____

Section 5	**11. CHECKING ACCOUNTS.** List all checking accounts. (If you need additional space, attach a separate sheet.)
Banking, Investment, Cash, Credit, and Life Insurance Information	

Section 5

Banking, Investment, Cash, Credit, and Life Insurance Information

*Complete all entry spaces with the most **current** data available.*

11. CHECKING ACCOUNTS. List all checking accounts. (If you need additional space, attach a separate sheet.)

	Type of Account	Full Name of Bank, Savings & Loan, Credit Union or Financial Institution	Bank Routing No.	Bank Account No.	Current Account Balance
11a. Checking		Name _____	_____	_____	$ _____
		Street Address _____			
		City/State/Zip _____			
11b. Checking		Name _____			$ _____
		Street Address _____			
		City/State/Zip _____	**11c. Total Checking Account Balances**		$

12. OTHER ACCOUNTS. List all acounts, including brokerage, savings, and money market, not listed on line 11.

	Type of Account	Full Name of Bank, Savings & Loan, Credit Union or Financial Institution	Bank Routing No.	Bank Account No.	Current Account Balance
12a.	_____	Name _____	_____	_____	$ _____
		Street Address _____			
		City/State/Zip _____			
12b.	_____	Name _____			$ _____
		Street Address _____			
		City/State/Zip _____	**12c. Total Other Account Balances**		$

ATTACHMENTS REQUIRED: Please include your current bank statements (checking, savings, money market, and brokerage accounts) for the past three months for all accounts.

13. INVESTMENTS. List all investment assets below. Include stocks, bonds, mutual funds, stock options, certificates of deposits, and retirement assets such as IRAs, Keogh, and 401(k) plans. (If you need additional space, attach a separate sheet.)

	Name of Company	Number of Shares / Units	⌄ Current Value	Loan Amount	Used as collateral on loan?
13a.	_____	_____	$ _____	$ _____	☐ No ☐ Yes
13b.	_____	_____	_____	_____	☐ No ☐ Yes
13c.	_____	_____	_____	_____	☐ No ☐ Yes
	13d. Total Investments		$ _____		

⌄ Current Value: Indicate the amount you could sell the asset for today.

14. CASH ON HAND. Include any money that you have that is not in the bank.

14a. Total Cash on Hand　　$ _____

15. AVAILABLE CREDIT. List all lines of credit, including credit cards.

	Full Name of Credit Institution	Credit Limit	Amount Owed	Available Credit
15a. Name	_____	_____	_____	$ _____
	Street Address _____			
	City/State/Zip _____			
15b. Name	_____	_____	_____	$ _____
	Street Address _____			
	City/State/Zip _____	**15c. Total Credit Available**		$

Section 5 continued on page 3 →
(Rev. 5-2001)

Collection Information Statement for Wage Earners and Self-Employed Individuals

Name_____   SSN_____

Section 5 **continued**	**16. LIFE INSURANCE.** Do you have life insurance with a cash value? ☐ No ☐ Yes (Term Life insurance does not have a cash value.) If yes: **16a.** Name of Insurance Company _____ **16b.** Policy Number(s) _____ **16c.** Owner of Policy _____ **16d.** Current Cash Value $_____ **16e.** Outstanding Loan Balance $_____ Subtract "Outstanding Loan Balance" line 16e from "Current Cash Value" line 16d = 16f $_____ **ATTACHMENTS REQUIRED:** Please include a statement from the life insurance companies that includes type and cash/loan value amounts. If currently borrowed against, include loan amount and date of loan.

☐ Check this box when all spaces in Sect. 5 are filled in and attachments provided.

Section 6 **Other** **Information**	**17. OTHER INFORMATION.** Respond to the following questions related to your financial condition: (Attach sheet if you need more space.) **17a.** Are there any garnishments against your wages? ☐ No ☐ Yes If yes, who is the creditor?_____ Date creditor obtained judgement_____ Amount of debt $_____ **17b.** Are there any judgments against you? ☐ No ☐ Yes If yes, who is the creditor?_____ Date creditor obtained judgement_____ Amount of debt $_____ **17c.** Are you a party in a lawsuit? ☐ No ☐ Yes If yes, amount of suit $_____ Possible completion date_____ Subject matter of suit_____ **17d.** Did you ever file bankruptcy? ☐ No ☐ Yes If yes, date filed_____ Date discharged_____ **17e.** In the past 10 years did you transfer any assets out of your name for less than their actual value? ☐ No ☐ Yes If yes, what asset?_____ Value of asset at time of transfer $_____ When was it transferred?_____ To whom was it transferred?_____ **17f.** Do you anticipate any increase in household income in the next two years? ☐ No ☐ Yes If yes, why will the income increase?_____ (Attach sheet if you need more space.) How much will it increase? $_____ **17g.** Are you a beneficiary of a trust or an estate? ☐ No ☐ Yes If yes, name of the trust or estate_____ Anticipated amount to be received $_____ When will the amount be received?_____ **17h.** Are you a participant in a profit sharing plan? ☐ No ☐ Yes If yes, name of plan_____ Value in plan $_____

☐ Check this box when all spaces in Sect. 6 are filled in.

Section 7 **Assets and** **Liabilities**	**18. PURCHASED AUTOMOBILES, TRUCKS AND OTHER LICENSED ASSETS.** Include boats, RV's, motorcycles, trailers, etc. (If you need additional space, attach a separate sheet.)

⊐ **Current Value:** Indicate the amount you could sell the asset for today.

Description (Year, Make, Model, Mileage)	⊐ Current Value	Current Loan Balance	Name of Lender	Purchase Date	Amount of Monthly Payment
18a. Year Make/Model Mileage	$	$			$
18b. Year Make/Model Mileage	$	$			$
18c. Year Make/Model Mileage	$	$			$

Section 7 continued on page 4 →

(Rev. 5-2001)

Collection Information Statement for Wage Earners and Self-Employed Individuals **Form 433-A**

Name_____ SSN_____

Section 7
continued

19. LEASED AUTOMOBILES, TRUCKS AND OTHER LICENSED ASSETS. Include boats, RV's, motorcycles, trailers, etc.
(If you need additional space, attach a separate sheet.)

Description (Year, Make, Model)	Lease Balance	Name and Address of Lessor	Lease Date	Amount of Monthly Payment
19a. Year				
Make/Model	$			$
19b. Year				
Make/Model	$			$

ATTACHMENTS REQUIRED: Please include your current statement from lender with monthly car payment amount and current balance of the loan for each vehicle purchased or leased.

20. REAL ESTATE. List all real estate you own. (If you need additional space, attach a separate sheet.)

Street Address, City, State, Zip, and County	Date Purchased	Purchase Price	⌑Current Value	Loan Balance	Name of Lender or Lien Holder	Amount of Monthly Payment	❋Date of Final Payment
20a.		$	$	$		$	
20b.		$	$	$		$	

ATTACHMENTS REQUIRED: Please include your current statement from lender with monthly payment amount and current balance for each piece of real estate owned.

⌑ **Current Value:** Indicate the amount you could sell the asset for today.

❋ **Date of Final Payment:** Enter the date the loan or lease will be fully paid.

21. PERSONAL ASSETS. List all Personal assets below. (If you need additional space, attach separate sheet.)
Furniture/Personal Effects includes the total current market value of your household such as furniture and appliances.
Other Personal Assets includes all artwork, jewelry, collections (coin/gun, etc.), antiques or other assets.

Description	⌑Current Value	Loan Balance	Name of Lender	Amount of Monthly Payment	❋Date of Final Payment
21a. Furniture/Personal Effects	$	$		$	
Other: (List below)					
21b. Artwork	$	$		$	
21c. Jewelry					
21d.					
21e.					

22. BUSINESS ASSETS. List all business assets and encumbrances below, include Uniform Commercial Code (UCC) filings. (If you need additional space, attach a separate sheet.) *Tools used in Trade or Business* includes the basic tools or books used to conduct your business, excluding automobiles. *Other Business Assets* includes any other machinery, equipment, inventory or other assets.

Description	⌑Current Value	Loan Balance	Name of Lender	Amount of Monthly Payment	❋Date of Final Payment
22a. Tools used in Trade/Business	$	$		$	
Other: (List below)					
22b. Machinery	$	$		$	
22c. Equipment					
22d.					
22e.					

☐ Check this box when all spaces in Sect. 7 are filled in and attachments provided.

Collection Information Statement for Wage Earners and Self-Employed Individuals

Form 433-A

Name_____ SSN_____

Section 8 Accounts/ Notes Receivable	**23. ACCOUNTS/NOTES RECEIVABLE.** List all accounts separately, including contracts awarded, but not started. (If you need additional space, attach a separate sheet.)

Use only if needed.

☐ *Check this box if Section 8 not needed.*

	Description	Amount Due	Date Due	Age of Account

23a. Name _____ $ _____ _____ ☐ 0 - 30 days
Street Address _____ ☐ 30 - 60 days
City/State/Zip _____ ☐ 60 - 90 days
☐ 90+ days

23b. Name _____ $ _____ _____ ☐ 0 - 30 days
Street Address _____ ☐ 30 - 60 days
City/State/Zip _____ ☐ 60 - 90 days
☐ 90+ days

23c. Name _____ $ _____ _____ ☐ 0 - 30 days
Street Address _____ ☐ 30 - 60 days
City/State/Zip _____ ☐ 60 - 90 days
☐ 90+ days

23d. Name _____ $ _____ _____ ☐ 0 - 30 days
Street Address _____ ☐ 30 - 60 days
City/State/Zip _____ ☐ 60 - 90 days
☐ 90+ days

23e. Name _____ $ _____ _____ ☐ 0 - 30 days
Street Address _____ ☐ 30 - 60 days
City/State/Zip _____ ☐ 60 - 90 days
☐ 90+ days

23f. Name _____ $ _____ _____ ☐ 0 - 30 days
Street Address _____ ☐ 30 - 60 days
City/State/Zip _____ ☐ 60 - 90 days
☐ 90+ days

23g. Name _____ $ _____ _____ ☐ 0 - 30 days
Street Address _____ ☐ 30 - 60 days
City/State/Zip _____ ☐ 60 - 90 days
☐ 90+ days

23h. Name _____ $ _____ _____ ☐ 0 - 30 days
Street Address _____ ☐ 30 - 60 days
City/State/Zip _____ ☐ 60 - 90 days
☐ 90+ days

23i. Name _____ $ _____ _____ ☐ 0 - 30 days
Street Address _____ ☐ 30 - 60 days
City/State/Zip _____ ☐ 60 - 90 days
☐ 90+ days

23j. Name _____ $ _____ _____ ☐ 0 - 30 days
Street Address _____ ☐ 30 - 60 days
City/State/Zip _____ ☐ 60 - 90 days
☐ 90+ days

23k. Name _____ $ _____ _____ ☐ 0 - 30 days
Street Address _____ ☐ 30 - 60 days
City/State/Zip _____ ☐ 60 - 90 days
☐ 90+ days

23l. Name _____ $ _____ _____ ☐ 0 - 30 days
Street Address _____ ☐ 30 - 60 days
City/State/Zip _____ ☐ 60 - 90 days
☐ 90+ days

☐ Check this box when all spaces in Sect. 8 are filled in.

Add "Amount Due" from lines 23a through 23l = 23m $ _____

Collection Information Statement for Wage Earners and Self-Employed Individuals

Form 433-A

Name _____ SSN _____

Section 9	Total Income			Total Living Expenses		
Monthly Income and Expense Analysis	Source	Gross Monthly		Expense Items [4]	Actual Monthly	
	24. Wages (Yourself)[1]	$		35. Food, Clothing and Misc.[5]	$	
	25. Wages (Spouse)[1]			36. Housing and Utilities[6]		
	26. Interest - Dividends			37. Transportation[7]		
If only one spouse has a tax liability, but both have income, list the total household income and expenses.	27. Net Income from Business[2]			38. Health Care		
	28. Net Rental Income[3]			39. Taxes (Income and FICA)		
	29. Pension/Social Security (Yourself)			40. Court ordered payments		
	30. Pension/Social Security (Spouse)			41. Child/dependent care		
	31. Child Support			42. Life insurance		
	32. Alimony			43. Other secured debt		
	33. Other			44. Other expenses		
	34. Total Income	$		**45. Total Living Expenses**	$	

[1] **Wages, salaries, pensions, and social security:** Enter your gross monthly wages and/or salaries. Do not deduct withholding or allotments you elect to take out of your pay, such as insurance payments, credit union deductions, car payments etc.
To calculate your gross monthly wages and/or salaries:
If paid weekly - multiply weekly gross wages by 4.3. Example: $425.89 x 4.3 = $1,831.33
If paid bi-weekly (every 2 weeks) - multiply bi-weekly gross wages by 2.17. Example: $972.45 x 2.17 = $2,110.22
If paid semi-monthly (twice each month) - multiply semi-monthly gross wages by 2. Example: $856.23 x 2 = $1,712.46

[2] **Net Income from Business:** Enter your monthly net business income. This is the amount you earn after you pay ordinary and necessary monthly business expenses. This figure should relate to the yearly net profit from your Form 1040 Schedule C. If it is more or less than the previous year, you should attach an explanation. If your net business income is a loss, enter "0". Do not enter a negative number.

[3] **Net Rental Income:** Enter your monthly net rental income. This is the amount you earn after you pay ordinary and necessary monthly rental expenses. If your net rental income is a loss, enter "0". Do not enter a negative number.

[4] **Expenses not generally allowed:** We generally do not allow you to claim tuition for private schools, public or private college expenses, charitable contributions, voluntary retirement contributions, payments on unsecured debts such as credit card bills, cable television and other similar expenses. However, we may allow these expenses, if you can prove that they are necessary for the health and welfare of you or your family or for the production of income.

[5] **Food, Clothing and Misc.:** Total of clothing, food, housekeeping supplies and personal care products for one month.

[6] **Housing and Utilities:** For your principal residence: Total of rent or mortgage payment. Add the average monthly expenses for the following: property taxes, home owner's or renter's insurance, maintenance, dues, fees, and utilities. Utilities include gas, electricity, water, fuel, oil, other fuels, trash collection and telephone.

[7] **Transportation:** Total of lease or purchase payments, vehicle insurance, registration fees, normal maintenance, fuel, public transportation, parking and tolls for one month.

ATTACHMENTS REQUIRED: Please include:

- A copy of your last Form 1040 with all Schedules.

- Proof of all current expenses that you paid for the past 3 months, including utilities, rent, insurance, property taxes, etc.

- Proof of all non-business transportation expenses (e.g., car payments, lease payments, fuel, oil, insurance, parking, registration).

- Proof of payments for health care, including health insurance premiums, co-payments, and other out-of-pocket expenses, for the past 3 months.

- Copies of any court order requiring payment and proof of such payments (e.g., cancelled checks, money orders, earning statements showing such deductions) for the past 3 months.

☐ Check this box when all spaces in Sect. 9 are filled in and attachments provided.

☐ Check this box when all spaces in all sections are filled in and all attachments provided.

Failure to complete all entry spaces may result in rejection or significant delay in the resolution of your account.

Certification: *Under penalties of perjury, I declare that to the best of my knowledge and belief this statement of assets, liabilities, and other information is true, correct and complete.*

Your Signature   Spouse's Signature   Date

(Rev. 5-2001)

Form 433-A Worksheet

Keep this worksheet for your records.
Do not send to IRS.

Use this Worksheet to calculate an offer amount using information from Form 433-A.

1. Enter total checking accounts from Item 11c

   A [_____]

2. Enter total other accounts from Item 12c

   B [_____]

   If less than "0", enter "0"

3. Enter total investments from Item 13d

   C [_____]

4. Enter total cash on hand from Item 14a

   D [_____]

5. Enter life insurance cash value from Item 16f

   E [_____]

6. Enter total accounts/notes receivable from Item 23m

   F [_____]

   Subtotal: Add boxes A through F = G [_____]

---

7. **Purchased Automobiles, Trucks, and Other Licensed Assets**

	Enter current value for each asset		Enter loan balance for each asset	Individual asset value (if less than "0", enter "0")
From line 18a	$_____ x .8 =	$_____	– $_____	= _____
From line 18b	$_____ x .8 =	$_____	– $_____	= _____
From line 18c	$_____ x .8 =	$_____	– $_____	= _____

   Subtotal = H [_____]

---

8. **Real Estate**

	Enter current value for each asset		Enter loan balance for each asset	Individual asset value (if less than "0", enter "0")
From line 20a	$_____ x .8 =	$_____	– $_____	= _____
From line 20b	$_____ x .8 =	$_____	– $_____	= _____

   Subtotal = I [_____]

---

9. **Personal Assets**

	Enter current value for each asset		Enter loan balance for each asset	Individual asset value (if less than "0", enter "0")
From line 21b	$_____ x .8 =	$_____	– $_____	= _____
From line 21c	$_____ x .8 =	$_____	– $_____	= _____
From line 21d	$_____ x .8 =	$_____	– $_____	= _____
From line 21e	$_____ x .8 =	$_____	– $_____	= _____

   Subtotal = J [_____]

| From line 21a | $_____ x .8 = | $_____ | – $_____ | = _____ |

   Subtract – $ 6560.00

   Subtotal = K [_____]

---

10. **Business Assets**

	Enter current value for each asset		Enter loan balance for each asset	Individual asset value (if less than "0", enter "0")
From line 22b	$_____ x .8 =	$_____	– $_____	= _____
From line 22c	$_____ x .8 =	$_____	– $_____	= _____
From line 22d	$_____ x .8 =	$_____	– $_____	= _____
From line 22e	$_____ x .8 =	$_____	– $_____	= _____

   Subtotal = L [_____]

| From line 22a | $_____ x .8 = | $_____ | – $_____ | = _____ |

   Subtract – $ 3280.00

   Subtotal = M [_____]

11. Add amounts in Boxes G through M to obtain your total equity and assets = 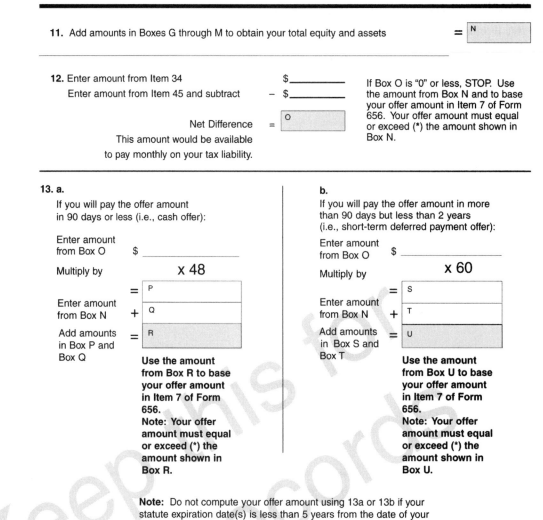 N

12. Enter amount from Item 34 $_____

Enter amount from Item 45 and subtract   – $_____

Net Difference = ☐ O

This amount would be available
to pay monthly on your tax liability.

If Box O is "0" or less, STOP. Use the amount from Box N and to base your offer amount in Item 7 of Form 656. Your offer amount must equal or exceed (*) the amount shown in Box N.

13. a.

If you will pay the offer amount
in 90 days or less (i.e., cash offer):

Enter amount
from Box O $ _____

Multiply by   **x 48**

= P

Enter amount
from Box N   + Q

Add amounts
in Box P and
Box Q   = R

**Use the amount
from Box R to base
your offer amount
in Item 7 of Form
656.
Note: Your offer
amount must equal
or exceed (*) the
amount shown in
Box R.**

b.

If you will pay the offer amount in more
than 90 days but less than 2 years
(i.e., short-term deferred payment offer):

Enter amount
from Box O $ _____

Multiply by   **x 60**

= S

Enter amount
from Box N   + T

Add amounts
in Box S and
Box T   = U

**Use the amount
from Box U to base
your offer amount
in Item 7 of Form
656.
Note: Your offer
amount must equal
or exceed (*) the
amount shown in
Box U.**

Note: Do not compute your offer amount using 13a or 13b if your
statute expiration date(s) is less than 5 years from the date of your
offer. Instead, refer to page 5 under "Deferred Payment Offer" options
1 through 3.

* Unless you are submitting an offer under effective tax administration or doubt as to collectibility
with special circumstances considerations, as described on page 3.

INDEX